The
Selected
Writings
of
A.R. Luria

The Selected Writings of A.R. Luria

EDITED WITH AN INTRODUCTION BY

Michael Cole

M.E.Sharpe INC.

WHITE PLAINS, NEW YORK

CONTENTS

vii   Introduction
      Michael Cole

I. Early beginnings

3   Psychoanalysis as a System of Monistic Psychology
    A. R. Luria

II. Developmental studies

45   A Child's Speech Responses and the Social Environment
     A. R. Luria

78   Experimental Psychology and Child Development
     A. R. Luria

97   Paths of Development of Thought in the Child
     A. R. Luria

145   The Development of Writing in the Child
      A. R. Luria

195   The Development of Constructive Activity in the
      Preschool Child
      A. R. Luria

229   The Formation of Voluntary Movements in Children
      of Preschool Age
      O. K. Tikhomirov

III. Neuropsychology

273   L. S. Vygotsky and the Problem of Functional
Localization
A. R. Luria

282   Two Approaches to an Evaluation of the Reliability
of Psychological Investigations
A. R. Luria and E. Yu. Artem'eva

294   Disturbance of Intellectual Functions in Patients
with Frontal Lobe Lesions
A. R. Luria and L. S. Tzvetkova

302   Neuropsychological Analysis of the Predicative
Structure of Utterances
A. R. Luria and L. S. Tzvetkova

319   Syndromes of Mnemonic Disorders Accompanying
Diencephalic Tumors
A. R. Luria, N. K. Kiyashchenko, L. I. Moskovichyute,
T. O. Faller, and N. A. Fillippycheva

330   Eye-Movement Mechanisms in Normal and
Pathological Vision
A. R. Luria, E. N. Pravdina-Vinarskaya, and
A. L. Iarbus

INTRODUCTION

The articles in this volume are a sample of the ideas constructed and facts collected by Alexander Romanovich Luria
(1902-1977) during more than half a century of psychological research. I became acquainted with parts of the work during the
late 1950s. I studied with Luria in 1962-63 and at various other
periods in the last 15 years. Despite this long association, the
scope of his contributions to our understanding of human nature
has been difficult for me to grasp. "Half a century" is an easy
enough concept to understand formally, but the living substance
of the phrase when applied to a scientist's work is rarely, if
ever, accessible to others. The exposition that follows is certainly incomplete and probably inaccurate; it is the best that the
facts at hand will permit.

Alexander Romanovich began his professional era at a tumul-
tuous moment in human history. The Bolshevik Revolution had
interrupted his high-school career, in the provincial Russian
commercial center of Kazan. Changes in educational regula-
tions and curricula left him free to accelerate his passage
through the accrediting process, and within three years he had
completed the formal requirements for a college degree.

With little guidance from a faculty in disarray (owing to the
abrupt change in the intellectual and political climate), Luria
was allowed to fashion his own education. The product may not
have been ideally systematic, but it represented a fascinating
amalgam of the leading ideas in the social sciences of the times.

Luria was interested in Utopian socialism and, particularly,

the problem of change: What was the source of ideas about society? How can one use such ideas to bring about social change?
His social thinking (and hence the medium for his social activities) was, from the beginning, focused on the individual. How
can the individual be linked to larger social units?

In his search for an answer to this question, Luria was drawn
to read the neo-Kantian social-science philosophers of the late
19th century - Dilthey, Richert, and Windelbandt, for whom the
relationship between psychology and history was a pivotal issue.
Although Wundt had set up a psychology laboratory in 1880, there
was nothing approaching a consensus about what kind of science
psychology could, in principle, represent. Even Wundt, who
maintained that the experimental method was an appropriate tool
of psychology, did not believe that laboratory methods were appropriate to all aspects of the science. Rather, experimental
methods could be used to study only elementary psychological
processes; folklore and ethnography had to be relied upon to
supply information about higher psychological functions.

Dilthey and his colleagues were not willing to concede this interpretation of either part of Wundt's enterprise. One of their
central questions was what kind of laws were possible from the
study of human psychological processes. Should one strive for
general ("nomothetic") laws that describe "Man" but are unable
to account for the specific behaviors of any individual "man"?
This was the model of the natural sciences (Naturwissenschaf-
ten) and the model adopted by Wundt for the study of sensory
processes. Or should psychology attempt only to describe the
intricate complex reality of individuals, providing "idiographic"
accounts in the tradition of the humane sciences (Geisteswis-
senschaften) such as history?

Luria's interest in these matters was not narrowly academic.
Caught up in the romantic enthusiasm of the revolution, he sought
a scientific basis for influencing human affairs. Perhaps for
this reason, he was not satisfied with the choice between an idiographic, descriptive psychology and a nomothetic, generalizing
psychology. The generalizing, "scientific" psychology of Wundt,
Brentano, and other laboratory psychologists seemed too remote

from any real-life process that one could observe outside the
laboratory. It was bloodless, artificial, and of no use whatever
in dealing with the problems facing humanity.

But the neo-Kantians offered no usable alternative. They
could, to be sure, provide much more illuminating descriptions
of recognizable psychological processes. But their method left
them handcuffed as scientists; they could not lawfully influence
the objects of observations. They were helpless to initiate or
guide change.

What the situation seemed to require was a new kind of psychology that could deal with the richness of individual psychological experience but admit of generalizations of the sort that
made the natural sciences powerful. For several years psychoanalysis seemed to Luria a promising basis on which to found
the kind of psychology he sought. Freud's writings were the
source of many interesting hypotheses about the motivational
sources of behavior, but his hypotheses about various symbolic
processes seemed overly abstract and difficult to study by objective means. Jung's studies using the free-association method,
however, appeared a promising tool that could make the motivational determinants of individual behavior accessible to analysis.
By elaborating the basic free-association technique, Luria hoped
to create an experimental science of individual mental life, a
science that would be both idiographic and nomothetic.

These early speculations about the future direction of psychology were never published, although Luria prepared a manuscript
on the subject, when he was 19 years old, that he kept throughout
his career. They did, however, guide his early clinical and experimental work. He spent time at Kazan's psychiatric hospital,
where, using Jung's free-association method, he interviewed patients. Accepting a position in a laboratory devoted to increasing the efficiency of industrial workers, he carried out studies
of the effect of fatigue on mental activity. It was in the course
of this work that he developed the first, rudimentary techniques
for combining experimental procedures with the free-association technique; he used an old Hipp chronoscope to measure the
reaction time of workers, at different levels of fatigue, who were

asked to associate to various verbal stimuli.

This very early activity would be of little interest if it were not so clearly and generally reflected in Luria's later work; but as the articles collected here attest, the basic techniques Luria developed while still a student were retained and applied through all the many phases of his career.

1923 was a turning point for Soviet psychology, a turning point that affected Luria almost immediately. Until that year, academic psychology remained relatively unaffected by the October Revolution. The leading Russian psychologist was G. I. Chelpanov, who had been the director of the Institute of Psychology in Moscow since its founding in 1911. Chelpanov was a psychologist in the tradition of Wundt and Titchener, a "brass instrument" psychologist for whom introspection under highly controlled conditions provided the essential data of psychology. His institute pursued pretty much of the same issues, by the same techniques, as those pursued in many laboratories in Germany and the United States.

By 1923 this approach to psychology was under attack for a number of reasons, many of which were similar to the reasons used in arguments against similar approaches to psychology in the United States. Introspectionist psychology was criticized for its methodological shortcomings; different laboratories could not agree on basic elements produced by trained introspectors. Arguments about the existence or nonexistence of imageless thought and "determining tendencies" had produced sufficient theoretical chaos to make many psychologists receptive to Watson's call for a psychology of behavior that eschewed the concept of conscious experience altogether. There was also widespread dissatisfaction with the very narrow limits of introspective psychology; it could not include the study of small children, of mental patients, or of people engaged in productive activity. To these complaints Soviet critics added the charge that introspective psychology was neither materialist nor Marxist.

The issue of the proper framework for Soviet psychology, especially for its titular leader, Chelpanov, came to a head at the First Psychoneurological Congress, held in Leningrad in 1923.

Chelpanov tried to defend the activities of his institute. He even admitted a role to Marxism as a set of ideas applicable to the social organization of human activity. His defense failed, and he was removed from his post and replaced by K. N. Kornilov, a former schoolteacher from Siberia, who had been on the staff of Chelpanov's institute for several years.

Kornilov was an advocate of a kind of objective psychology that was similar in many respects to Watson's behaviorism, although he did not reject discussion of mental states in the same, thoroughgoing way as Watson. Kornilov called his approach "reactology," which he took to mean the study of mental effort as reflected in peripheral motor activity. He "measured" mental effort by studying the reaction time and strength of simple motor responses, assuming that the more strength spent on the motor component of a response, the less remaining for the "mental" component. Confirmation of this generalization was seen in the fact that the strength of simple reactions was greater than the strength of complex reactions. Kornilov pointed to his method as manifestly a materialist interpretation of mind; and with this achievement as a rallying point, he was able to gather a group of young scholars to undertake the reconstruction of psychology along materialist and, he asserted, Marxist lines. One of those invited to the institute in Moscow was A. R. Luria, whose research on worker fatigue using reaction-time methods made him a pioneer reactologist in Kornilov's eyes.

The essay in the first section of this collection dates from this very early period in the history of Soviet psychology (and Luria's scientific career), when the proper subject matter and theoretical stance of psychology in the USSR were very much a subject of debate. Only a very few propositions were generally accepted: Psychology should be an objective science, based wherever feasible on experimental methods; it should be consistent with the principles of Marxist dialectical materialism.

Agreeing on these principles and implementing them turned out to be two very distinct tasks. It was not clear what ideas and techniques from previous psychological research could be retained. Neither was it clear what Marxist writing implied for psychology (a problem that existed for many branches of Soviet science, and was to be the source of repeated disputes over the years). In this atmosphere of uncertainty and change, a wide variety of scientific programs were offered, among them Luria's suggestion that psychoanalysis be used as a model upon which to build a materialist, Marxist psychology. Although this suggestion did not prevail, the terms in which Luria made it are clearly prophetic of both his own later work and those influential movements in psychology that attempted to incorporate psychoanalytic notions of motivation into experimental psychology.

The publication in which "Psychoanalysis as a system of monistic psychology" appeared, Psychology and Marxism, contained papers from the Second Psychoneurological Congress. Kornilov, who wrote the lead essay, was its editor. This volume contained contributions from several branches of psychology, all of them offering programs of research for a reconstructed Soviet psychology. Most interesting from the vantage point of history was an essay by a former schoolteacher, Lev Semyonovitch Vygotsky, who had begun to do research on problems of education, especially education of the handicapped and retarded. On the basis of his presentation, which treated consciousness as the internalized modes of behavior from one's social environment, Vygotsky was invited to join the staff of Kornilov's institute. This event became the central organizing point of the remainder of Luria's scientific career.

Although Vygotsky became a major figure in Luria's life almost from the outset of their acquaintance, his influence on Luria's research and writing came about more slowly. There were reasons for a gradual, rather than an abrupt, change in the course of research. As the initial essay in this volume suggests, Luria had already evolved a rationale for research, which was operative when he met Vygotsky at the beginning of 1924. The extent of the research completed by Luria and his colleagues in the early 1920s is difficult to judge, because there were few journal outlets for Soviet psychologists (Luria enjoyed telling how he got the paper for printing research carried out in Kazan from a soap factory); but Luria's (1932) monograph The nature

of human conflicts contains several studies that appear to have
been carried out in 1923 and 1924. (That monograph is worth
reading both for the intrinsic interest of the research it reports
and for fascinating glimpses into the history of Luria's career
and Soviet psychology.) The early chapters explain "the combined motor method," in which the subject had to carry out a
simple movement in response to verbal stimuli while reaction
time and the dynamics of the movement were being recorded.
Using this technique, Luria (assisted by Alexei N. Leont'ev, his
lifelong colleague and current Dean of the Psychology Faculty
at Moscow University) studied the influence of motives on the
organization of voluntary motor activity. This academic research was carried out in such real-life settings as a purge of
Moscow University (where students with inadequate academic
records or "undesirable" family backgrounds were appearing
before a board of examiners). It not only was relevant to an experimental psychoanalysis (an idea Luria was no longer pursu-
ing when the book was written in 1930) but had promising potential for application, which Luria pursued in the criminal justice
system, where he developed the combined-motor method into the
prototype of the modern lie detector. The very popularity of the
research seems to have extended his participation in it.

It is important to keep in mind that when Vygotsky appeared
on the scene he was still a very young man, a 26-year-old who
had been a philologist until a very few years earlier, when his
attention was drawn to problems of psychology. By no means
was the sociohistorical school of psychology he pioneered a finished product. It was no more than a schema, a point of view
that had to be fleshed out in theory and experimental practice.
In the years between 1924 and 1934 (when Vygotsky died of tuber-
culosis) the "troika" of Vygotsky, Leont'ev, and Luria began to
carry out its reconstruction of psychology from first principles.
It was a slow task, and Luria was not a man to put all else
aside while waiting for new ideas to ripen when he had not finished harvesting the fruits of his previous labor. Instead, he
seems to have applied his prodigous energy to both tasks simultaneously: he continued to extend his original methods to new

problems while slowly changing their content and contexts to incorporate the ideas that were growing out of the continuous interactions with Vygotsky.

It is within this context that the essays in the second section
of this book should be read. Progressively, as the years pass,
we can see the central ideas of the sociocultural approach coming to dominate Luria's research.

The first essay in this section reports one of several large
research projects using the free-association technique to determine how a child's social environment affects the form and content of his/her linguistic and cognitive processes. In this use
of the free-association technique, Luria is applying his notion
that Jung's method for studying the dynamics of individual behavior can also reveal social determinants of mental life. But
the theoretical rationale for this work no longer retains any
references to Jung (in part, most likely, because Luria was severely criticized for his earlier advocacy of psychoanalytic
ideas). Instead, we see the prototype of ideas that were to be
made famous by Vygotsky in his book Thought and language,
first published in 1934: language is the product of sociohistorical circumstances and the forms of interaction between child
and adult; it is a vital tool of thought and is susceptible to specific influences, which differ in their cognitive impact depending on the social context in which they are imbedded.

Perhaps because these ideas have remained very much alive
in our own psychological tradition, the research Luria reported
retains considerable relevance. His insistence that the street
urchin is not generally more backward, but certainly less educated, than children raised in normal families is as contemporary as any current journal article discussing the education of
"culturally different" children ("He is not more backward than
the schoolchild ... He is just different. ...."). His demonstration
that a given child will be at different "stages of development"
with respect to familiar and abstract (school-based) words and
that schooling "levels" different cultural experiences is an extremely important finding that seems to have been lost by the
time cross-cultural research came into vogue in the 1960s.

The next two articles in this section review research on intellectual development in children as it was then being carried out
in the Soviet Union, Western Europe, and America. It was characteristic of both Luria and Vygotsky that they attempted to
place their research within the general circle of contemporary
scientific ideas influencing psychology. In order to be maximally persuasive, they sought to demonstrate both the correctness
of their own approach and the points where it made contact with
(and then diverged from) the ideas of their contemporaries.

These articles show, even more clearly than previously translated works, Luria's early and pervasive interest in the development of behavior. They show, too, the strong influence of
Piaget, Werner, Karl and Charlotte Bühler, and William Stern,
both as positive contributors to an eventual psychology of higher
psychological functions and as foils against which Luria, Vygotsky, and their colleagues pitted their own theories.

Of special interest in terms of current research is Luria's
report on the development of writing, a topic that has emerged
in the mid-1970s as a major area of concern in educational research and practice. His study of written language represents
a rejection of notions (such as De Saussure's) that writing is
simply language written down or the contention of the Prague
linguistic circle that writing is merely the graphic representation of language elements that are reacted to in a static way for
purposes that are almost entirely restricted to language's communicative function. Rather, he subsumes language under the
general category of a mediated psychological activity whose
specifics are determined by the activities that implement the
purposes of writing in the first place. Thus, instead of beginning with a study of writing as a way of representing language,
Luria traces the "prehistory" of writing back to primitive mnemonic activities whose purpose is the representation of past
events in the present. This approach to writing (see also Vygotsky's article "The prehistory of written languages," in Vygotsky,
1978) suggests interesting ways to introduce writing into young
children's school activities and serves the more general purpose
of motivating studies of the relation between writing and talking

in the course of human development.

The next essay in this second section is a description of one of a series of studies Luria and his colleagues carried out with identical and fraternal twins during the mid-1930s. Very little of this work was published in either Russian or English. In 1935 and 1936 a few articles were published in the Works of the Medical-Genetic Institute (the institution in which the work was carried out); and one article, on the comparative development of elementary and complex mental functions in twins, was published in the now-defunct American journal Character and Personality (Luria, 1937). With the exception of the current contribution, it was not until the late 1950s that more accessible accounts of this work appeared in Russian; and when they did, the study of twins as a means of differentiating biologically and culturally determined psychological processes (which was the impetus for the work) had disappeared entirely. In keeping with this de-emphasis on the significance of twins in cognitive research, no mention is made in the title of the article of the fact that the subjects in Luria's studies of constructive play were identical twins. Selecting them for study is justified only on the grounds that their identical heredity and similar home environments make it easier to discern the effects of planned environmental (educational) intervention.

This discussion of constructive play is an excellent example of the way in which Luria linked basic, theoretically oriented research with problems of broad social concern. The article appeared in a publication devoted to educational applications of research, and Luria places the problem squarely in the context of conflicting programs of pedagogy. But the intervention experiment he describes is firmly rooted in the sociohistorical theory of mental development. This is evident in his discussion of the conceptual underpinnings of the different approaches to organizing preschool curriculum units devoted to constructive activities. In his rejection of the highly structured approach attributed to Montessori and her followers or resort to totally unguided free construction, we see reflected Vygotsky's insistence on a distinction between elementary functions, involuntari-

ly applied, and higher functions that incorporate planning elements in a deliberate manner. It is the task of the educator to
create an environment to move the child from the spontaneous
application of elementary skills to the deliberate application of
higher, analytic skills. The test of the effectiveness of such a
program of instruction is more than the satisfactory completion
of the instructional task itself. If the educational program is
really successful, it will result in qualitative changes in the
structure of the child's activity in a variety of seemingly remote
tasks that, theory dictates, bear a specific analogy to the instructional tasks. The latter part of the paper, which assesses
the children's ability to handle a variety of perceptual and clas-
sificatory tasks, represents the more general test of the conse-
quences of differential tuition in the block-building task, and a
test of the basic theory as well.

The final article in section two is the only selection in this
volume not written by Luria. Rather, it represents one of the
seminal pieces of research in his well-known program of experiments on the role of speech in the development of mental
processes, which was initiated in the late 1940s and carried into
the late 1950s. The contribution here is by Oleg K. Tikhomirov,
a student of Luria's who is currently on the faculty of Moscow
University.

The reader will quickly discern that the data base and theoretical terminology in this article represent a sharp departure
from the earlier contributions in this section of the volume. The
data consist of kymographic recordings of the simple motor responses of very young children, along with their elementary verbal responses to instructions by adults. The language is largely
Pavlovian, providing a description of the children's behavior in
terms of interactions between hypothetical inhibitory and excitatory processes taking place in the nervous systems of individual subjects. But the true conceptual discontinuity with the earlier articles is not so great as these differences suggest. Instead we see a highly skilled and imaginative effort on Luria's
part to mold the style of his research to the social/political
realities within which he worked.

Already in the article on constructive play we see changes in
style of exposition in comparison with earlier selections: there
are fewer explicit references to foreign authors, almost all of
which are polemical, and a general down-playing of the links between this work and efforts to develop the sociohistorical approach to higher psychological functions. Indeed, the central
role of Vygotsky in providing the conceptual foundations of this
later work is by no means clear. These changes reflect the fact
that the adherents of the sociohistorical school, Luria and Vygotsky in particular, had been severely criticized in the early
and mid-1930s. These criticisms arose from at least two
sources: unhappiness with careless application of standardized
ability tests (which Vygotsky and Luria strongly disapproved of,
but which they were accused of fostering via Vygotsky's association with the Institute of Pedology), and disagreement about the
significance of observations that Luria had made in Central Asia
concerning the intellectual changes wrought by the introduction of
literacy and collectivization (see Luria, 1976). Between 1934 and
1956, Vygotsky's writings were generally unavailable in the USSR.

During the first decade of this period, there was a general
hiatus in psychological publications, owing both to the official
disfavor into which psychology in general, and the sociohistorical approach in particular, had fallen and to the crisis of World
War II, during which psychologists contributed their skills to the
war effort.

In the late 1940s psychology again came under attack, but this
time in a way that involved the direct and active intervention of
the Central Committee of the Communist Party and its chairman,
Joseph Stalin. This is not the place to review the reasons for
Stalin's interest in psychology or its overall impact on the science (see, for example, Graham, 1972, or Tucker, 1963). It suf-
fices to say that Stalin strongly favored adoption of Pavlovian
psychophysiology as a model upon which all of psychology should
be built. All other approaches were considered erroneous, and
their adherents were put under tremendous pressure to renounce
their previous activities and join in the reconstruction of psychology along Pavlovian lines.

Luria was not exempted from this general requirement, all the more so since he had been associated with a school of psychology that had come under special scrutiny in the past. From approximately 1937 through 1947 he left the study of cognitive development and embarked on a career as a neurologist (the fruits of this work are surveyed in the third section of this book). About 1948, however, he was told to leave the Institute of Neurosurgery, where he had been working for several years, and was assigned to the Institute of Defectology, an institution that had been founded by Vygotsky about twenty years earlier. There he turned once again to the problems that had occupied him earlier in his career, but it was not possible to approach them in the style he had come to adopt in the 1930s.

What Luria fashioned was an experimental approach that has its closest parallel in studies contained in The nature of human conflicts, but with a conceptual structure that grew directly out of the basic principles of the sociohistorical school and a language that was thoroughly Pavlovian. Thus, the basic method is the combined-motor method, but with a very careful concentration on the way the verbal and motor components of a child's response enter into complex functional systems to enable the child to meet the requirements of the task. Critical here is the issue of whether speech comes to precede and guide the motor response (which is possible only when its excitatory and inhibitory components are well integrated) or whether it only accompanies action. This issue has its direct parallel in the studies of writing, carried out 20 years earlier, in which it was important to discern when the child's writing came to precede and guide his activity instead of following or accompanying it.

It is somewhat ironic that this work, which in some respects camouflaged Luria's main lines of concern, generated enormous interest in his work among American psychologists. One cannot be certain, but I suspect that the Pavlovian framework Luria used to describe and motivate this work, especially the promise that reflex theories could be extended to the study of language (Pavlov's "second-signal system") were the cause of the work's popularity in the United States. The late 1950s and early 1960s were the high watermark of neobehaviorist theorizing about language, and many psychologists found an obvious parallel between Luria's view that language responses come to mediate motor responses and various lines of mediational stimulus-response theories that had been elaborated here on the conditioning models of Hull, Spence, and Skinner. This was also the period when experiential studies of children's intellectual development within a learning-theory tradition were just beginning to come into vogue, and Luria's ideas about the role of speech in this process were exceedingly congenial.

But as events turned out, no sooner did American and English psychologists "discover" Luria than he reverted to the line of work that forms section three of this book and that occupied most of his working career between 1937 and his death in 1977 — the study of the brain's organization of higher psychological functions. During the last decade and a half of his life he published several books summarizing his work on this topic, a body of learning he liked to call neuropsychology.

Although Luria did not complete his medical training and start to specialize in neurology until 1937-38, involvement in medicine began when he was an undergraduate in Kazan. Luria's father, who became a prominent physician following the revolution, had wanted his son to be a doctor from the outset, and was not particularly happy when Luria failed to complete his medical training before moving to Moscow. Luria did begin his medical training in Kazan, and he retained an active interest in the analytic potential of pathological cases for illuminating general psychological functions. He completed his medical degree in 1937. But except for limited studies conducted in the late 1920s to test certain implications of Vygotsky's theories, he undertook little systematic research in clinical neuropsychology until after the outbreak of the war.

So many volumes of Luria's research in neuropsychology have appeared in English during recent years that systematic coverage in a book such as this would be impossible. The selections we have chosen give the flavor, but neither the breadth nor depth, of his effort to use experimental/clinical neuropsychology as a basic tool of psychological analysis.

The first article in the third section of the book begins, very fittingly, with an overview of Vygotsky's theory and its implications for the study of brain-behavior relations. This article certainly deserves study by anyone interested in Luria's approach to neuropsychology (and, I would argue, anyone interested in the study of human cognition) because it lays out in capsule form his general enterprise, of which neuropsychology was only one aspect. It is, in fact, as fitting a summary of the second section, on cognitive development, as it is an introduction to the third section, on neuropsychology.

This suggestion is completely consistent with Vygotsky's view that "localization of higher nervous functions can be understood only chronologically, as the result of mental development." American colleagues have often bridled at Luria's characterization of their neuropsychology as "atheoretical." They correctly point to the theories of brain function that guide their work and their meticulous attempts to establish the reliability and validity of their tests. Unfortunately, Luria and his Western counterparts never really understood each other on this point. Luria's summary of Vygotsky's views (which he had a large role in shaping) makes it clear that his idea of theory is an enterprise infinitely more ambitious than all those undertaken by any but a handful of psychologists from other countries. He often said that in order to have a theory of brain-behavior relations, it is necessary to have a theory of both the brain and behavior. As the remaining articles in this section indicate, Luria, like his colleagues, concerned himself with the minutiae of experimental detail. What the introductory article on Vygotsky makes clear is that all of the detail work was done in a ceaseless effort to carry out a bold program conceived in the enthusiasm of youth, his own and his government's.

References

Graham, L. R. Science and philosophy in the Soviet Union. New York: Knopf, 1972.

Luria, A. R. The nature of human conflicts. New York:
    Liveright, 1932.
Luria, A. R. The development of mental functions in twins.
    Character and personality, 1936-37, 5, 35-47.
Luria, A. R. Cognitive development. Cambridge, Mass.:
    Harvard University Press, 1976.
Tucker, R. C. The Soviet political mind. New York:
    Praeger, 1963.
Vygotsky, L. S. Thought and language. Cambridge, Mass.:
    MIT Press, 1967.
Vygotsky, L. S. Mind in Society (M. Cole, V. John-Steiner,
    S. Scribner, & E. Souberman [Eds.]). Cambridge, Mass.:
    Harvard University Press, 1978.

                                             Michael Cole

PART ONE

Early Beginnings

A. R. Luria

PSYCHOANALYSIS AS A SYSTEM
OF MONISTIC PSYCHOLOGY

I

Every major scientific achievement, regardless of the science in which it occurs, always introduces a number of new methodological principles that also become binding for any other, related domain of inquiry.

After Comte's work in positive philosophy, uncritical application of metaphysical principles in scientific investigation became impossible. The dynamic principle presented in the works of Darwin, replacing the earlier, static view that the various species had an unchanging, self-contained existence, subsequently became binding on all biological sciences.

Even major achievements concerning narrower problems have had an influence on the evolution of the set of principles that we may call the leading methodology and that are binding

From K. P. Kornilov (Ed.) Psikhologiya i Marksizm [Psychology and Marxism]. Leningrad: Gosizdat, 1925. Pp. 47-80.

This paper also constitutes the first chapter of a book entitled [Principles of psychoanalysis and modern materialism]. [Editor's note: This book was never written.]

Russian editor's note: The question of the relationship of some aspects of Freud's theory to Marxism has been, and remains, a much disputed one. This paper ... considers the meeting points of the two systems.

3

in equal measure on all sciences of the epoch. Pavlov's work
on conditioned reflexes, the latest studies of endocrine activity,
Einstein's theories based on his analysis of the speed of light
— all these achievements share the basic methodological postulates of the period. Marxism, which aside from being a
revolutionary doctrine is a tremendous scientific achievement
in its own right, has been especially valuable for its methodology, which first entered science under the term dialectical
materialism, and may now be considered as absolutely binding on many related fields of knowledge. We believe, therefore, that the methodology of dialectical materialism may
be demanded not only of economics and the social sciences
but of the biosocial (and this includes psychology) and biological sciences as well. Dialectical materialism rests on
two major premises, forming one strong fundament and coming together in a resolute determination to study objectively,
with a sharp line drawn between the imaginary and the real,
the true relationships among perceivable events; and this
means to study them not abstractly, but just as they are in
reality, to study them in such a way that the knowledge we
acquire will help us later to exert an active influence on them.

This last practical touch has had an extremely salubrious
effect on all of Marxist philosophy and has helped it formulate
two postulates that today are fundamental and applicable to all
positive sciences. The first of these is materialist monism,
which constitutes the basis for any approach to the phenomena
of nature and society.

Marxism regards as absolutely false the distinction, cultivated by idealistic philosophy, between two fundamentally
unique classes of phenomena having different origins, such as,
for example, mind and matter, substance and spirit, etc. For
Marxism the only possible point of view is that the world is
one, that it is a single system of material processes, and that
the mental life of human beings is only one of its many aspects;
for Marxism, the human mind is a product of the activity of the
brain and, in the final analysis, of the effects of the social environment and the class relations and conditions of production

underlying it on the brain and on each individual human being. Any attempt to isolate "thought" or "mind" as some discrete class of phenomena Marxism regards as an unscientific and patently idealistic approach to things. Marx and, especially, Engels, and after them many of their followers, clearly stated the necessity of this monistic approach to the study of any problem. The monistic approach was especially prominent in the attitude of Marx and Engels toward the mind, which they saw as a property of organized matter, rooted in the activity of the human body and in the influence of the social conditions of production on it. With this, the problem of mind immediately shifts from the realm of philosophical speculations about the "reality of consciousness," etc. (there is nothing more alien to Marxism than such blatantly metaphysical, absolute philosophizing), to the level of a monistic elucidation of mental phenomena and the reduction of the mind to a set of more elementary and fundamental material processes.

We might sum up this first postulate of Marxist methodology as the requirement to examine the things and events of the world objectively and not to refer to "man" as the ultimate cause of phenomena (cognition, social phenomena, etc.), as did the thinkers of the 18th and 19th centuries, but to explain man himself in terms of the phenomena of the world outside him, his external, material conditions of existence.

The second basic premise of the materialist method is that phenomena must be approached dialectically. Here, Marxism draws a sharp distinction between itself and metaphysical materialism in that it looks on material conditions as something constantly changing, ceaselessly in movement, although this movement sometimes experiences leaps, breaks, discontinuities, as it were, and most often unfolds in a series of shifts or swings from one extreme to the other rather than proceeding uninterruptedly in one continuous direction.

This is where Marxism introduces its dynamic view of things and events as a necessary principle and draws a

firm line between itself and a static, metaphysical view of
things that tends to see phenomena as discrete, isolated,
unchanging essences, not as processes. Metaphysical reasoning was absolute and static and seriously impeded the
development of a positive scientific approach to knowledge
of phenomena, creating a system of philosophical abstrac-
tions instead of a system of positive scientific concepts.

Thus, in studying integral, concrete, vital processes, science should take into account all the conditions and factors
acting on the thing or phenomenon on which it has focused its
attention and, instead of looking for absolute and eternal truths,
should proceed from the principles of objectivity and dialectical materialism. These basic postulates have been elaborated
in Marxism into a number of more specific methodological requirements.

Since the material environment acting on man is in most
cases predetermined by the conditions and relations of production, any science that studies man must take into consideration these external material factors, which set the conditions
for mental activity, i.e., such a science must have one foot in
biology and the other in sociology. Hence, any science of man
cannot be a metaphysical science of man in general, but must
be a positive science of man as a social or, more precisely, a
class being. Only such a perspective will ensure that scientific
results are correct and objective.

On the other hand — and this is the epistemological principle of Marxism — if the mental apparatus that creates a system is influenced by social and class factors, then any thought
must contain some mixture of subjectivity, consciously or unconsciously giving a class or socio-economic coloring to the
system it has created. Therein lies the reason for the Marxist doctrine that complex sociopsychological phenomena must
not be taken as givens: they must not be "believed literally,"
but explained in terms of other, more elementary principles;
and the social and class factors that underlie them must be
brought to light.

We call this principle the analytical principle (1); it acquired its importance in the analysis of "ideological superstructures" and is a powerful weapon in the struggle for a real and objective knowledge of things, untainted by "personal distortions," i.e., knowledge of things as they really are.

In these respects the Marxist system is profoundly and fundamentally different from other metaphysical and naïve empirical philosophical systems and, in contrast to the naïve empirical method of idealistic philosophy, may be wholly described as a system of scientific analytical methodology.

Every modern science, in our opinion, should conform to this basic premise of Marxist method. This, of course, includes psychology; and if psychology has, in fact, not always measured up to this requirement, it is only because it has been more closely allied to the principles of idealistic philosophy than to the fundamental tenets of a scientific, materialistic outlook. It is just these shortcomings that psychoanalysis strives to overcome.

II

In one sense, psychoanalysis is a reaction to the old empirical psychology (2), just as the latter, in its time, was born of the reaction to rationalist psychology.

Psychoanalysis may also, however, be regarded as a protest against the shortcomings and errors of a narrow, empirical psychology and an attempt to avoid its mistakes.

From either standpoint, psychoanalysis draws a sharp line between itself and aspects of the dominant psychology, which a dialectical materialist method should also particularly oppose.

Operating mainly with the introspective method, complicated only by empirical controls, classic, "general" psychology was perforce limited to study of the "phenomena of consciousness" or, more precisely, the "phenomena of one's own consciousness"; this, of course, turned it into a science that was subjective and naïvely empirical, as opposed to a purely empirical science.

The concern of this psychology was to study in a more pre-

cise manner those conscious processes the investigator was
able to note in himself through attentive observation of the
phenomena of "subjective experiences," "thinking," etc., taking
place within him. All sorts of experimental conditions were
contrived to make it easier to observe these processes; the
real nature of these "experiments" was brilliantly exposed by
the Wurzburg school, which showed that in the introspective
method, these conditions played only a subsidiary role.

Because of this naïve, empirical approach to mental life,
empirical psychology was forced to repudiate any scientific
materialist foundation of mental phenomena (in empirical psychology this aspect was usually limited to comments added in
passing about "body" and "soul," which are obviously idealistic
concepts). It was forced to limit its field of inquiry to the, from
a scientific viewpoint, patently pernicious sphere of subjective
phenomena, i.e., the indications or statements made by subjects concerning the processes they observed taking place in
themselves, and to take them at their word without making any
adjustments for the "subjective factor" (3), only occasionally
correcting experience with essentially naïve physiological
studies (e.g., a study of respiration and pulse accompanying
consciously evoked emotions). At the same time, the richest
domain of unconscious mental processes, which underlay the
"bare facts" to which naïve empirical scrutiny had access, remained a closed book to the investigations of classic psychology.

Because of these flaws in its basic methods, psychology remained predominantly a descriptive science, concerned with
describing and classifying the phenomena of consciousness and
hardly daring to venture to explain them or analyze the conditions under which they occurred.

These conditions, which in part ordinarily lie hidden in the
lower, unconscious reaches of mental life and in part are to be
sought in external conditions, had perforce to remain beyond
the scrutiny of general psychology.

All these features defined the clearly idealistic and naïvely
empirical nature of the old psychology. (4)

The naïve empirical data obtained in its contrived experiments were responsible for a second fundamental flaw in the classic empirical psychology.

Since it was unable to undertake a scientific explanation of mental phenomena, experimental psychology took another route: it broke down its findings into discrete, minute elements, "atomic facts," as it were, and studied each of these hypothetical elements of the mind separately. (5)

The tendency to construct mind out of such isolated, static elements is by no means a new phenomenon (6); indeed, it is particularly characteristic of that kind of thinking Engels [in Anti-Dühring], called metaphysical, and is fundamentally at variance with a dynamic, vital, dialectic concept of things.

But this was the metaphysical error to which psychology fell prey when it drew such a rigid distinction between "reason," "senses," and "will" or distinguished sensations and feelings as the most rudimentary elements of mental life, or, finally, when it concentrated on the study of the elementary processes of sensation, perception, memory, attention, ideas, etc., in isolation.

All these elements, viewed as discrete, static phenomena, are, of course, not real-life processes. Even though their study in isolation may, in its time, have been useful to psychology, it has now unquestionably become a hindrance to its further development, and we may with justification call this "subject matter of psychology," which psychologists themselves admit to be a product of abstraction, metaphysical fictions, and the system that studies them, a metaphysical system to the core.

Of course, a system of psychology built in this way was not even able to begin the study of something such as an integral psychoneural process, the real basis of human activity, characterizing man's behavior, motives, responses, etc. The old psychology, which rested on principles such as those enumerated above, had long since given up studying the whole man, to say nothing of man as a creature shaped by the specific conditions of his socio-economic and, above all, his class situation. Even the most recent works of general psychology, often reviving the old traditions of "faculty psychology," have not been able to

create a system that would help elucidate the complex structure
of the human personality, let alone influence it.

It should be clear from the above discussion that the main
principles on which classic psychology was based cannot meet
the methodological requirements laid down by the positive scientific thought of the present period; and, of course, they do
not at all meet the prerequisites of the dialectical materialist
method.

Moreover, almost the whole of modern psychology may, as
far as its basic premises are concerned, be characterized as
a system of metaphysical idealism built on the basis of naïve,
empirical investigations.

Of course, such a state of affairs precludes from the outset
any possibility of a sociobiological explanation of mental phenomena, and it does not allow for influencing the mind in any
organized or systematic way. The question then arises whether
psychology may not stand in need of a radical reworking in
terms of the scientific method of dialectical materialism. We
thus come to the problem of the relationship between the psychology and philosophy of Marxism and psychoanalysis.

III

In establishing its concepts, psychoanalysis proceeds from a
number of fundamental postulates that are often entirely different
from those of general experimental psychology mentioned above.

Instead of studying discrete, isolated "elements" of mental
life, psychoanalysis attempts to study the whole personality,
the whole individual, his behavior, inner workings, and motive
forces (7); instead of describing individual subjective experiences, it endeavors to explain the different manifestations of
the individual personality in terms of more basic, more primary
conditions of the person's existence and environment; instead
of a covertly dualistic approach to mental life, which often falls
into idealism, it proposes a monistic, dynamic (8) approach to
the personality; instead of studying "things" in isolation, it
would study continuous processes that reflect the organic conti-

nuity between the life of the child and the mind of the adult human being; instead of "extrasocial" man in general, studied in abstraction from the social conditions forming him, psychoanalysis endeavors to link many of the deepest-lying workings of the human mind to the influences of social groups; and finally, instead of naïve, empiricist satisfaction with a description of the phenomena of consciousness "as they are given to us," it starts out with the principle that the internal, hidden factors determining phenomena must be studied analytically "not as they are given to us," but as they become accessible to us through methods of objective analysis.

Proceeding from these principles, psychoanalysis constructed its system of psychology; and this system is, in our view, incomparably more in line with the methodological requirements of positive science, which dialectical materialism has formulated in their clearest form.

Let us take a look at the foundations of psychoanalysis from the viewpoint just described to determine where its method coincides with the method of Marxism.

In their reaction to atomizing, experimental psychology, applied psychology, and psychoanalysis (9) have come forward with the resolve to study the whole human personality, and in this respect are following in the footsteps of Marxism, which had expressed the same intention earlier.

True, in its early stages Marxism did not have a finished, pure, psychological theory of the personality; its interests lay elsewhere, mainly in the problems of society and the development of the various forms of society. The problem of the personality, the motive forces underlying individual behavior, and the interests impelling people to create ideological systems for themselves were all questions with which the founders of Marxism were intimately concerned, perhaps because of their tremendous practical importance. One need only throw a cursory glance at the major works in Marxist philosophy to see how interested Marx and Engels were in these topics. (10)

We need only look a bit more closely at the premises of the Marxist approach to personality to see that with respect to problems of the mind, this approach really does postulate an integral, concrete person as its subject matter, not isolated functions of the mind, as had been the practice in general psychology.

Marxism sees the individual as an inseparable element of and an active force in history. It is interested in such questions as the motive forces of the personality or the individual, of the individual's needs and drives, and how the real conditions of social and economic life, so inseparably linked with the personality, are reflected in the individual's behavior or, as we would say, elicit the appropriate responses from the organism (11); and it is interested in discovering the laws governing individual behavior, i.e., in uncovering them objectively and scientifically, and in knowing the individual personality not as it sees itself, but "as it is in fact."

To this integral, monistic approach to the personality Marxism owes another of its tendencies, an extremely important one: having nothing much in common with pure, speculative philosophizing, in its constructs Marxism starts with the problems of practical life (and in this respect is fundamentally different from all metaphysical philosophy). Its purpose is to study the world so as to be able to change it; and this activist, practical orientation runs like a lifeline throughout its system.

This standpoint of practical activism especially requires that man be studied as an integral biosocial organism, so as to be able to exert a molding influence on him; in this respect there is nothing more alien to the spirit of Marxism than an approach directed toward the study of the isolated "phenomena" of man's mental life rather than toward real, historical man. Finally, this standpoint ascribes central importance to questions about the motives of human behavior, the way biological and social forces act on the individual and his responses to them.

All these demands Marxism places on modern psychology may be summed up in one general requirement, namely, that instead of high-flown speculations about the essence of mind and its relationship to body, a monistic approach be employed in the study not of "mind in general," but of the concrete psychoneural activity of the social individual as manifested in his behavior.

This is what we mean by a monistic approach to the study of mental phenomena. Though it proceeds from the premise that mental phenomena are ultimately reducible to complicated material phenomena, dialectical materialism cannot on that account demand a materialist formulation for any mental process. Being dialectical it can make only one demand: that the workings of the brain, the means by which the environment exerts its influence, and outward behavioral manifestations be studied simultaneously. This, indeed, is the only way that psychology can, instead of taking the philosophical and metaphysical road toward constructing a monistic theory of personality, set out along the promising path of science toward mastering this problem, namely, by linking the specific motive forces of the organism and its behavior with processes taking place in the nervous system and the body's organs, and by ascertaining the role of these organs in psychoneural activity.

Perhaps there should be a return of sorts to the ideas of Feuerbach and, before him, to the French materialists of the 18th century, who started out by studying the whole, feeling human being (i.e., a being knowing objectively through the senses) and discarded any concept of a "soul" that existed apart from the objective processes taking place in the individual.

The philosophy and psychology of Feuerbach and the materialists (the "anthropologists") were, of course, immeasurably nearer to Marxism than the concepts of psychologists of the subjective, empiricist, and experimental schools. (12)

*   *   *

In contrast to scholastic, atomizing psychology, psychoanalysis starts out with the problems of the whole person; it proposes to study the person as a whole, and the processes and mechanisms that shape behavior. (13) It perhaps owes these principles to the fact that its first point of reference was the ill personality, the person out of alignment with the social structure; and its paramount task, as it saw it, was the active treatment of this person. This practical, activist orientation is perhaps what led psychoanalysis to construct the system of cognitive, explanatory psychology we find in Freud's theory.

We may take this as a fundamental and primary postulate of psychoanalysis: psychoanalysis is primarily an organic psychology of the individual; its major objectives are: to trace the determining factors of all aspects of the concrete individual, living under definite sociocultural conditions, and to explain the more complex structures of that individual's personality in terms of more basic and more primary unconscious motive forces. (14) This individual personality, which psychoanalysis takes as its starting point, is not regarded by it — and this is especially important — as a purely psychological concept similar to the concept of "soul" and "person" in the old psychology. Despite the forced psychological terminology of psychoanalysis, which strikes the eye at first glance, it approaches the individual as an integral organism, in which the anatomical structure and the functions of the individual organs, the drives, and higher mental activity are all integrally interrelated. This is why in the psychoanalytic approach to the individual we often encounter discussions, sounding strange to the old psychology, about organ functions, zones of the body, etc., as factors having a direct, explanatory value for specific psychoneural processes. This concretely organic approach to psychology is especially characteristic of psychoanalysis.

Psychoanalysis is not much concerned with providing a theoretical elucidation of the "essence of the mental" or the "reality of mind." Suffice it to say that in the psychoanalytic literature one almost never comes across definitions of "the mind" and "the mental" such as those so characteristic of every philosophical psychology; the question of "the mind's reality," which is essentially a metaphysical, philosophical question, almost completely disappears from the picture in psychoanalysis (15), giving way to concrete study of processes and mechanisms within the individual himself.

The fact that psychoanalysis has systematically abstained from answering questions about the essence of the mind once more underscores its dialectical — we could even say practical — point of view.

The path it has chosen — instead of beginning with a complete, monadic formula and materialist explanation of the essence of mental phenomena, proceeding first to describe, and then to interpret, the behavior and reactions of the individual, drawing connections between these reactions and processes taking place in the organism and its component parts — is unquestionably scientifically valid and, in fact, the only one that can bear fruit.

We do, of course, encounter a number of difficulties when we attempt to come up with a clear-cut philosophical system based on psychoanalysis, for such a system is just what psychoanalysis is not. But we hope to show that in studying individual behavior, the unconscious drives underlying it and their connections with organic states, psychoanalysis is heading in the direction of a monistic theory of individual behavior.

Without interrupting the thread of our argument, we should like to touch briefly on some of the basic features of mental life as psychoanalytic theory conceives it, for the purpose of illustrating its fundamental monism.

The first (purely negative) feature we have already mentioned. Psychoanalysis denies the property of consciousness to the mind, and instead suggests that this property is inherent in only a small class of mental phenomena.

Facing the question of unconscious mental activity squarely, psychoanalysis discards the subjectivism inherent in any attempt to isolate the mind as a special sort of phenomena, distinct from physical phenomena. Unconscious mental activity becomes the entire focal point, whose symptoms are easier to ascertain objectively than to perceive in oneself by means of introspection, which places them on a level with other processes in the organism from which they are functionally, but not fundamentally, distinct (we should be more inclined to say that they differ from the latter in their relationship to social stimuli, which is sustained by a complex system of receptors and effectors, and in the way external influences from the environment shape them, rather than in any fundamental way). This is already a considerable step on the way toward constructing a system of monistic psychology.

Further, in its view of mental activity as an energy process not different in principle from somatic processes, psychoanalysis provides us with a purely monistic, developed conception of this energy, stipulating that it may quite easily assume psychic forms or patently somatic forms.

For the most part, the system of psychoanalysis is based on the premise that "psychic energy" is wholly subject to the laws governing any other form of energy; it cannot disappear, but it can be transformed into another kind, assume other forms, or be channeled in a different direction.

For example, a severe mental trauma a person has suffered but almost completely forgotten or a strong impulse a person has brought under control cannot disappear without a trace. If conditions prevent the free unfolding of such processes, they are replaced by others, which may just as well be mental processes as somatic processes. For instance, the energy linked to a mental trauma may be converted into somatic energy and show up in a number of somatic symptoms (this is especially apparent in the case of neurotic illnesses, particularly hysteria) such as functional disorders of the heart, the stomach, etc., all of which are based on disorders in innervation, or various "hysterical stigma," even to the point of signs of burns, wounds, and structural changes in organs.

These symptoms, which mark the conversion of energy from mental forms into purely somatic forms, are by no means a rarity in psychoanalytic practice; and some psychoanalytic writers, Groddeck, for example (16), have provided us with a number of descriptions of such phenomena.

These phenomena, which in psychoanalysis are referred to as conversions, are not, in principle, different from others in which particular drives are frustrated and disappear, as it were, from the mental sphere while their energy is transformed into another form of psychic manifestation, e.g., into fear. The conversion of one kind of mental energy into another or its conversion into a somatic process represents phenomena of basically the same order, demonstrating the essential organic unity between these two kinds of energy.

This is surely a tremendous step toward a monistic psychology; and what has been said (although it is not a definition of mental phenomena) is of much greater help for understanding mental phenomena and their relationships to somatic phenomena than the dualistic explanations about "soul" and body one finds in the old psychology.

Finally, one of the positive characteristics of the mind, its capacity to react to complex internal and external (social) stimuli and to give birth to complex reactive structures, will be discussed further on.

*   *   *

It goes without saying that in approaching the study of such a complex system as the whole person, psychoanalysis must first discriminate certain basic determining aspects of the individual's overall organization and begin by investigating them.

We will not be far from psychoanalysis's view of the individual if we say that it regards the individual personality as an organized whole that reacts to numerous internal and external stimuli and in its study places primary emphasis on these two groups of processes as basic to any description of the overall structure of the mind and as the key to an understanding of the whole person. (17)

Indeed, responses to such stimuli are a manifestation of the whole reacting person, reflect all its most important features, and provide us with a general idea of how the individual personality is structured.

Sherrington (18) and Loeb (19) discussed these kinds of reactions, calling them total reflexes and tropisms; the behaviorists and writers such as K. N. Kornilov (20) also had them in mind in discussing integral reactions involving the whole organism.

Thus, the problem of the individual personality is, on the whole, reduced to the question of the stimuli affecting the organism and, particularly, the organism's response to them.

As we have said, psychoanalysis endeavors to distinguish
between two types of such stimuli: external stimuli, coming
from the biological and social environment, and internal stimuli,
originating in physiological processes taking place in the body
and its various organs.

Stimuli of the former kind, preeminently social, exert a
shaping influence essentially on the entire mind; we shall come
back to them a little later. The constant stimuli of the second
kind, specifically, the way they are reflected in man's mental
apparatus, are described by psychoanalysis as drives.

But we should stress immediately that psychoanalysis does
not, in principle, make any distinction between the two (21), although its main concern is with the influence of internal stimuli,
drives, which have been very little studied, despite their fundamental importance.

Herein lies the core of the psychoanalytic system (22) and
the point at which it differs radically from classic scholastic
psychology.

Its concept of drive is rigorously monistic, as is its view of
the individual in general. Indeed, a drive is not a psychological
phenomenon in the strict sense, since it includes the effects of
somatic and nervous stimuli and of the endocrine system and
its chemistry, and often has no clear-cut psychological cast at
all. We should be more inclined to consider drive a concept at
the "borderline between the mental and the somatic" (Freud).
(23) The dualism of the old psychology is thus completely discarded. Whether or not the particular person is or can be conscious of drive is entirely of secondary importance, depending
on a number of minor details in the development of drive. Moreover, all the hypotheses about the relationship between soul and
body, their psychophysical parallelism or interaction (so necessary to the old psychology), are also left by the wayside. Psychoanalysis has shifted the problem to an entirely new plane —
a monistic approach to the mind. This approach is somewhat
reminiscent of a statement by LaPlace, who, after constructing
a system to explain the creation of the world on the basis of the
mutual attraction between the heavenly bodies, responded to his

patron's question about the place of God in his system with the observation, "Your Excellency, I am able to do without this hypothesis."

This approach has enabled psychoanalysis to reexamine the question of individual mental functions and to place them in their organic relationship to the individual as a biological being.

A few examples will show how psychoanalysis, from the very outset, began to depart from the doctrines of classic psychology.

In their very first investigations some psychoanalytic thinkers noted that the strict isolation of discrete acts and states as either purely active or purely passive was a flaw in classic psychology that rendered it incapable of understanding a number of phenomena.

For example, it was observed that even in such an ostensibly simple function as memory other functions of the mind also played a part, regulating the overall process of remembering, retention, and recall of accumulated experience.

It turns out that not everything is remembered, retained, and recollected with the same degree of facility; items (we should say stimuli) unrelated to a person's interests are not retained as vividly as others that clearly bear the marks of this personal interest.

Items that are patently opposed to the interests of the person are remembered with more difficulty and are erased from memory very swiftly (although they are still retained in the unconscious, as was discovered later) through the active intervention of personal interest, which acts as a kind of self-censor. This explains cases of repression or forgetting of names, actions, etc., that serve no purpose for the individual and would be difficult to explain otherwise. (24)

Thus, psychoanalysis arrived at a concept of drive that made it an active ingredient of all the mental manifestations of the individual, selecting from among the multitude of stimuli only those that are suited to it and in this way enabling the organism to adapt actively to the environment.

The controlling influence of drives shows up just as clearly in the act of attention, in which they effect an automatic selection that diverts the attention in the direction in which it may consciously absorb the stimuli most in accord with conscious or unconscious drives. (25) The controlling role of drives is especially apparent in associations; most studies have found that associations are steered by affect and that drives interfere with this process. (26) Finally, even processes that were especially dear to the old psychology, e.g., thought and its allied process of cognition, have proved to be largely determined by the direction of drives.

In the light of these observations, psychoanalysis took an initial step that bore substantial fruit for its subsequent development: it took sharp exception to the study of discrete mental phenomena in isolation and, once it discovered what all drives had in common, shifted the question to the plane of studying the interaction among mental functions and the interrelations of the different aspects of the mind, thus laying the cornerstone for positive holistic psychology.

Hence, the concept of drive as a guiding and determining factor grew out of psychoanalytic theory and helped it take the second step toward a monist approach to the study of the whole person.

We shall not dwell on the question of drives; for our purposes it was important only to show the unique approach of psychoanalysis to this question.

We have already mentioned the point that was most important for our purposes: that for psychoanalysis, drives are not a purely psychological concept, but have a much broader sense, lying at "the borderline between the mental and the somatic," and are more of a biological nature.

Thus, psychoanalysis attaches special importance to the de-

pendence of mental functions on organic stimuli. It makes mind
an integral part of the organism's system; it can hence no longer
be studied in isolation. This is what sets psychoanalysis apart
from the old scholastic psychology, which attempted to depict
the mind as something with no connection at all with the overall
life of the organism and studied the brain quite apart from any
influence other organs of the body might have on it (e.g., the
endocrine glands) and the general dynamics of the organism as
a whole. Indeed, the outstanding merit of psychoanalysis has
been that it situates the mind within a general system of interrelations of organs, views the brain and its activity not in isolation, but on a level with the other organs of the body, and attempts to give psychology a solid biological foundation and to
effect a decisive break with the metaphysical approach to the
study of the mind. (27) I should not be wide of the mark if I
said that in doing this, psychoanalysis took an important step
toward creating a system of monistic psychology. (28)

Let us take a look at this point in a little more detail, despite
the ambiguous formulations presented in psychoanalytic systems
(a feature, we might add, of all systems of empirical rather than
philosophical knowledge [29]) and despite the subjective terminology, which Freud himself said was provisional and needed to
be replaced by an organic terminology. (30)

We should first of all be interested in knowing what class of
drives, i.e., those constant stimuli originating within the body,
psychoanalysis deals with.

It tends roughly to distinguish between two classes of drives:
one kind has to do with personal interests, i.e., the interests of
the individual concerned with self-preservation; the other includes drives that are biologically related to the continuation of
the species and are called sex drives. The first, which psychoanalysis calls ego drives for short, are based on what is
conventionally referred to as the instinct for self-preservation
and are associated with the alimentary and defensive reactions
of the organism. (31) They often play a dominant role in the
life of the organism, in the fate of stimuli from without, in individual illness, etc. It is this class of drives that plays the

greatest role in defining the unique, whole person psychologists
are just now getting around to studying, and so these drives are
ordinarily defined as the interests of the particular person.

The sex drives have been studied much more thoroughly by
psychoanalysis. This has been due principally to the fact that
psychologists of the classical school, who studied the mind in
isolation, in abstraction from the various bodily functions outside the brain, paid little attention to the influence of sexual
activity on the mind. Perhaps what was partly to blame here
was some false sense of shame that previously hindered an objective approach to the study of human sexual experience. On
the other hand, we owe the especially well developed theory of
sexual drives in psychoanalysis to the fact that the whole of
psychoanalysis was based primarily on a study of nervous diseases (conversion neuroses), in which sex drives play an especially
important role and are particularly accessible to inquiry. (32)

This group of drives, which is doubtless of endogenous origin
(33) and hence is one of the most rudimentary aspects of the
personality (34), is, again, not regarded by psychoanalysis as a
purely mental phenomenon, but rather as being of an organic
order and, indeed, rather alien to the conscious mind in the
strict sense of that term as understood by ordinary psychology.
These drives exert their influence on the conscious mind only
in closest connection with various other bodily functions.

In its definition of sexual drives, psychoanalysis includes
factors that quite patently demonstrate the organic nature of
psychoanalytic psychology, which we shall now discuss.

Sexuality has not been exhaustively defined by Freud. (35)
He does, however, distinguish the following components of it:
functions associated with the differentiation of the sexes and
with the perpetuation of the species, although the latter are not
necessary (36); the pleasure derived from functions associated
with this organic drive; a certain attraction to objects stimula-
ting this drive; in brief, the relation to things that we call love
and that, by analogy with hunger, is given the narrower label of
"libido" in psychoanalysis (37) is accorded a central place on a
par with that of an organic substrate. We have already pointed

out that the sex drive has a very clearly nonpsychological and
biological sense in psychoanalysis. In comparing the theory of
the libido with biological theories of sexuality, Freud discovered
the close affinities this theory had with the findings of some of
the most recent studies in the area of sexual biology, especially
those stressing the influence of sexual secretions on the brain
and the nervous system (in particular, the findings of Steinach
and his school). This leads us to presume that the time is not
far off when psychoanalysis will be able to operate with a terminology of sexuality and sex drives that will include the real
content of the specific sexual chemistry distinguishing these
drives from others, e.g., ego drives. . . .

What do we really mean when we say that pleasure is an essential feature of the sex drive? Is not this factor extremely
psychological, subjective? And if not, how does psychoanalysis
conceive it? Is it in this pleasure principle that we shall find
that organic objectivity of which we spoke earlier, or does it
indeed represent an ultrapsychological teleology, a theory that
these drives are created with the purpose of striving to attain
pleasure? Let us try to outline briefly the place that pleasure
occupies in the general system of psychoanalysis.

The doctrine of pleasure doubtless occupies a central place
in psychoanalysis. It is viewed as a principal determining factor, a major tendency, a principle of the organism's viability.
The entire organism, both its conscious and unconscious parts,
is guided by this inclination to seek maximum pleasure by satisfying drives.

But in this respect the pleasure principle plays a very specific role. We know that subjectively gratification, pleasure,
is only a state of conscious mental activity. But with its pleasure principle psychoanalysis goes far beyond the limits set on
the concept by the subjective "psychology of consciousness" and
transforms pleasure into an organic concept, into a universal
biological principle of the functioning organism.

What appears to consciousness as pleasure conceals deeper-
lying organic impulses; the organism follows these impulses
in its struggle for existence and self-preservation. Psychoanal-

ysis leads us back to the organic sources: psychological causality is transformed into organic causality. (38)

Indeed, as we have already pointed out, the human organism
is under the constant influence of continual internal stimuli,
drives; if to these we add the external stimuli that impinge
ceaselessly on the organism, we can get a good idea of the level
of tension that must build up in the organism. And from this
tension arises the biological impulse to lower the level of stimulation, which appears to consciousness as something unpleas-
ant, which must be avoided. (39)

A need to release this built-up excitation, of both internal
and external origins, is created. To reduce stimulation coming
from without, to block access to the organism, and, finally, to
reduce the tone of stimulation from drives — these are the tasks
the mental apparatus takes upon itself. In fact, the most recent
psychoanalytic works define the mental apparatus as an "organ
of inhibition." (40) The basic impulse of the overall organism,
which is also reflected in the pleasure principle, if we may
borrow this vocabulary, is thus reduced to an impulse to control and release the body from these external and internal stimuli and excitations (41) and to achieve a state of minimum tension. (42)

Hence, the concept of drive is given a quantitative formulation, in energy terms, and processes taking place in the mind
are reduced to energy processes of stimulation and reactions
to them; with this, the psychological, subjective features the
pleasure principle as the major impulse of the organism seems,
at first glance, to have, disappear. We should also point out
that the apparent teleology to which psychoanalysis seemed to
subject the organism also disappears, to be replaced by a strictly biological causality; and, of course, not a trace remains of
any kind of voluntaristic striving for gratification. Psychological teleology gives way to organic causality. (43)

The organic nature of drives should be clear. We must now,
however, try to get a better notion of their organic sources,
which brings us to the second question we have posed. Accordingly, we shall have occasion to consider again the second im-

portant step taken by psychoanalysis toward the construction of a materialist monist psychology for the whole organism by integrating the brain and the mind along with it into an overall system of the body's organs and their interrelations.

Psychoanalysis quite early noted that some parts of the body are especially responsive to different external and internal stimuli and that their stimulation has a particularly powerful influence on the brain and the entire psychoneurological system. For example, it proved completely impossible in studying the mind to disregard the sources of its driving forces, that is, the different organs of the body; the brain could not be studied independently of the system of interrelations it has with other organs. (44)

This raised the problem of the organic sources of drives and the responses of the individual; and, accordingly, psychoanalysis developed the theory of the psychological significance of the various organs of the body. Later this theory was molded into a rigorous system in the doctrine of erogenous zones (Freud, 45) and of deficit organs and their mental compensation (Alfred Adler, 46) and found lucid confirmation in the physiological theory of the interrelations of organs and the influence of the endocrine system on the brain and its functions.

Alfred Adler was the first to take up the question of the importance of the body's organs and their function for psychology, and created a structured system to deal with the question. According to him, we frequently find organs with a relatively depressed functional capacity, which are weak, and which are hyperexcitable. (47) Adler called these organs deficit organs and claimed that their deficiency was the basis of their morbidity. It is biologically impossible, however, for an organ with depressed activity not to be compensated for from some other quarter, which would take over for this weak spot in the body; thus, if one of the dual organs (lungs, kidneys, brain hemispheres) is deficient, some of its functions are taken over by the other — e.g., if one lung is deficient, the second one undergoes a compensatory development. The picture is somewhat different in the case of a single organ; in that case, the central nervous system takes over for the deficient organ and performs its function by blocking the stimuli addressed to that organ and creating a mental superstructure over and above the function of the deficient organ to serve as an auxiliary apparatus in fulfilling the tasks imposed on it. When an organ is deficient, the task of compensation becomes a major motive force for the mind; the organ becomes a focal point of interests and attention and in this way becomes a point of origin for all of the individual's systemic responses. This, in general outline, is how Adler's theory of the role of the organs in performing mental functions looks. (48)

This brings us to Freud's theory of the organic basis of drives, which furnished a firm, positive groundwork for the whole of psychoanalysis. Of the ideas touched on in the foregoing, we shall be dealing primarily with the organic sources of sex drives.

Freud's great merit was unquestionably to have called attention to the role played by the organs and zones of the body in mental life; each of these zones and organs has its own specific hypersensitivity, which we have described above as a basic feature of drive. These zones, whose stimulation produces what we above called pleasure (in the specific sense given to it), are also sources of drives. They are, of course, the genitalia and, in addition, the oral mucosa, the anal opening, and in the very broadest sense, even the skin and muscles.

All these regions, which psychoanalysis calls erogenous zones (49), constitute a single powerful system that acts on the mental apparatus, guides its activity, and controls and directs its striving to reduce the level of tension and to attain pleasure.

These zones, in which endogenous excitation has the possibility of receiving external gratification, have a definitely sexual nature, although they are not limited to the area of the genitals. The erogenous function may often be linked to the ordinary functions of an organ. (50) This introduced a complication into one of the earlier concepts of psychoanalysis, namely, organ pleasure. An erogenous zone may be any zone of the human body and, conversely, "There is no area of the body that is totally devoid of erogenicity."

All of these positions are based on study of infantile, pregenital forms of sexuality, the sexuality of neurotics, and sexual perversions. The findings of these studies underscored that erogenicity was diffused throughout the organism and that erogenous functions are no more than concentrated in the genitals, which therefore must be viewed not as the only erogenous zone, but merely as the one that is ordinarily dominant. (51)

This state of affairs, in which the diffuseness of erogenous functions among the various organs of the body is a primary premise, underscores the tremendous importance of erogenous zones for the mind. In guiding the functioning of the mental apparatus in accordance with the pleasure principle, the erogenous zones regulate the child's relationship to the external world as well, obliging him to distinguish erogenous stimuli from others, and in this way condition the child's various responses to the external environment.

We need not deal particularly with the view that when the mother's breast touches the infant's mouth and stimulates the oral mucosa, it concentrates on itself (just as do other stimuli having no alimentary value, for example, a nipple or the thumb) all of the child's interest or, as we would say, his responses; later, specific stimuli applied to the skin or muscles, the activity of the intestines, stimuli associated with the excretory orifices (52), etc., do the same.

It is therefore not surprising that the erogenous zones are able to influence the entire further development of the personality; and the problem thus posed of the interrelations between the mind and other organs shifts such psychological questions as the formation of personality, etc., to a completely new plane.

The theory of personality formation has not yet been sufficiently developed by psychoanalysis on this new organic basis, but even the little it does give us helps us to understand the human mind immeasurably better than the old, subjective, empirical psychology was able to do.

If the functions of the erogenous organs do indeed occupy such an important place in the child's life, then it is reasonable that they should contain the roots of many traits of the human personality. We have already said that during certain periods of development, the functions of these organs concentrate around them the greater portion of a child's interests; stimulation of them and the responses such stimulation produces are perhaps the most important factor in the primitive life of the child, still in the process of being organized; no wonder, then, that these responses often serve as a prototype to which later forms of mental life revert. In analyzing specific personality traits and their origins in primitive responses to organ stimulation, we find at least three paths by which primitive drives and types of organic reactions may be transformed into complex personality traits: a personality trait may simply reproduce the earlier response, as it was, reproduce it in a modified, more complicated, sublimated form, or, finally, may be shaped as a reactive structure to this form of primary gratification and accentuate features that are the opposite of those that existed in childhood.

Earlier we noted in passing that the development of the child's organism passes through a series of stages in which the different erogenous zones predominate, one after the other, until they are finally replaced by the genital system as the sole, dominant one, with a powerful influence on mental activity.

Psychoanalysis has singled out, especially, three of these stages of erogenous zone predominance: the stage of oral eroticism (in which the oral cavity acquires an erotic significance associated with eating), then the anal stage (associated with the digestive and excretory system), and, finally, after other zones briefly enjoy this dominant role, the genital stage. (53)

No wonder, then, that the predominance of each of these zones should leave its mark on the formation of the personality, their overall influence on mental organization taking any one of the three aforementioned paths.

For example, one of the most important stages in the development of the child is the anal stage, during which the anal mucosa are hypersensitive, all reactions associated with this zone assume paramount importance, and the child strives continually to stimulate it. In the child's outward behavior this is manifested in a heightened interest in defecation, a tendency to retain the feces as long as possible, and a refusal to defecate and hence to stimulate the intestines.

Freud, and after him other authors, describes a number of personality traits that are unquestionably traceable to these primitive reactions associated with the anal stage.

For example, the recurrence of these reactions later on may show up in traits such as stubbornness, in indecisive pondering over one's responsibilities and the performance of one's duties, followed abruptly by impulsive action, etc. (54) In this case, a person is just repeating in other spheres of life the stubbornness and the effort to put off the final act (defecation) that once played an important role at the very beginnings of his life, when he was still a primitive being, and when the focal point of his interests was the activity of the intestines and stimulation of the zones associated with them. (55) The way these personality traits and habits are formed thus coincide completely with the way conditioned reflexes are formed on their rudimentary organic base.

Examples of personality traits formed through the transformation or sublimation of primitive anal erotic functions are punctiliousness and stinginess, as an attempt to retain one's feces, which later assumes more social forms and is transferred to another object, i.e., things collected, money, etc.

Finally, the primitive features of anal eroticism may be inhibited or repressed during the subsequent development of the organism as socially unacceptable, or they may even be replaced by other socially colored traits quite the opposite of them. According to Freud and his followers, the characteristics of bodily cleanliness and punctiliousness, which develop as a reaction in place of an inhibited and repressed impulse to filthiness, to soil oneself by smearing one's feces all over oneself, etc., are impulses associated with anal eroticism.

However incomplete these examples offered by psychoanalysis are, and however odd they may seem to us (56), one thing must be stressed: in psychoanalysis we have the first attempt to construct a theory about the development of the human personality not on the basis of some subjective mental qualities, not by means of a purely external analogy with biological laws (57), but on an organic basis, by tracing the primitive foundations of complex personality traits to the activity of the organs of the human body and their effects on man's mental makeup.

The principle of the interrelation of the organs, including the brain, is a component part of this theory and makes it possible to materialize, to use Binswanger's term (58), the theory of personality and to place it on a positive foundation.

*   *   *

These, then, are the main outlines of a psychology constructed on the basis of materialist monism, which views phenomena of mental life as one of the various kinds of organic phenomena and draws no principled distinction between processes taking place in the organs of the human body and psychological responses to them.

Psychoanalysis, which shifted the theory of mental phenomena to an entirely new plane, the plane of the theory of organic processes taking place in the human organism as a whole, made a decisive break with the metaphysics and idealism of the old psychology, and has laid the first solid foundation (together with the theory of human responses and reflexes) (59) for a materialist, monistic psychology that takes a positive approach to the mind of the whole person.

This is psychoanalysis's answer to the leading problem posed to modern psychology by the most important philosophy of the age, dialectical materialism, the problem of finding a materialist approach to the whole personality and the motive forces of the individual psyche.

Psychoanalysis has made an important contribution to the resolution of this problem in that it has taken two major steps: it has affirmed the interrelatedness of individual mental functions, and it has reintegrated the mind into the overall system of organs and their biologically determined activity.

In doing this it has opened up an entirely new biology of the mind (60) and taken some major steps toward the creation of a coherent, objective, monistic system (61); and we can whole-heartedly concur with Pfister's statement that "Freud was the first great positivist in psychology."

If the system of psychoanalysis is to measure up better to the requirements of dialectical materialism, however, it must develop fully the dynamic dialectic of mental life and take a third step toward a holistic approach to the organism: it must now integrate the organism into a system of social influences. (62)

It is with these aspects of psychoanalysis that we shall be dealing in later work.

Notes

[Editor's note: The original text contains 120 notes, most of them citations to very old works or to Russian versions of Marx, Engels, and Freud. We have retained only those that include personal comments by Luria, quotations, or references that seem particularly relevant.]

1) We want to point out here only the inherent similarity between the analytical method of Marxism, which looks beyond the surface of things to their real roots, and psychoanalysis, which is more specialized in its area of application, but is just as important in terms of its basic approach.

2) A note on terminology: we use the terms "empirical psychology," "general psychology," and "the old psychology" (despite a certain inaccuracy) to denote the school of psychology, which has typified and in fact even become classic for a whole epoch, that has developed along the lines laid down by most empirical psychologists of the last quarter of the 19th century.

3) Any study of purely experimental psychology can serve as an example; in Russia there are the studies of Chelpanov's school.

4) L. Feuerbach gives a brilliant description of this weakness in psychological methods in his essay "Against the dualism of mind and soul," in which he writes: "In psychology, roast pigeons fly into our mouths, while into our consciousness and senses fall only conclusions, no references, results only, and not the processes of the body...." ([Works]. GIZ, 1923. P. 148).

5) See, for example, the criticism of mosaic psychology in W. McDougall's An outline of psychology. 1923. Pp. 16-17. See also the works of a number of psychologists representing new trends (a detailed list will be found in my pamphlet [Psychoanalysis in the light of the principal tendencies in contemporary psychology]. Kazan, 1923. Pp. 10 ff.).

6) See Bonnet, Essais analytiques sur les facultés de l'âme, 1769, according to whom the task of psychology was to "analyze each fact, breaking it down into its simplest elements." Quoted in Boltunov, [The concept of empiricism in German psychology of the 18th century]. Vop. Filosof. Psikhol., 1912, Book 111, p. 50. The same tendencies are found throughout English associationism and are also reflected in some of the most recent systems of experimental psychology. See the definition of the subject matter of psychology in Tichener, Uchebnik Psikhologii. Moscow, 1917. P. 37.

7) Elsewhere I have called attention to the fact that one of the most important psychoanalytic journals, the Psychoanalytic Review, bears as a subheading the very appropriate motto: A journal devoted to understanding human conduct. This sums up very well the intent of psychoanalysis.

8) As I shall try to show later on, this view does not at all contradict the apparent teleological nature of psychoanalysis.

9) For how modern psychology deals with this question, as well as its general trend, see my pamphlet [Psychoanalysis in the light of the principal tendencies in contemporary psychology].

10) Marx and Engels were especially interested in the human personality and the higher products of human activity, as is evident from a number of passages in their writings. See, for example, Marx's The 18th brumaire of Louis Bonaparte and The German ideology, and Engels's L. Feuerbach....

Masarak was not far from the truth when he commented, "According to Marx, the tasks of scientific history consist in studying the driving causes reflected in the minds of the active masses and their leaders as conscious motives" ([The philosophical and theoretical foundations of Marxism]. Moscow, 1900. P. 156).

11) An examination of the writings of Marx and Engels clearly reveals that in Marxist theory, the mind is conceived as a reflex to social stimuli. Aside from the cited writings of Marx and Engels and of Plekhanov (especially Marx's Theses on Feuerbach), there remains only one reference to the Marxist Voltmann, [Historial materialism]. St. Petersburg, 1901. Pp. 258, 262, 266, etc.

12) Feuerbach brilliantly anticipated many of the concepts of the new psychology. His arguments for a monistic approach to the individual, about feelings, about the relationship between cerebral activity and the activity of the organs of the body were altogether a classic prototype of a sound and profound approach to the problem of the individual personality. See especially his essay "Against the dualism of body and soul, flesh and spirit," in [Works]. GIZ, 1923. Vol. 1, pp. 146 ff.

13) This principle is expressed especially well in the writings of American psychoanalysts. See, for example, W. White, Foundations of psychiatry. 1921. Chapt. 1.

14) For the concept of psychoanalysis as the psychology of the whole person, see also O. Pfister, Zum Kampf um die Psychoanalyse. 1920. Pp. 27-28 (Psychoanalyze, als eine System der organischen Psychologie). L. Binswanger, Psychoanalyse und klinische Psychiatrie. Int. Z. Psychoanal., 1921, pp. 147 ff.

15) See S. Freud, The ego and the id. (On the psychic nature of the unconscious). It should be noted in general that the biological and the sociological approach, but not the logical-philosophical approach, to the mind is close to psychoanalysis.

16) G. Groddeck, Über Psychoanalyse des organischen in Menschen. Int. Z. Psychoanal., 1921, p. 252. S. Ferenczi, Hysterische Materialisationsphänomene. (Hysterie und Pathoneurosen, 1919). F. Deutsch, Experimentelle Studien zur Psy-

choanalyse. Int. Z. Psychoanal., 1923, pp. 484 ff. Many of Freud's writings are devoted to this subject (see Kleine Schriften zur Neurosenlehre). For nonpsychoanalytic writers dealing with the same question, see Charcot, Janet, Déjérine, P. Dubois, the earlier Carpenter, and many others.

17) After describing its foundations, I shall have occasion to return to this, in my view, fundamental postulate of psychoanalysis more than once. For the time being, I refer the reader to studies in which the mind is regarded as a system reacting to stimulation and drives. See Freud, Jenseits des Lustprinzips (1921), especially pp. 21 ff., and W. White, op. cit., especially pp. 2, 4, 5 ff.

18) See Sherrington, The integrative function of the nervous system.

19) See Loeb, The organism as a whole from a physiological viewpoint. London, 1916.

20) K. N. Kornilov, [The theory of human reactions]. Moscow, 1922.

21) Freud, Jenseits des Lustprinzips. See also F. Alexander, Metapsychologische Betrachtungen. Int. Z. Psychoanal., 1921, p. 181: "These two sources of stimulation, the internal and the external, have a common origin."

22) L. Binswanger, Psychoanalyse und Klinische Psychiatrie. Int. Z. Psychoanal., 1921, p. 153, says: "The concept of drive constitutes the real core of Freudian theory, the foundation of the whole edifice."

23) See Freud, Drives and their fate. [Psikhol. i Psikhoanal. Bibliotek]. Moscow, 1922. Vol. III, pp. 107 ff. See also his "Psychoanalytic comments on an autobiographic description of paranoia." Jahrbuch f. Psychoanalyse, II, p. 65: "We regard drive as a borderline concept between the mental and the somatic and see in it the mental representation of organic forces." On the theory of sexual drive, see Vol. VIII of the cited Bibliotek; L. Binswanger, op. cit., pp. 153, 155; W. White, Foundations of psychiatry. New York, 1921. Pp. X and 1. Here the question of the soul and the body disappears once the problem of mental life is shifted to a plane studying the mind as a

"finite expression of the integration of the individual into an organic unity...." White correctly observes, "The only way to approach psychology properly is to do away with all metaphysical speculation about the essence of the soul and its relationship to the body and to proceed on the basis of the premise that what we have become accustomed to calling the mental is a manifestation of the organism as a whole."

24) In addition to Freud's classic works (see his The psychopathology of everyday life, Introductory lectures on psychoanalysis, Vol. 1, and his writings on the theory of neurosis — Minor writings on the theory of neurosis), see E. Jones, The repression theory and its relation to memory. Brit. J. Psychol., VIII (2); and T. Loveday, T. W. Mitchell, T. H. Pear, & A. Wolf on this theme, The role of repression in forgetting. Brit. J. Psychol., VII (2).

25) The first approach to this problem was made in the literature on witnesses' testimony, which shed light on the role interest plays in directing attention and screening perceptions. (See W. Stern, H. Gross, and others.)

26) The literature on this question is vast. I shall deal in detail with the question of complex associations (or responses) elsewhere. Let me point out only that the problem was first posed and examined by Jung. See his Diagnostische Assoziationsstudien. 1910-11. Vols. 1-2.

27) The clearest statement of this need to integrate the brain and the mind into an overall system of the body's organs may be found in Feuerbach. In his essay "Against the dualism of body and soul" (Works, 1923, Vol. 1, p. 157), he says: ".... It is not the soul that thinks and feels, because the soul is a personified and hypostatized function, transformed into a discrete entity; it is a function or manifestation of thought, sensation, and desire; and it is not the brain that thinks and feels, because the brain is a physiological abstraction, an organ riven loose from its totality, from the skull, from the head, from the body, and fixed as if it were a self-contained entity. The brain can function as the organ of thought only in connection with the human head and the human body." Unfortunately, this essen-

tially simple truth has long been forgotten by general psychology.

In this respect psychoanalysis is right in step with the latest theories on endocrine glands and their influence on the mind; these theories also attempt to integrate mental life into the system of the body's organs. Of writings following this line of thought, I shall mention only the new book by N. A. Belov, [Physiology of types]. Orel, 1924.

28) Aside from Freud, a number of other writers have pointed out the monistic materialist nature of psychoanalysis, e.g., Bleuler, Physisches und Psychisches in der Pathologie. Z. Ges. Neurol. Psychiat., 1916, XXXI; W. White, Foundations of psychiatry; L. Binswanger, Psychoanalyse und klinische Psychiatrie. Int. Z. Psychoanal., 1921, p. 155 (in connection with personality theory); J. Meagher, Psychoanalysis and its critics. Psychoanal. Rev., 1922, No. 3, p. 326; and S. Ferenczi, a number of writings.

29) "The fact that certain concepts of psychoanalysis are unclear," stated Freud, "draws the dividing line between speculative theory and science, which is built on the basis of empirical data. Science willingly leaves to speculative, contemplative philosophizing the advantages of a smooth, logically unimpeachable soundness, and is prepared to be satisfied with obscure, elusive, basic propositions." On narcissism. [Psikhal. i Psikhoanal. Bibliotek]. Moscow, 1923, Vol. VIII, p. 121. In another place Freud adds, "I myself have an aversion to simplification at the expense of truth." Introductory lectures on psychoanalysis. 1922. Vol. II, p. 71. This makes the interpretation of the basic principles of psychoanalysis extremely difficult.

30) See Freud: "We must bear in mind that all the psychological propositions we have allowed for the time being must sooner or later also be translated to an organic foundation." On narcissism. Op. cit., Vol. VIII, p. 122; See A. K. Lents on the outwardly psychological terminology of psychoanalysis: [Conditioned reflexes and the construction of modern psychiatry]. In [New ideas in medicine]. St. Petersburg, 1924. No. 4, p. 69.

31) This class of drives takes an especially active part in processes such as inhibition of stimuli coming from without (repression, censor) and in the formation of narcissistic neuroses. More on this later.

It should be pointed out that in psychoanalysis, this class of drives, despite its apparent simplicity, has been very little studied. See Freud, Introductory lectures (Drives and their fate), and ... The ego and the id.

32) Freud, Introductory lectures ... The charges of pansexualism and narrow sexual monism against psychoanalysis are very reminiscent of the charges made against Marxism of paneconomism and of elevating the economic factor to the status of the sole determining factor in history. Engels, in his letter to Bloch of September 21, 1890, deals brilliantly with this misunderstanding and the reasons for giving priority to the study of the economic factor....

33) See F. Alexander, op. cit. Only the sex drive has an endogenous origin; all others originate outside the body, from environmental stimuli.

34) See I. C. Flügel, On the biological basis of sexual repression. Int. Z. Psychoanal., 1920, p. 324. "Sexual drives are the oldest and most primitive form of vital energy."

35) In the psychoanalytic system, the mind in the narrow sense is frequently regarded as something opposed and hostile to sexuality. The definition of the mind often includes the notion of the mind as an "inhibiting organ," regulating the inflow of stimuli. This is especially clear when applied to one of the major aspects of the mind, consciousness. See Freud, On narcissism; F. Alexander, op. cit., p. 273; S. Ferenczi, Die Psyche als Hemmungsorgan. Int. Z. Psychoanal., 1922, p. 4.

36) Freud examined a broad class of sexual phenomena in which sexual activity is not associated with the procreative function (perversions, infantile sexuality, neurotic symptoms, etc.). Thus, his concept of sexuality is much broader than just genital sexuality....

37) This way of formulating the question brings into sharp relief the importance ascribed by psychoanalysis to sexuality....

38) See L. Binswanger, op. cit., p. 152. "While for Kretsch-
mer and the psychologists the forces determining mental life
come from the mind, for Freud they are rooted in the biology
of the organism." G. Jelgersma, Psychoanalytischer Beitrag
zu einer Theorie der Gefühle. Int. Z. Psychoanal., 1920, p. 8.
"Thus, in psychoanalysis we have concepts that are of a purely
natural science order and not a psychological order." See F.
Alexander, op. cit., and others. I have recently encountered
the pleasure principle in biology (see Ferenczi, Versuch einer
genital theorie, 1924) and even in reflexology (see the interesting paper by V. I. Boldyrev, Two new laws of brain function.
Bulletin of the Battle Creek Sanitarium and Hospital Clinic,
1924, XIX(2) (March); Pfister, op. cit., pp. 247 ff.; W. White,
op. cit. pp. 10-11).

39) See Freud, On narcissism: "Dissatisfaction is an expression of higher stress, i.e., it is a material process that
has reached a certain level (my emphasis — A. R. L.) resulting
in the accumulation of an internal tension perceived mentally as
a feeling of discomfort, of displeasure." See also Freud, Theory
of the sex drive. Jenzeits des Lustprinzips, pp. 3 ff.; Jelgersma,
op. cit., pp. 1-2 ff.

40) See Freud, On narcissism. "The affective apparatus is
the instrument with which we cope with stimulations.". . .

41) Freud, Introductory lectures; also Jenseits des Lustprinzips, p. 62: "The pleasure principle is an impulse serving
a function whose task is to make the affective apparatus free
of excitement or to maintain the amount of excitation in it constant or as low as possible.". . .

42) See, especially, Freud, The ego and the id, and Jelgersma, op. cit. It is curious that the psychoanalytic system coincides with Avenarius's theory of vital differences. (See Avenarius [Critique of pure experience], for example, in Lunar-
charsky's interpretation. Moscow, 1909. Pp. 24 ff.)

43) See Alexander, op. cit., pp. 270-71, and L. Binswanger,
op. cit., pp. 153-54. At this point it is perhaps especially op-
portune to state the dialectical approach to the question of teleology: What appears to us as a striving toward a goal (pleasure)

is only the realization of a biological necessity. The contradiction between causality and teleology is here reduced to nil.

44) See Alfred Adler, Studie über die Minderwertigkeit der
Organe. 1907. P. 59, in particular. W. M. Wheeler, On instincts. J. Abnorm. Psychol., 1920-21, XV, 295 ff. "A typical
psychologist does not study his material (as he should, that is)
by comparing it and collating its different parts as the natural
scientist does; instead he limits his inquiry to the head, ignor-
ing the other parts of the organism.".... L. Binswanger, op.
cit., p. 153. N. A. Belov [Physiology of types]. Orel, 1924.
The foundation for mental and somatic phenomena in Freud is
not the brain in isolation, but drives, a borderline concept between the mental and the somatic and signifying organic forces
(my emphasis — A. R. L.).

45) The theory of erogenous zones, one of the cornerstones
of psychoanalysis, was elaborated in "The theory of the sex
drive"; an abundant literature has been devoted to this subject.

46) This theory was presented by Alfred Adler in his
classic Studie über die Minderwertigkeit der Organe and developed further in his later works on the nervous personality,
1912, Praxis und Theorie des Individualpsychologie, 1920, and
others.

47) Some authors call attention to the similarity between
the concept of a deficit organ and the concept of an erogenous
zone in the light of this definition of deficiency. See E. Wexberg,
[Two psychoanalytic theories]. (Russian trans.) Psychotera-
piya, 1912. O. Hinrichsen, [Our concept of affective processes
in relation to the theories of Freud and Adler]. Ibid, 1913,
No. 6. See also Adler, op. cit., p. 25.

48) I have not touched on a number of important aspects of
this original theory, for example, the theory of stigmas of deficit organs (organic and psychological), the theory of the paths
and outcome of central compensation, and last but not least,
Adler's individual psychology, which rests entirely on these
foundations. I hope to be able to return to these themes later.

49) The concept of erogenous zones has its own history.
Charcot called attention to their hypersensitivity and specific

properties, calling them hysterogenic zones. Chambard (1881) saw them as centres érogènes connected with sexual functions. Féré (1883) noted the similarity between the two; and the theory of erogenous zones has been dealt with in detail by Binet and Féré, H. Ellis, and finally, Freud. See H. Ellis, The doctrine of erogenous zones. Medical Review of Reviews, 1920, April, p. 191.

50) See Freud, Introductory lectures ..., and other works. On this point Freud's theory of erogenicity is very close to Adler's theory of organ functions.

51) The evolution of the primacy of the genital erogenous zones fits in completely with the concept of a dominant as a sphere of maximum excitability, attracting to itself all stimuli, even those meant for other organs; the concept of a dominant was developed by A. A. Ukhtomskii and his school. See the articles by him and his followers in Russk. Fiziol. Zh., 1923, Book VI. See, with this, Ferenczi's description of the evolution of genital primacy in Hysterie und Pathoneurosen. 1919. P. 11. Genital primacy is manifested in the fact that every excitation of the erogenous area is immediately drawn into excitation of the genitals as well.... As the central erogenous zone, the relation of the genitals to the other erogenous zones corresponds to the relation of the brain and the sense organs. See also Freud, The theory of the sex drive.

52) See, for example, E. Jones, Anal erotic personality traits: "In the first years of life of the infant, the act of defecation is one of his chief interests."

53) See Freud, The theory of the sex drive; Introductory lectures. See also D. Forsyth, The rudiments of character. Psychoanal. Rev., 1921, pp. 117 ff. Forsyth distinguishes three basic phases of pregenital organization: (1) autonomic; (2) differentiation of the erogenous zones connected with the alimentary system; (3) dermal eroticism. These phases of pregenital organization influence the subsequent fate of the "sexual constitution."...

54) E. Jones sees this interesting trait in the curious habit of putting off answering letters, the avoidance of household

chores, etc. See op. cit., pp. 29-30.

55) I have described only two personality traits, omitting an extremely interesting study of other aspects.

56) ... E. Jones, op. cit., p. 24: "The most striking result of Freud's studies, which has perhaps caused the most doubts and provoked the most protests, is his discovery that certain character traits depending on sexual stimulation of the anal zone produce such profound changes in very early infancy."

57) See, for example, Fouillée, Temperament and personality, in which a theory of temperament is constructed by analogy with biological processes of integration and differentiation.

58) "In psychoanalysis, personality is something fixed, materialized, and dynamically enlightened" (L. Binswanger, op. cit., p. 155).

59) On the fundamental similarity between the respective approaches of psychoanalysis and reflexology, see Bekhterev, [Foundations of human reflexology]. GIZ, 1923 (1st ed., 1918, Chapt. 38), and books by his pupils Ivanov-Smolensky and Lents in the journals Psikhiat. Nevrol. Eksp. Psikhol. and Novye idei v Meditsina, Vol. 4. See also G. Humphrey, The conditional reflex and the Freudian wish. J. Abnorm. Psychol., XIV, 338.

60) O. Pfister, op. cit., p. 247: "A complete new world of psychology has opened — a biology of affective life, new in all its major features."

61) See A. K. Lents, [Conditional reflexes and the development of modern psychiatry]. Novye idei v Meditsina, 4, 69: "The psychoanalytic system is psychological in name only; in reality, it is objective and physiological."

62) Only then will the theory of psychoneural activity advance from mechanical materialism to dialectical materialism.

PART TWO

Developmental Studies

A. R. Luria

A CHILD'S SPEECH RESPONSES
AND THE SOCIAL ENVIRONMENT

The Influence of the Environment in Speech Responses

Modern psychology has come to the firm view that human
personality is shaped by its concrete sociohistorical circumstances. We can think of no form of behavior that can be studied
in isolation from this historical context, by itself, independent
of the specific sociohistorical conditions determining it.

The dialectical method obliges us to reject a static concept of
behavior in which the various types of behavior are studied independently of the environmental conditions and general context
within which they develop. Both our theoretical premises and
practical experience have brought us to the definite conclusion
that no psychological function can be understood except in terms
of its development (the genetic approach) and its particular social conditions (the sociological approach). Only by tackling the
problem of the role played by concrete sociohistorical and cultural conditions in transforming behavior can we hope to arrive
at an adequate appreciation of how behavior patterns are shaped.

In the first part of this study (1), in which we undertook a
genetic analysis of a child's speech responses, we attempted to
trace the general lines of development of children's speech. In

From Rech' i intellekt derevenskogo, gorodskogo i bespri-
zornogo rebenka [Speech and intellect among rural, urban, and
homeless children]. Moscow-Leningrad: Gosizdat RSFSR, 1930.

this second part, our aim will be to shed some light on the social factors involved in this process. Again, our emphasis will be on the psychological aspects of speech rather than on its phonetic and grammatical aspects. We shall attempt to explore the psychological aspects of the speech of children from different social groups, and on the basis of this material we hope to be able to ascertain some of the distinctive features of the speech pattern (and to a certain extent the thought patterns) of children reared in different social environments.

More than any other aspect of our behavior, speech is the product of the specific historical circumstances in which it develops. Since its primary function is to promote communication, an individual's speech develops under conditions of maximum interaction with others. The more intimate, the more lively this interaction, the more rapidly will speech develop, and the richer will be its content. Drawing its content, as it does, from direct social experience, speech naturally reflects the richness or barrenness of the social environment in which the experience takes place; accordingly, it should not be surprising if the speech of children from different social classes were not at all similar. Indeed, if we examine the speech of these children, we find that it faithfully reflects the distinctive features of the environment from which it has sprung.

Social conditions play a tremendously important role in shaping speech; indeed, speech is social in nature, and communicative in both function and origin. But this is not the only reason why speech is so dependent on social factors; it is, in fact, also an extremely vital tool of thought; it is intimately involved in all of a child's intellectual operations — indeed, in all his intellectual experience. And since this intellectual experience is directly linked with specific features of the social environment, it is reasonable to assume that the particular environment in which a child grows up also plays a maximum role in the development of speech, which in turn gives shape and form to the individual's social experience. Accordingly, it should occasion no surprise that the speech of a working-class child in a large city, the speech of a child from a backward country area, and the speech of a homeless urchin who has been deprived of a stable social environment should be radically dissimilar.

Finally, there is one other factor that deserves detailed scrutiny in this study. If we are right in saying that speech is thought's most vital cultural tool, it should follow that it is one of the most readily influenced of psychological processes. Any structured pedagogical environment or, to put it in other terms, any placement of a child in a structured social situation will stimulate and structure that child's speech, which will then serve as a vehicle for the subsequent transformation of his intellectual operations. Conversely, any inadequately structured environment will lead to the opposite result: if special intellectual uses of speech are not developed, it will remain entrapped in its rudimentary state. Speech may fulfill its communicative functions quite adequately, yet be poorly suited for complex intellectual activity. We therefore thought it might be instructive to compare the speech and intelligence of a child who had been exposed to structured pedagogical influences over a prolonged period with the speech and intelligence of a child who had been deprived of an adequately structured environment within which to grow and develop. By carefully comparing and contrasting children in these two categories we hoped to shed light on some of the specific features of the speech and intelligence of children brought up under different circumstances and to clarify the role played by a structured pedagogical environment in the transformation of a child's psychological processes.

Our subjects in this study were schoolchildren and homeless urchins.

Our method was extremely simple, but adequate to our purposes. We had decided to investigate what direct speech responses children from different social groups would give to various verbal stimuli. In emphasizing the immediacy, the spontaneity even, of a child's speech responses, we of course there-

by excluded any direct study of knowledge learned in school.
We decided to limit ourselves as far as possible to an investigation of the natural course followed by associative processes when they were not influenced by the particulars of any specific situation. We therefore neither asked the children any questions, assigned them problems or tasks, nor imposed any restrictions on their intellectual activity during the experiment by giving specific instructions. The three groups — urban children, rural children, and homeless children — were placed in a situation in which their intelligence had free play. Our goal was to obtain an "intellectual profile," an "instantaneous portrait," so to speak, of the natural associative processes of children living in different social environments.

This obliged us to employ a simple association experiment as our method; and the results, which we shall analyze in detail in the present essay, demonstrate that this method was quite suited to describing the specific features of the speech and intellectual activities of children from different social environments. Indeed, if we took a rigorously deterministic position, we would have to concede that ideas that cropped up "spontaneously" in our minds were actually a long way from being spontaneous. Their occurrence is determined wholly by our previous social experience, and the "spontaneous" ideas of an urban, a rural, and a homeless child will be entirely different. A person's class and his particular social experience fill his mind with a quite specific content, and the study of this content not only is of considerable interest for the infant science of psychology of classes but is also of indisputable pedagogical interest, since it sheds light on specific features of the intellectual resources of the children from different social environments with whom our pedagogue will come into contact.

What we here mean by intellectual resources has nothing whatever to do with the skills a child learns in school. If we analyze these resources we can get an idea what associations are the most vivid for a child of a given social background and what his socially shaped experience has been. Thus the indices we worked out for assessing this general experiential background

first of all characterized the environment in which the child was
brought up and only secondarily reflected the child's stage of
development. We should be prepared to find that the results
obtained in a study of children of different ages but the same
social backgrounds would have much more in common than the
corresponding information obtained about children of the same
age but different social backgrounds.

However, we undertook the series of involved experiments
and calculations that such a study requires not just because we
wanted to analyze the elemental content of the intellectual resources of children from different social environments. A
peasant child's richest and most vivid associations will be rooted
in his rural environment, and it is just these associations that
will be the most barren in the urban child; on the other hand,
in the schoolchild these differences will tend to be evened out
by what he learns in school, gaps in his experience will be
filled, his experience will become more harmonious, and his
intellectual resources will become richer — these observations
certainly did not require any deep and detailed investigation.
But the fact is that we expected our experiments to yield other
data as well.

We do not believe that the social environment supplies merely
the content of every individual's experience and nothing more;
on the contrary, it determines a vast range of characteristics
inherent in the basic mechanisms underlying a person's reactions and, ultimately, the overall pattern of the reactions of the
social group to which the individual belongs.

Let us consider each of these factors individually and attempt
briefly to explain just what we mean by these statements.

Associative Mechanisms and Environmental Influences

First, the social circumstances in which a child grows up will
inevitably leave their mark on the mechanisms underlying complex psychological processes, not just on the content of those

processes. This is especially true of associative processes, which in both their genesis and their function are the most directly exposed to the influence of environmental factors acting on them.

Let us take a relatively simple example. A child's speech responses occur at a definite pace or speed; this speed corresponds both to the customary pace of his intellectual activity and to the extent of his command over his linguistic and associative processes. (2) We may even go one step farther. There can be no question that the particular social conditions in which the child has had to develop are also inevitably reflected in the pace and the extent of his command of his language. It is quite understandable that the relatively slow and quiet pace of country life is hardly conducive to the development of quick and lively behavior; and the behavior of a person living under the conditions of an individual household economy, often even in an almost natural economy, with very few surplus items available to be marketed, a sparse population, and a very low cultural level, will always be somewhat slow and relatively relaxed. And if on top of this we consider the fact that, because of the relative lack of tension in social relations and the cultural backwardness of country life, the speech of a child from this environment will begin to develop six months — sometimes even a year — later than that of a city child, we will not be surprised if the figures obtained in our experiments quite faithfully reflect the slower pace of speech and intellectual activity of the rural child compared with his city peer.

Table 1 gives us a comparison of such figures.

Table 1
Average Speed of Speech Responses in Children
of Different Social Environments

Subjects	Response time (sec)
City children 9-12 years (44 subjects)	1.9
Rural children 10-12 years (40 subjects)	2.34
Homeless children 10-12 years (46 subjects)	3.01

We see that the average response time (regardless of the difficulty of the test word and the content of the association) of the rural child is much slower than that of his urban counterpart. Later we shall see that in a formal sense the complexity of the associative processes we observed in either case was in general of about the same level; hence the speed of associative processes, which is quite different for the rural and the urban child, is really in this case a reflection of the distinctive pace (primarily the speed of association and speech) of behavior patterns shaped under conditions of different social tension.

One figure, in particular, strikes our attention: the mean reaction time for homeless children was 3.01 sec compared with 1.9 sec for ordinary children (i.e., approximately 60% higher than that of a schoolchild of the same age). This figure has implications that provide some interesting clues to the specific mechanisms concealed behind the bare statistical data. The fact that the reaction time of homeless children was quite long is by no means attributable to the same factors that are responsible for the slower reactions of the rural child; these phenomena, outwardly similar, actually conceal factors that are radically different from one another. In fact, to say that the urchin lives at a depressed, slowed pace is misleading; all the evidence indicates that the direct opposite is the case. However, at this point we come up against two other factors that influenced the results of our experiments with the homeless children, and in the light of which the overall slowness of this group becomes clear. The street child is deprived of the training other children receive in school. He is a stranger to everything associated with study or with the knowledge and skills acquired in schools. He is not more backward than the schoolchild; this we know from the facts. He is just different: he does not know how to reason formally — that is taught in school. Anything even resembling a problem divorced from real life is a novelty to him. His linguistic experience has had nothing to do with abstract logical operations of the type cultivated in school. This is why the urchin, who is quick and deft in coping with the situations of everyday life, becomes quickly disoriented and pro-

ceeds slowly in the contrived situations of an experiment, in
which, moreover, we employed abstract linguistic (associative)
operations.

However, there is also another factor that will help us solve
the puzzle of the urchin's slow performance and throw the contours of his mind into relief. Not only is he a stranger to abstract, formal operations but when he is suddenly exposed to
the unnatural conditions of a test, he displays a marked emotional tension indicating acute and complex affective reactions that
he conceals from outside view. The urchin has had to wage a
bitter struggle with life, and that struggle has left its specific
emotional traces on him. A strong inner discipline (especially
in his relations with his closest comrades) and an equally strong
distrust of everything coming from without have left their mark
on his overall behavior. In our experiments the urchin was not
the average experimental subject, embarking on a test half confident, half unsure; from the very beginning he adopted an attitude of mistrust and hostility toward the experimenter; he was
afraid to let fall an improper word, to give something away —
and all the more so considering that many of these children had
any number of questionable deeds in their past that they did not
want to reveal and hence carefully shielded from discovery.
The affective complexes associated with the past experience of
these children had left their mark on their behavior and caused
them to hold back in their responses in our tests. A close analysis of the reactions of these children will demonstrate the tremendously important role played by the affective traces of their
past experience.

But we might first ask ourselves whether the rural child or
the homeless child is backward in terms of the indices we used.
Indeed, just such a view is quite widespread even to this day
among many levels of educators and educational and experimental psychologists, and, moreover, is considerably reinforced
by the results of certain tests that seem effectively to demonstrate that rural children and street children are quite backward. But is this really the case? If we ask ourselves on exactly what these evaluations are based we immediately encounter

a serious discrepancy. Although the street child may score an average of 69 on the Binet-Burt intelligence tests, this is not in itself a sign of his deficient intelligence. We can expect the street child to be quite backward in any school-acquired skills; and a set of tests designed to evaluate school development rather than natural development will of course give us comparatively low scores for both the street child and, frequently, the rural child as well. But a completely different picture is obtained if we take more than just a formal approach to the scores, in particular, if we compare the associative patterns of these children's thought processes.

A study carried out by A. N. Mirenova gives a detailed and qualitative analysis of data obtained on Binet test scores for street children. This analysis convincingly demonstrates that these children are different, not mentally retarded, and that instead of defective intelligence, they have abilities that have evolved along unique and independent lines.

The result of our study of speech responses just as clearly bears out our claim that there are no grounds whatsoever for attributing some form of mental retardation or backwardness to rural children as far as their natural, spontaneous thought processes are concerned.

Table 2 gives a summary of these results. We see that the reactions of both the street child and the rural child are not radically different in form from those of schoolchildren of the same age. If we compare these figures with the results of a study of urban children we will find them very similar. Thus, rural children gave an average of 65% appropriate responses, which is roughly normal for their age; it was typical of them that only a small number of inappropriate responses were totally alien to the test stimuli. Fifteen percent of rural children gave appropriate responses (not at all a high figure for the age group in question). Most of the inappropriate responses were auditory association responses, which, as a rule, are very typical for first- and second-graders, who have only recently begun formal study of language.

The responses of our homeless children were similar. In any

Table 2

Types of Speech Responses
of Children of Different
Social Groups (in %)

Subjects	Inappro-priate respon-ses (groups 1, 2, 3)	Appro-priate respon-ses (groups 4 and 5)	Refusals	Extra signal	Audi-tory	Predica-tive	Appro-priate associ-ations
Rural children 10-12 yrs	35	65	C	15	20	30	35
Urban children 8-10 yrs	42.5	52.5	2.5	27.5	12.5	24.5	23.5
Urban children 13-16 yrs	11	83	1.6	5.8	1.7	51.7	35.2
Homeless children 10-12 yrs	20.4	76.4	1.7	15	3.7	31.5	39.9

event, it would be absolutely wrong to say that the free associations of these children were in any sense backward; 76.4% of all their responses were quite appropriate; 15% of the extraneous responses occurred in cases in which the stimuli touched some sort of affective scars. Primitive auditory responses, echolalia, and stereotypes, which are so characteristic of the mentally retarded child, are almost completely absent; and there is no basis whatever for assuming that we are here dealing with oligophrenic children.

The psychological resources of these children are quite specific and qualitatively different from those of a child from another social group. They may perhaps be retarded in terms of formal learning, but in potential they are fully normal; and under the right conditions, they could develop into complete, highly productive, human beings.

Although for different reasons the rural child and the urchin are less quick in their speech responses than the average urban child of the same age, their responses are just as complex,

so that in terms of potential the psychological development of
these children is in no sense subnormal.

Environmental Influences and the Level of Socialization of the Fund of Associations

Our data not only afford us an opportunity to pinpoint those
specific features in the speed and form of associative processes
that are influenced by the social environment in which a child
has grown up: they also provide us with a rough idea of the
associative patterns characteristic of the group as a whole and
hence enable us to draw certain general conclusions about the extent and direction of the organizing influence of the environment.

A child's entire experience, all of his intellectual resources,
are environmentally determined. This we have already stated.
However, the environmental factor is by no means the same in
all cases. If the environment is unchanging, stable, and comparatively barren in stimuli, if the entire social group of children experiences roughly the same, rather monotonous situations, then a certain percentage of children will respond with
the same (or almost the same) word to a particular test stimulus; and there will be relatively few different responses derived
from different areas of experience. Quite the opposite picture
is obtained when a child's environment has been rich and varied,
when the social group of children is exposed to a variety of different influences, or, finally, when the children have not yet
been completely assimilated into a broad, structured, social
environment and instead have had their behavior shaped primarily by individual, spontaneous experience (family, environment, etc.) rather than by the organizing influences of a group.
The variety of responses will in this case be rather large; and
the index for socialization, i.e., the sameness of group experience, will be low. Thus, our experiment enabled us not only to
ascertain the extent to which a child's experience has been
shaped by his environment but also, indirectly, to determine
some of the characteristics of the environment itself, i.e., its
sameness, richness, and uniformity.

T. Ziehen (3), relatively long ago, called attention to the fact that the associations of small children more often are of quite an individual nature and that responses common to all or at least a large number of children are much rarer. Ziehen thought that this characteristic was peculiar to childhood and noted that the number of like responses increased with age, indicating a uniformity of group experience.

Kent & Rosanoff (4) obtained similar data in their experiments. With many children as subjects, they compiled indices reflecting the frequencies with which certain responses were encountered in different age groups. They, too, observed an increase in common responses and a decrease in individual responses with age.

All these observations have been dealt with in the works of Piaget (5), who has found that the socialization of speech is a gradual process in a child's development and that speech plays a completely different role in young children: it is egocentric, and only loosely connected to the outside world. Only later, as the child grows older, does speech begin to acquire its communicative functions.

Thought in general assumes a social character as part of the same process, and begins to subserve social goals and reflect socially acquired experience.

In the light of these considerations, it should be clear why our predecessors have found that the responses of children tend to become increasingly uniform as they grow older.

The similarity and homogeneity of children's associative responses increase with age. This trend is abetted by the growing socialization of the child's behavior and by the fact that children in a given social group tend to acquire a standard fund of knowledge in school or in the course of everyday life. Of course, as a child acquires this knowledge, his responses tend to become not only more like the responses of others in his social group but also richer and more varied. Thus, along with a decrease in the number of individual responses, we find that associative responses begin to move more and more along channels common to the group as a whole.

The developmental differences we noted in our children were superimposed, so to speak, on underlying class differences of a more basic nature. This is reflected in the fact that children of consecutive age groups from the same social group were much more alike in the sameness of their collective experience than children of the same age from different social strata.

Indeed, the barren and monotonous environment of the rural child shows clear-cut differences from the rich, rapidly shifting environment of the urban schoolchild and homeless waif. The uniformity and sameness of the responses of the group of rural children were in sharp contrast to the richness and variety of the responses of urban children. But the problem goes even deeper: a detailed analysis reveals notable differences between these groups of children not only in the general nature of their responses but also in the different degrees of socialization exhibited in various areas of childhood experience.

It was comparatively easy to quantify this observation and to work out relevant indices for the level of socialization of childhood experience. The simplest approach was the following: taking all the subjects belonging to one homogeneous group, we recorded all the responses they gave to each of the test words. This approach gave us the "response lexicon" of our children.

In examining this, we immediately perceived that the number of different responses given to each word varied; some answers were given frequently by the children (for example, 50% of all the children gave the word "father" in response to the word "mother"), whereas other words occurred only once. The fact that most of the subjects gave identical responses in this case of course indicates that all the children of this social group had a homogeneous experience with respect to that particular association. On the other hand, a large number of nonrecurring answers, some given only once, meant that a particular area of experience was poorly socialized and that accidental, individualized memories predominated over routine associations common to the entire group.

We also worked out certain average indices extending beyond individual, concrete spheres of experience; these indices measured the degree of sameness of responses characteristic of a group and the average level of socialization of associative processes in each particular group. For this we needed only to take the average indices for the entire group of children on each of the tests rather than averages for the particular words.

These indices will provide us with some indirect idea of the characteristics of the environment operating on the child, its relative richness or barrenness, its constancy, and its variety. Actually, the fact that a good number of responses were identical for the entire group indicates that the environmental influences operating on these children have been largely the same for the entire group. A predominance of individual responses, given only by some subjects, indicates the opposite.

We decided on three principal indices we thought would give a fair idea of the factors in which we were interested.

1. The index of commonality (uniformity) of collective experience. This index was computed from the maximum number of identical responses given to a test word and was expressed in terms of the number of subjects whose responses to a particular stimulus were the same. (6)

2. The index of diversity gave us the opposite picture. It was the total number of all different responses given to a stimulus (or the corresponding average number of different responses for the given group). Of course, the index is inversely proportional to the first. We can expect that a more austere and unchanging environment will produce a less variegated experience than a rich and changing environment. Finally, this index provides a rough idea of the proportion of individual associations, atypical for the group as a whole, in a child's total responses. The next parameter is especially useful in providing this information.

3. The index of individual responses, i.e., the number of individual responses encountered in a given group only once. This index has a particular importance also because usually a large number of identical responses was given by two or three chil-

dren in our group, i.e., they showed a relatively low level of socialization. Without this index the degree of heterogeneity of the responses of the particular group could not have been determined, and we would have lost a very important index for characterizing the group.

As we shall see, all these parameters were relevant to our analysis, and help us to delineate the specific features of the collective experience of the children of different social groups.

Table 3 gives a summary of the average values of these indices for each of the groups of children we studied.

Table 3

Homogeneity of Collective Experience of Children from Different Social Groups (in %)

Subject	Homogeneity of collective experience	Variety	Individual Responses
Rural child	35.7	49.6	15
Urban child (younger)	16	67	54
Urban child (older)	19.2	47.5	33.9
Homeless urchin	17	56	41

Even a superficial glance at the figures in this table invites some very interesting inferences. Our attention is drawn especially to the fact that the first of our indices — the homogeneity of collective experience — was very high for the rural children: whereas an average of only 16% of the young urban children gave common responses, this figure for rural children was approximately twice as high (35.7%). We consider this figure one of the most important in the entire study. Indeed, we can imagine how unchanging and monotonous their environment must have been for one-third of the children to have responded identically to the test words! Of course, such an unusual homogeneity of responses is possible only when the environment in

which the child grows up is relatively austere and remains the
same, year in and year out. Urban conditions, which are richer,
more varied, and more subject to change, will not, of course,
produce such uniform responses; and the figures clearly bear
this out. The figures showing the number of purely individual,
solitary responses given by our subjects are especially demon-
strative of this fact. The rural child gave very few (only 15%)
of these one-time responses deriving solely from personal, random experience, whereas more than half of the urban child's
responses (54%) were of this type; even for the older schoolchild the number was still 33.9%. These figures are, moreover,
extremely typical. The unchanging and relatively austere environmental influences of country life do not leave very much
opportunity for the chance, individualized experiences that differentiate one person from another. Even though the rural child may
think that the word association he gives as a response is out of
his own head, in actual fact it is merely the environment speaking through him; and he himself unconsciously responds in a
way typical for his group as a whole. Although we like to refer to the peasant's individualism, it is by no means the kind of
individualism that strives to maintain some of those unique features that distinguish one person from another. In fact, it is
precisely these unique features, these specific differences, that
are rare in the associations of the rural child. These associations are to a great extent the reflection of the concrete environment in which the rural child grew up.

In our data for rural children, the figures for individual responses diverge radically from the corresponding figures for
the other social groups, thereby serving as further evidence
that developmental differences are manifested only against a
background of class differences.

We have some interesting data that show us the tremendous
significance of the concrete sociohistorical conditions for the
development of a child's psychological experience and for the
level of socialization attained by this experience. The material
obtained with rural children in our experiments was gathered
in a typical rural village, very quiet, remote from the city,

from the district capital, and from the railroad. The environment in such a village is characteristically monotonous and unchanging, and these conditions will yield results like those just
discussed.

We were also able to make another study, not included in this
essay, on children of a large village located near a railroad and
of a regional city on which the economy of the village was eco-
nomically dependent. This difference was enough to give us a
completely different picture. Instead of 35% uniform responses,
we obtained a figure of only 24%; on the other hand, the variety
of the responses increased sharply. Of course, our uniformity
index of collective experience was still higher than that of the
urban schoolchildren, but it was far lower than that obtained
for children from a typical country village, isolated from the
influences of the city.

However, we may go even further in our analysis. We may
ask ourselves whether all spheres of experience are of equal
social significance for children. Will we find that the percentage of responses that are the same for the entire group is the
same for every test word, regardless of from what area of experience that word has been taken? Or, on the contrary, will
we find that conditions to which the children of the group are
accustomed and which influence the entire group in the same
way will give us the maximal number of uniform responses whereas
words taken from strange areas of experience to which not all
the children have been exposed will give the most individual
responses, showing a wide range of variation and randomness
for the group as a whole? It is reasonable to assume that where
environmental influences are restricted to a narrow range of
situations, such a difference will be great and that, on the other
hand, if the child's environment has provided him with a sufficiently rich and varied experience, these differences will be
minor.

To begin, we shall compare the responses of rural children
with those of the older urban children, on the one hand, and with
homeless children, on the other.

Table 4 shows us the indices of sameness of collective exper-

ience for children from different social groups, but this time
the figures refer to the values obtained when the test words are
taken from different areas of social experience rather than to
the aggregate indices. The question we posed for ourselves
was: How uniform will the children's (rural, urban, homeless)
responses be when they are given test words from home, school,
city life, etc.?

Table 4

Uniformity of Collective Experience as Reflected in
Responses to Different Types of Stimuli (in %)

Subjects	Home	School	City	Social life	Nature
Rural children	40	40	16	20	16
Urban children (older)	16.5	14	14	12.5	16.5
Homeless children	19	20.8	18	16.3	12

The data in Table 4 give us an interesting picture.

We see that when presented stimuli taken from home and
school life, the group of rural children had an extremely high
uniformity index: 40% of all rural children gave identical responses; in the sameness and uniformity of their experience,
these subjects far outstripped the others. But if we look at the
figures for test words associated with city life, we find that the
number of children who responded with identical answers decreased to 16%, i.e., more than twofold. The figures here show
that everything associated with a primitive home and school environment was part of the collective experience of rural children
and that the monotonous environment was a major influence for
all of them. None of the responses to test words associated with
the city and with social life derived from such a uniform experience, and hence the number of identical responses was considerably less.

But city children and homeless urchins did not exhibit such

sharp differences in the sameness and uniformity of their collective experience of different types of test words. The lives of both of these groups were sufficiently rich and varied that in no case was the number of identical responses very high. But their experience was rich and varied in all spheres: the indices for even the most varied types of test words did not differ as widely as in the case of the peasant children. The indices for the different types of test words differed very little; in fact, only one decrease was noted, and that was by only about 33% for the urchins' responses to test words associated with nature (one could, of course, expect that street children would have a minimum of collective experience in this area).

We observed an analogous but inverse picture when we analyzed the number of individual (single) responses given by our subjects to analogous test words. Table 5 summarizes the results.

Table 5

Number of Individual (Nonrecurrent) Responses
to Different Sets of Test Words (in %)

Subjects	Home	School	City	Social life	Nature
Rural children	22	20	48	44	24
Urban children (older)	42	50	50	48	42
Homeless children	55	53	60	59	54

We see that the number of responses occurring only once in rural children was comparatively low for test words associated with the home and school and quite high when the children's experience was of a highly individual nature (city, social life). The children had not yet been exposed to structured collective experience in these areas, so that the high number of purely individual responses should not surprise us. The urban schoolchild gives us a different picture. Although the number of individual responses is higher for these children than for the rural children, the differences in indices obtained for different types of test words are not at all great. Obviously, school studies and the influences of city life expose the child to experiences in all spheres of life, and there is practically nothing that is totally foreign to him. The material to which he is exposed in his schoolwork makes nature and society just as accessible to him as the direct impressions he receives from his environment. For the city child the world of immediate impressions begins to give way to more mediated forms of experience, to a world of facts assimilated through communication, books, and cultural influences.

It is enough to compare the responses of the rural child with those of the older urban schoolchild to observe this phenomenon directly. Let us dwell on a few examples in which the responses of a city child who has already had long exposure to the influences of school are compared with those of a 10-12-year-old rural child to the same test words.

Table 6

Analysis of Responses to the Word "School" (in %)

Subjects	Index of commonality	Index of diversity	Index of individual responding
Rural children	37-50	15	5
Urban children (younger)	14	60	46
Urban children (older)	11	61	53

Our first example is the word "school" itself; the indices for this word showed a wide range of variation for the rural, urban, and street children. Table 6 presents a summary of these data; we see essentially opposite pictures for urban and rural children: whereas most of the responses of the rural children to this word were of two kinds ("a building," "learning") and, moreover, a total of only 6 different responses were given (in a group

of 40), among the younger urban children (44 in all) we obtained
27 different responses, and the same word was given by only 7
subjects. The results were the same for the older schoolchildren: 22 different responses from a total of 36 subjects, the
same word being given in only 4 cases.

Table 7

Breakdown of Responses to the Word "School"

Rural children	Older urban schoolchildren	
1. Building 15	1. Pupil 4	12. Shelf 1
2. Learning 20	2. Good 3	13. Grade 1
3. Hut 1	3. Desk 2	14. Window 1
4. Barn 2	4. Class 1	15. Five 1
5. Is standing 1	5. Map 1	16. Pretty 1
6. Teacher 2	6. Teacher 1	17. Organized 1
	7. Children 1	18. Children's home 1
	8. Building 1	19. Group 1
	9. Wall 1	20. No. 16 1
	10. Floor 1	21. Assignments 1
	11. Stove 1	22. Big 1

Table 7 is an excerpt from some specific experiments listing
the responses to various test words.

The uniform, almost stereotyped responses of the rural children and the wide range of responses of the urban schoolchildren are strikingly apparent, and no laborious analysis is necessary to demonstrate that the foregoing data reflect quite specific environmental influences. As an illustration, let us take
two types of response to words rooted in the experience of the
rural child but known to the urban child only through indirect
experience; these examples will demonstrate the specific differences in the responses in the two cases: our test words are
"rake" and "cart."

Do we even need to point out how fundamental are the differences in the distribution of these responses? Both the concreteness of the responses of the rural children and the sometimes

Table 8

"Rake"		"Cart"	
Rural children	Urban school-children	Rural children	Urban school-children
1. To rake 20	1. Shovel 5	1. To ride 21	1. Squeaks 6
2. Pitchfork 2	2. Pitchfork 5	2. Wheel 2	2. Goes 5
3. Hail 1	3. Iron	3. Plow 1	3. Wood
4. Mow 2	(adj.) 2	4. Horse 2	(adj.) 3
5. Plow 2	4. Wood	5. Sleigh 3	4. Sleigh 3
6. Shovel 2	(adj.) 2	6. Is there 3	5. Horse 2
7. Sickle 2	5. Lies	7. Harrow 1	6. Firm 1
8. Tree 1	there 2	8. Hitched 1	7. Loaded 1
9. Axe 1	6. Sharp 2	9. Barn 1	8. To ride 1
10. I'm carry-	7. To rake 2	10. Harness 1	9. To carry 1
ing 2	8. Sickle 1	11. Hay 1	10. Squeaky 1
11. Hay 1	9. Saw 1	12. Roll 2	11. Good 1
	10. Hay har-		12. Log 1
	vest 1		13. Peasant 1
	11. Mower 1		14. Big 1
	12. Hanging 1		15. Black 1
	13. Hammer 1		16. Wheel 1
	14. There is 1		17. Coachman 1
	15. Stick 1		18. Axle 1
	16. Peasant		19. Stands
	girl 1		there 1
	17. Big 1		
	18. Rake 1		
	19. Is bro-		
	ken 1		

quite general tone of the responses of the urban children stand out. (The use of a large number of adjectives is characteristic of literary associations and the low level of concreteness of the object for the child doing the associating.) The unusual concentration of the rural child's responses was significant: when 20-21 children respond as one voice, "rake" — "to rake" and "cart" — "to ride," two things stand out: the primitive action-word type of response manifested here, and — more important — the high degree of sameness in the nature of the responses for the entire group. We almost never find such uniformity among urban children. Such results can be generated only by a primitive and unchanging environment. In these cases the rural children typically had an unusually small number of nonrecurrent answers (only 4 for "rake" and only 6 for "cart"), whereas the number of such answers among the urban children was far higher (12 for "rake" and 14 for "cart").

However, we find a completely different picture when we look at the responses to words not derived from the immediate experience of the rural child, i.e., words that are still largely strange to him. Let us again take two words — this time "union" and "truth" — to illustrate what we mean. The first of these is from social life, whereas the second is an abstract term for the rural child.

The marked differences between the two cases are obvious. The rural children displayed an extremely varied pattern of responses to both words. Thirty different answers to the word "union" were obtained from 40 children, and 22 of these occurred only once; about the same picture is seen in the case of the word "truth."

The content of the responses in the two instances is also quite typical. The rural children understood the word "union" in the sense of a cooperative union, a shop, where they could buy calico, boots, etc., whereas the urban children, without exception, understood union to refer to a social or political organization. The responses of the rural children to the word "truth" were also inappropriate in the vast majority of cases, whereas those of the urban children clearly demonstrated that they had an adequate grasp of the word's meaning.

But in this study we were not interested in the children's ideas; we wished only to point out the considerable value of an association test for the purposes we had set forth inasmuch as

Table 9

"Union"		"Truth"	
Rural children	Urban children	Rural children	Urban children
1. I sell 1	1. Youth 6	1. I tell 4	1. Untruth 16
2. Members 1	2. Workers 4	2. I read 2	2. Lie 3
3. Shop 6	3. Councils 4	3. Dove 1	3. Crooked-
4. Coopera-	4. Soviet	4. Crooked-	ness 3
tive 1	(adj.) 2	ness 2	4. Good 2
5. Meeting 1	5. Workers	5. I love 1	5. To speak 2
6. Trade 3	and peas-	6. Samovar 1	6. Stupidity 1
7. Proletar-	ants 1	7. Cat 1	7. Newspaper 1
iat 1	6. USSR 2	8. Was justi-	8. Bitter 1
8. Moscow 2	7. Workers 2	fied 1	9. Party 1
9. We buy 2	8. Trade	9. Rails 1	10. My 1
10. Shopping 1	unions 1	10. Grandpa 1	11. Pupil 1
11. Council 2	9. Far away 1	11. Goes 2	12. Not ful-
12. Calico 1	10. Worker 2	12. Purpose-	filled 1
13. Boots 1	11. Unity 1	ly 1	
14. I sit 1	12. Peasant	13. Barn 1	
15. Goods 1	(adj.) 2	14. I be-	
16. The boys 2	13. Alliance 1	lieve 1	
17. Rufusal 1	14. Milk	15. Earth 1	
18. I don't	(adj.) 1	16. Was 2	
know 1	15. Ally 1	17. Untruth 1	
19. School 2	16. VLKSM 1	18. My 1	
20. Building 1		19. Brother 1	
21. Goats 1		20. Old lady 1	
22. Boat 1		21. I hear 2	
		22. Book 1	

"Union"		"Truth"	
Rural children	Urban children	Rural children	Urban children
23. We holler 1		23. I wrote 1	
24. Teacher 1		24. School 1	
25. Pencil 1		25. Songs 1	
26. Let's go 1		26. Sleep 1	
27. Hand 1		27. Teacher 1	
28. School 1		28. Right 1	
29. Together 1		29. I think 2	
30. Necessary 1		30. I don't know 1	

it made it unnecessary to pose questions directly to the subjects and ensured that the results would be less arbitrary and more objective.

As we have seen, different areas of experience revealed different levels of socialization for the rural and the urban child. Moreover, the empirical facts show that pedagogy has completely different tasks to perform in the city and in the country, i.e., each of these environments has its own specific problems when it comes to specifying and ordering the fund of social ideas possessed by children reared in these two environments.

We have intentionally omitted discussing how the collective experience of the homeless urchin is ordered and structured. His responses display a whole array of specific features, and will be dealt with separately elsewhere.

But our numerical data alone are enough to point out a number of features peculiar to the associative processes of these children. We are struck first of all by the wide variety of their responses. As a rule, we found no test words to which the group of 46 urchins gave less than 18-19 different answers, and usually the figure was much higher.

The reasons for this are not hard to understand: on the one hand, the experience of the homeless urchin is incomparably more diversified than that of a rural child or even of an urban schoolchild of the same age. On the other hand, his individual

responses, which are connected with specific emotional config-
urations, give the urchin's associations an even more specific
character, and hence a greater variety.

However, it should be clear that against this general background of wide diversity, in which it is frequently impossible to
find any reaction distinct from the others that is peculiar to any
number of subjects, large or small, there are certain major
areas of experience which are extremely diversified and with
respect to which a collective experience common to the entire
group is nonexistent.

This brings us to one of the most interesting findings of our
study: the areas of experience that are most commonly part of
the collective experience of the normally developing child are
the least common for the homeless urchin. What could be more
intimate and more familiar to a child than his home? There is
surely no other area of experience in which responses are likely
to be more invariable and uniform. The group of 40 rural children gave only 11 different responses to the word "house," and
2 (hut and barn) accounted for 27 anwers. This could hardly
have been otherwise: for these children the household is the
focal point of their lives, and it is not surprising that the most
similar aspects of the home situation produce the stablest and
most uniform impressions on the minds of the children in this
group. The exact opposite was the case with our street children.
Whereas the rural children gave the most uniform responses
to the word "house," the street children gave the most varied
answers, and in this respect behaved quite true to form.

Only three answers were given by as many as three street
children, and these were extremely typical for them: "is burn-
ing" (a response that, however strange, we did not encounter
in any of the other groups of subjects), "bed," and "cow." The
first answer's association with the street experience of the urchin, and the latter's association with vestiges of a rural relation to the home (the farm unit of house and cow) are quite obvious. Characteristically the test word "home" provoked 84%
different responses, and of these, 70% (31) were purely individual, occurring only once.

Table 10

"House"

Street children		Rural children
1. Cat 1	20. Mama 1	1. Barn 14
2. Room 1	21. Garden 1	2. Shed 13
3. White 1	22. Cow 3	3. Garden 2
4. Is burning 3	23. Horse 1	4. Drying barn 1
5. Lamp 1	24. Hut 1	5. Stands there 1
6. Where one	25. Porch 1	6. Home 1
lives 1	26. Wood (adj.) 1	7. Village 1
7. Tables 1	27. Bench 1	8. Where you live 1
8. Roof 1	28. Yard 1	9. Hut 1
9. Fence 1	29. Wall 1	10. Our 1
10. Church 1	30. People live	11. Wood (adj.) 2
11. Black 1	there 1	
12. Windows 2	31. Stone (adj.) 1	
13. Red 1	32. Barn 1	
14. Class 1	33. Clock (ex-	
15. Stairs 1	traneous) 2	
16. Chair 1	34. I don't know 1	
17. Frying pan 1	35. Books 1	
18. Street 1	36. Home 1	
19. Bed 3	37. Knob 1	

It is quite understandable that this extreme variety in the responses given by the street children is tied in with the high degree of variability and diversity of the experience of these children, who have grown up without any direct exposure to the influence of stable, familiar, more or less unchanging circumstances; instead, the situations in which they find themselves change rapidly and unexpectedly, literally kaleidoscopically.

Some test words have completely different meanings for the street child and for the child growing up in a home environment,

and hence will illustrate specific differences in the psychological relief, so to speak, of these two social groups. The word
"kettle" or "boiler" [kotel] is just such a word (Table 11).

Table 11

"Kettle"

Street children		Rural children
1. Boils 2	19. Iron (adj.) 1	1. I cook 12
2. You cook 6	20. Porridge 1	2. Cast iron 8
3. You must boil	21. Trunk 1	3. Father 1
it 1	22. Pot 1	4. Stir 1
4. Grounds 1	23. To be heated 1	5. Water 3
5. Urchins 2	24. Fire 1	6. Fill up 3
6. Lye 1	25. Stove 1	7. Put on 4
7. Cart 1	26. Potbelly	8. Pot 2
8. Kitchen 1	stove 1	9. Cup 1
9. Steamship 1	27. On the train 1	10. Oven tongs 1
10. Big 1	28. Little kettle 1	11. Window 1
11. Ring 1	29. Boilers 1	12. Samovar 1
12. Basin 1	30. Table 1	13. Iron 1
13. Rails 1	31. Shop 1	14. Jar 1
14. Soup 3	32. Goat 1	
15. Steering	33. Spring 1	
wheel 1	34. Kettle	
16. Cube 1	(echolalia) 1	
17. Water 1	35. I'll tell you in	
18. Floorboard 2	a minute (re-	
	fusal) 1	

Even a quick glance at Table 11 is sufficient to reveal that the
two groups have drawn their responses to this word from two
completely different areas of experience. All the responses of

the rural children are associated with eating and the preparation of food (I cook, fill it up, put it on, etc.) whereas for the street children we can distinguish at least three completely different situations with which the word was associated (eating, street kettles around which the homeless and abandoned gather to keep warm; travel — the boilers or kettles on a ship or train, the "section" into which they get stuffed, and numerous other situations specific to their lives). On the other hand — and this should even go without saying — the street child and the rural child are direct opposites as far as the uniformity of collective experience is concerned. A constant environment identical for all the rural children and a kaleidoscopically changing, individual, unstable, and diversified yet organized environment for the street children are the distinguishing marks of the two groups. This is why the diversity of the responses of the street children is two and a half times greater than that found in the corresponding group of rural children.

We shall not dwell further on the street child, his collective experience, and his individuality; that will be dealt with elsewhere.

Let us merely make one comment of a methodological nature: it is absolutely meaningless to study children divorced from the environmental factors that shape their mental makeup. However, most of the methods used in such studies have not been sufficiently objective. The questionnaire, the survey, the interview, or studies of the "set of ideas" of a group have always yielded results whose objectivity is open to serious question. A study of a child's fund of associations such as we have carried out, an evaluation of his collective experience and level of socialization, and the uniformity of the responses of his entire social group give us a good idea of those aspects of a child's experience that are socialized and allow us at least to make indirect inferences about the nature of the environment that has shaped the child. We have gathered all our information from "nonarbitrary" data rather than by posing questions to the child directly; this of course enhances the clinical value of our data

and illustrates the importance of an associative experiment.
As a method it enables us to study the degree of socialization
of the content of a child's mind and thus indirectly to explore
the intellectual "capital" of a given social group of children.

Speech Responses and the Pedagogical Process

It remains for us to say a few words about the implications
of our study for pedagogy.

The stimuli to which children will give the most invariable
and identical responses and to which their responses will be
most varied, more or less unsocialized, and individual are certainly relevant to education. The issue is what stimuli will provide the soundest underpinnings for educative processes.

However, one other question should be added: Which stimuli
are sufficiently understood by a child, and which have become
a stable and permanent part of the structure of his experience?
A serious examination of this problem can provide us with some
basic guidelines for mapping out school curricula, and will help
us to guard against the premature inclusion in a teaching program of certain elements that will actually only complicate the
normal learning of school material.

An associative experiment conducted with a particular group
of subjects could be a direct source of abundant material for
solving this problem. A particular example will illustrate what
we mean: The rural children used in our experiment were giv-
en the word "threshing floor" [gumno] as one of their test
words.

This word was chosen because it is specifically a rural word,
and the experimenters thought it would be understood by all the
children. However, it turned out that the peasants in the region
where the experiment was conducted did not use this word, and
in fact did not even know what it meant, or at least had only a
vague idea of its meaning. The results revealed this immediately, and the pattern of responses is shown in Table 12.

We see that the responses to this stimulus differed radically
from the average responses of the rural child in two respects:

First, they were much more diversified: there were 30 different responses, 28 of which occurred only once, the other 2 occurring six times each ("I don't know," and "To ride"). This is certainly curious, but a look at the content of the responses will clear the matter up. At least 17-18 of all the responses were inappropriate; they were entirely unrelated to the test word. We can safely say, therefore, that at least half of the children did not understand the test word, and that while 6 children refused to answer ("I don't know"), 18 gave inappropriate responses in an effort to lend this strange word some familiarity.

Table 12

Responses of Rural Children to the Word
"Threshing Floor" [Gumno]

1. I go 6	11. Manure 1	21. Iron 1
2. To me 1	12. Plow 1	22. Please 1
3. Paper 1	13. Smooth out 1	23. Dove 1
4. Herd 1	14. Meeting 1	24. We thresh 1
5. Hay 1	15. On the border 1	25. Our 1
6. Shed 1		26. Clock 1
7. Raise a fuss [gomonyat] 1	16. Let's take 1	27. Man 1
	17. Was 1	28. Mother 1
8. House 1	18. Oats 1	29. Jackdaw 1
9. Ears 1	19. Nose 1	30. I don't know 6
10. They say 1	20. City 1	

We obtained such results only when words not used in the particular region were presented, as in the case just described. A number of especially abstract words (e.g., truth, freedom, thought, number, etc.) produced very similar results in rural children.

Table 13 is a summary of results obtained on rural children presented with such unfamiliar test words compared with results obtained with common and easy words.

The picture is very clear-cut and well defined.

Table 13 (in %)

Nature of test word	Index of diversity	Index of uniformity	Inappropriate responses	Appropriate responses
Familiar words	30	62.5	7.5	92.5
Abstract words	71	12	69	31

Whereas 62% of the answers to easy, ordinary stimuli were the same, this figure (uniformity index) decreased to 12% for difficult test words, for which instead we observed highly diversified, variable, and very individual answers. Further, whereas 92.5% of the answers to easy, common test words were appropriate, only 31% were appropriate for difficult and poorly understood words. It is therefore quite natural that under such conditions no correctly conceived approach to teaching can afford to neglect the "index of accessibility" of each stimulus used in the teaching process; we can therefore surmise that the educational system of the future will employ accurately measured indices of accessibility for all the stimuli a teacher might have occasion to use. Only if this condition is fulfilled can the teaching process hope to be sufficiently effective, and only then will methods and techniques of teaching acquire precise foundations.

Of course, this "index of accessibility" will vary for different ages and social groups. A quick glance at our material tells us that words that are quite within the grasp of the urban child are largely out of the reach of the rural child, and that words not understood by younger children are easy and simple for older children to understand.

These observations are all obvious, and their detailed analysis can await the place set aside for them in the present book. An analysis of all aspects of our findings is beyond the scope of this succinct outline.

We should once again stress that under certain conditions, a precise, experimental, psychological experiment will be a necessary stage in any concerted effort to improve the effectiveness of education; and if such an experiment is performed, it goes without saying that the child-subjects should not be isolated from their general historical circumstances. Education is always group oriented, and the teacher should focus on the socialized aspects of his pupils as individuals.

A study of how a specific historical environment is reflected in a child's mental makeup, how this environment helps to shape the child's intellectual assets, how it determines certain forms of complex associative speech processes, and, finally, how certain class traits are created and leave their imprint on the concrete psychological characteristics of children growing up in different environmental conditions — such a study will be successful only if a correctly conceived, experimental approach is used. We shall consider this array of problems in later studies; but the present book, with its modest examples of speech and associative processes, is at least a beginning.

Notes

1) [Speech and intellect in child development]. Moscow, 1927.

2) For a detailed treatment of this question, see [Speech and intellect], Vol. I.

3) Th. Ziehen, Die Ideenassotiation des Kindes, I-1898, II-1900.

4) Cf. Whipple, Manual, Vol. II.

5) J. Piaget, Le langage et la pensée de l'enfant. 1924.

6) In some cases, this index, which takes into account only the maximum number of coincident responses, is replaced by the sum of all responses that were repeated at least three to four times (in 8-10% of the cases) in the given group.

Translated by
Michel Vale

A. R. Luria

EXPERIMENTAL PSYCHOLOGY
AND CHILD DEVELOPMENT

It was not so long ago that investigators of human development thought that the empirical study of the child was almost
completely impossible. The child was considered too variable
a creature, during his first years of life, to conduct experiments
on, so that one could assess child development in the best of
cases only by observations, by keeping diaries and such.

There has been a change in attitude in recent years in this
respect, however. It has not only proven possible to carry out
psychological experiments on children but indeed this has been
found to be the only way to arrive at any deeper understanding
of the broad outlines of child development or to study in their
developmental aspects the sources of those extremely important forms of behavior that achieve their fullest development in
the civilized adult.

The work of Köhler, Lipmann, Bogen, and others on the first
manifestations of intelligent behavior in the child, of Jaensch and
his school on the primitive forms of perception in children, of
Katz, Kuenberg, Eliasberg, and Weigl, on juvenile abstraction,
of Ach, Rimat, and Bacher on concept formation, of C. Bühler on
group responses of small children, and, finally, the outstanding
studies of Piaget on primitive thought in the child and of Lewin
on child behavior in a natural environment have all had an im-

From Nachnoe Slovo, 1930, No. 1, pp. 77-97.

portant part in promoting the experimental study of children; Volkelt's review at the Ninth Congress of Experimental Psychology was able to present a rather impressive list of experimental studies of early childhood that are of unquestionable value.

We shall be dealing with two problems that may be counted among the most timely topics in modern scientific study of the child: the development of a child's perception of the external world, and the formation of cultural skills.

The first topic concerns the ways a child establishes contact with the external world and how he becomes part of the system constituting his environment. The second deals with how a child gradually assimilates cultural experience and becomes an active member of a cultural, laboring community....

In this paper we have not wished to restrict ourselves merely to presenting what Western European psychology has already achieved. All this has already been analyzed, criticized, and defended by studies conducted by Soviet psychologists. The findings we shall present below are the results of our experimental research at our laboratory at the Krupskaya Academy of Communist Upbringing.

Development of a Child's Perception of the External World

How does the young child perceive the external world? Research psychologists have been able only to venture good guesses as to what processes may be regarded as characteristic of a child's primitive perception of the external world.

Whatever we perceive of the world is perceived in a structured fashion, i.e., as a pattern of stimuli. We react and adapt to these external stimuli, and indeed our entire behavior amounts essentially to some more or less apt accommodation to the diverse structures of the external world. To adapt effectively to these conditions the individual must perceive the various situations of the external world in as clear and as differentiated a manner as possible, distinguish among them, and single out from among the whole complex system of forms acting on him those that for him are the most essential. The more differentiated and subtle are our mental capacities in this respect, the more our minds will be able to discriminate among the forms perceived.

May we reasonably expect to find in the infant any measure of distinct perception of situations or of clear discrimination of forms? There are no grounds to assume so, and indeed everything indicates that the world of a child's perceptions differs quite sharply from ours as adults and that, during the first months of life, an infant does not perceive distinct forms and hence is unable to accommodate his behavior to them in any way.

Actually, a number of objectively and carefully performed studies have shown that a child passes the first weeks of life in a diffuse state between sleep and wakefulness. This primitive, semisomnolent state and the child's total isolation from the outside world are further exaggerated by the fact that the receptors necessary to perceive the external world do not begin to operate until rather late. For example, a child does not begin to fix his gaze on shining objects until the age of 3 weeks, the eye begins to follow a moving object only at about the 4th-5th week, and active eye movements and search for an object that has vanished do not appear until the age of 3-4 months (Blonsky). The upshot is that until the age of 3 or 4 months, a child is sort of mentally blind and does not perceive the external world in any distinct forms. In fact, this chaotic, blurred nature of infantile perception still lingers on for many months. The first thing to penetrate the shroud separating the child from the outside world seems, judging from experimental findings, to be color and discrete colored spots. In a series of ingenious experiments Katz showed that a child of 3-6 years may still completely ignore shape and give marked preference to colors. In his experiments Katz gave his child subjects a number of shapes (circles, triangles, squares) of different colors and asked the children to match them. Remarkably enough, in almost no case did the young children match shapes, but matched colors instead. Apparently, this color response is more elementary and manageable for the child than a response to shape. In his inkblot tests Rorschach (1) found that both children and primitive peoples saw mainly combinations of shades of color in the blots and that only

subjects with a more differentiated mental makeup saw structures in them.

All these considerations indicate that the perception of colors
and colored spots is a more primitive, or elementary, and earlier process than perception of structure, and that there is a period in an infant's life in which all that he perceives of the external world consists of spots of light and color arranged in no particular pattern or structure. As time passes, however, the child
begins to perceive shapes and form; and this capacity then becomes one of the most important conditions for the organism, adaptation, without which any further progress would be impossible.

But when does the external world begin to acquire a structured appearance for the child? At what point do discrete, defined structures begin to crystallize out of the chaos of different
shades and hues? This question is central not only for the psychologist but also for the epistemologist who wishes to build his
theory of knowledge on positive foundations.

Obviously, experiments aimed at penetrating the fundamental
mechanics of infantile perception are hardly simple, and a great
deal of ingenuity is required to deal with this problem in the indirect way required.

In the following we shall describe some experiments carried
out in our laboratory to illustrate the degree to which infantile
perception is structured. (2)

To find some objective measure for ascertaining whether a
child perceived a figure as a discrete shape or as some jumbled
chaos of lines and dots we proceeded from the assumption that,
when developed, the mind perceives shape and form as a whole
and that it rather strongly resists breaking it down. If this were
the case and we constructed a shape from individual, separable
elements, a child who did not perceive the shape as a whole
would respond to it as an unorganized collection of individual
elements, whereas a child with a relatively developed, structured
perception would relate to it as a whole, undissociable figure.

We had two groups of blocks. One we arranged in a square,
and the other we spread about at random (Figure 1). Obviously,
a person with a developed and differentiated perception would

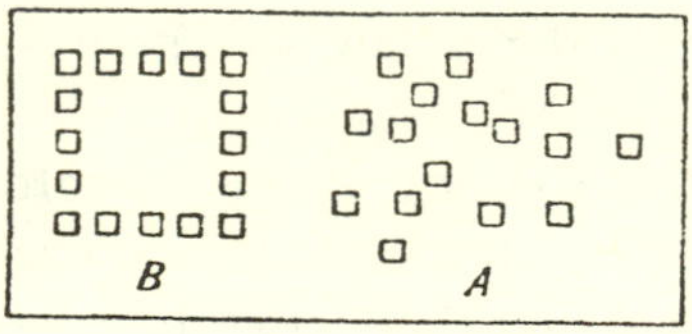

Figure 1

see these two figures as two basically different structures: one would
have no order to it at all, and the observer could remove one, two, or
even three pieces from it without
harm, whereas the second would be
a self-contained whole, in which the
elements were arranged to form one
single structure that in a sense resisted any attempt to break it
up, i.e., the Gestalt factor, linking the elements into one single
integral system, would be operative.

Does a child perceive a square of this sort as an integral
structure, or is it still for him nothing more than a group of random pieces? Would we be able to observe the same resistance
to breaking up an integral figure in a child as in an adult?

Let us find out. In the course of play, we had a child find
from among the others a block onto which we had pasted red paper on the bottom, promising him a piece of candy if he found it.
We arranged the blocks in such a way that together they formed
a specific structure, one block being "extra."
Figure 2 shows this arrangement. We then began our game.

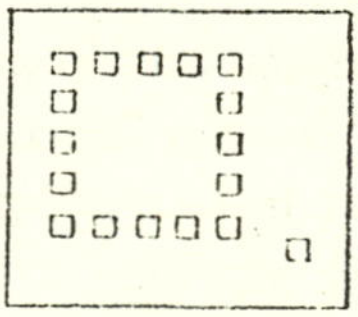

It is evident that if the blocks arranged in
a square were not perceived by the child as a
regular structure, the choice of the one block
with the concealed mark on it would be completely random, and each block would have an

Figure 2

equal chance of being picked. But if the child perceived all 16
blocks as a square and the 17th as an extra one, then the relative stability of the square alone would make the child tend to
pick the extra one standing alone. This would be a persuasive
demonstration that he perceived these elements as a structure
with its own intrinsic consistency, existing as a separate, discrete entity.

Our experiments showed (3) that children of different age
groups responded in opposite ways to this task. Almost all children $1\frac{1}{2}$ to 2 years old picked up blocks indiscriminately, break-

ing up the square as they did so.   Children $2\frac{1}{2}$ to 3 years old or
more, on the other hand, without exception picked the extra block.
These children evidently found it very difficult to break up the
figure. No matter how many times we repeated the experiment,
placing the extra block in different positions, we obtained the
same results: the square remained intact, and the children always picked the extra block that was not part of it. Even our attempts to check the impulses inclining the child toward the extra
block (by removing the rewards attached to it) altered the course
of events for only a short time. Thus, it seemed that for this
age group the square was a unified structure, difficult to break
up, and that all the child's attention was concentrated on the extra block off to the side. This conclusion was further reinforced
in our experiments by the fact that even if we took one of the
blocks that was part of the square and placed it
so that the identifying mark was face up (Figure
3), the child would disregard it and still reach
immediately for the block standing alone, not-
withstanding the fact that he could have gotten
his reward simply and easily by picking the
block lying there with the mark face up. That
is how strong the Gestalt factor, the discrete-
ness factor, was as a determinant and organizer
of the child's entire behavior.

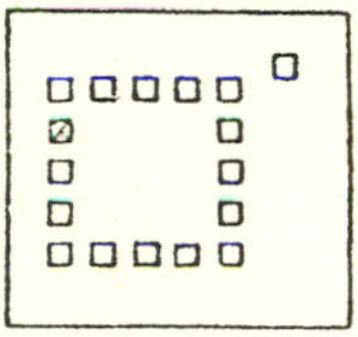

Figure 3

We observed a profound and fundamental difference between
the behavior of $1\frac{1}{2}$-2-year-olds and that of 3-4-year-olds. The
behavior of the younger children was ill defined and unorganized
and appeared to be governed wholly by the child's diffuse and
chaotic perceptions. . . . The world first ceases to appear chaotic and unstructured to the child some time between the ages of
$1\frac{1}{2}$ and 2 years. The first foundations for an organized perception of the world, which subsequently transforms the child's behavior so thoroughly, are laid down during this time. (4)

Psychologists have known that at about this time a child's behavioral processes begin to be organized, the first signs of organized attention appear, and the child begins to single out particular objects in the external world and fix his gaze and, if one may

use the term, his entire behavior on them. This process is now much more intelligible to us. Indeed, it is at about this time that the outside world begins to be perceived by a child as something with a definite structure; and it is quite clear that a child's perception begins to discriminate certain structures in it that are the most prominent while others that are less structured begin to function as background. These structures, which emerge from a general background and coordinate the child's behavior around them, stand out as a "field of clear consciousness," if we may use a subjective phrase. Only when certain stimuli of a situation are singled out in this way does organized accommodation to them first become possible.

But what we have just described here are nothing other than the characteristic features of attention. It is characteristic of attention that it singles out some elements from a general background and allows others to recede; attention is marked, above all, by the replacement of unorganized, diffuse behavior by organized responses concentrated on specific stimuli. Indeed, some psychologists have correctly observed that our attention is only the subjective expression of the organization of our perceptions into particular structures.

For instance, let us take a set of lines arranged parallel with one another, as in Figure 4A, and compare them with the configuration in Figure B; in both cases, A and B, the number of lines is the same; but in A they are laid out in a uniform way, whereas in B a certain structure has been given to them. As a result, a peculiar change takes place in perception: whereas in A our gaze

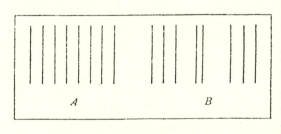

Figure 4

glides smoothly over the pattern, discriminating nothing against the background of these monotonous lines, in B it concentrates on the two middle lines, which appear as a kind of pathway at the

center of a structured field, and we could say that our attention
is optimally concentrated on them. We are dealing with a similar process in the child, except that objectively one and the same
figure is first perceived by the child as an undifferentiated collection of elements, and only later does he begin to perceive it
as an integral structure. Of course, either the figure itself or
whatever is interfering with it (depending on the conditions of
the experiment) begins to attract the child's attention; in our experiment, specifically, the separate, extra block served as a focal point against the background of the structure as a whole and
attracted the child's elementary attention to it. . . .

After such tests we may distinguish two fundamentally different stages in the development of a child's perception; a chaotic
and diffuse stage, and a stage of structured perceptions, in which
the external world first assumes distinct contours for the child.
These findings agree well with the observations of Major (5),
who distinguished three stages of perception in experiments in
which he showed children colored pictures.

In the first stage the pictures appeared to the child as merely
chaotic combinations of colored spots; he evidently did not notice
the figures shown in them (at this stage a child will tear up pictures like any other piece of paper). In the second stage the
child began to discriminate the figures in the pictures, but from
all appearances did not differentiate between the picture of an
object and the object itself: the child would try to grab an apple
in a picture, tussle with a cat in a picture, etc. He began to distinguish between an object and its image only much later. This
naïve relationship to shape remains a typical feature of a child's
perception for some time.

We noted the same features in the development of a child's
active behavior as in the development of his perception. Experiments we performed with children of different age groups will
illustrate the two stages a child passes through in his relation
to the things of the external world: first, a diffuse, unordered
stage, and, second, a stage in which naïve perception of shape
predominates.

We made a cross out of blocks (Figure 5) and asked our sub-

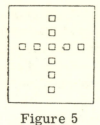

Figure 5

jects to count all the blocks. We were not particularly interested in the actual counting (calling out the numbers), but in the order in which
the child moved his finger from one block to the
next. The degree and nature of the order in this
process would show us, we thought, how a child
accommodated to a regular but relatively complex structure at different stages of development,
i.e., how this structure determined the child's actions.

We gave 2-3-year-olds this task. We immediately noticed that
a regular structure still did not elicit methodical, ordered behavior at this age: when he counted the blocks, a child would point
to one block and then another in no order, jumping from one row
to another, leaving out some and counting others twice. His adaptation to structure was clearly unsystematic. We have observed
the same type of behavior in many retarded children of much
older age, but at lower levels of development. This unordered,
unsystematic accommodation later gives way to regular, organized, systematic forms of behavior, although not all at once;
one may say that first only the simplest structures begin to
elicit organized forms of behavior. A child of 3-4 years is able
to count a series of blocks arranged in a straight line correctly
and systematically (Figure 6A), but still cannot respond in any
organized fashion to the structure of a broken line (Figure 6B);
and the ability to respond
correctly to the structure of
a cross, which requires a
systematic switchover from
one intersecting line to another, appears even later.

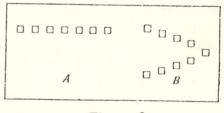

Figure 6

What we found especially
interesting, however, was that
a child would not directly
acquire this ability to cope with a complex structure, but would
pass through a certain intermediate stage. Whereas for a 2-3-
year-old the structure of the perceived figure exercised no noticeable influence on how he organized his behavior, in the next

stage the structure wholly determined the child's behavior. The example of the cross shows this with special clarity. A 5-6-year-old child would comply with our instructions to count the blocks in the cross by doing so in the order in which he perceived them in the cross arrangement. But since the cross consisted of two intersecting lines, the child would count each line separately, so that the block in the middle would be counted twice. Whereas in the first stage each block constituted a separate, independent item for the child, in this second stage his orientation was determined by his perception of the overall shape, and counting became a function of shape. Only much later would this simple determining role of shape be overcome; and then, at the same time as the child perceived an integral structure, he would begin to discriminate the individual elements as well. Thus we come to the third stage, in which the ability to accommodate to a structure in an organized fashion goes hand in hand with the critical use of such a comparatively complex process as elementary counting. In this third stage the individual elements are differentiated from the whole, and behavior begins to assume a complex and mediated nature; a direct reaction to shape gives way to complex, acculturated perception, linked with abstraction of individual elements. This differentiation of individual elements in a shape has quite definite age limits, which although they depend to a considerable extent on the complexity of the structure itself, are still quite constant.

Thus, we found (in an experiment done by the students Novitskii and Elmenev) that 62.5% of 4-5-year-old preschoolers made mistakes in counting a cross owing to holistic perception of structure; in another group, of 8-9-year-olds, mistakes of this type were made in only 6.2% of the cases. When a more complex figure (Figure 7: blocks arranged as two intersecting squares) was given to the children, the number of mistakes made (counting the blocks at the intersections twice, or counting unsystematically, in no order) increased to 100% for the preschoolers (5-6-year-olds) and remained at a high level even for the

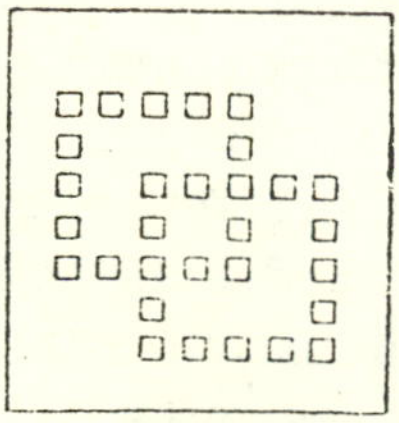

Figure 7

older group (87.5%). The ability to discriminate an individual
element within a perceived shape is a rather complex task for
children; it is clear, however, that only after such an ability
has developed will a child be able to utilize complex forms
of thought requiring the ability to isolate individual elements
at will, abstract them, and operate with them with relative ease.

Thus we see that the path traversed by a child's perception
leads from chaotic, diffuse perception, to a simple, holistic relationship to shapes, to a complex, mediated accommodation to
them, combining holistic features with relative ease of discrimination of individual elements.

The Development of Cultural Skills in the Child

An adult possesses a number of cultural skills. All are acquired in the process of growing up and learning; and by the time
a child reaches school age, these skills are already to a considerable extent automatic. When we read or write we do not really
carry out any complex psychological actions, but only automatically reproduce techniques we learned at earlier stages of development. If we wish to find out how cultural skills are developed, we must go back to the earliest stages of their history and
describe the path they traversed in the child's mind. Let us take
the two perhaps most important cultural abilities, counting and
writing, to see how they develop in the child.

The Development of Counting

How does a child learn to count? Posing the question in this
way will help us to follow the development of counting processes
in the child. We know that the abilities and abstract concepts
necessary for counting develop quite late, after a child has begun school. But we also know that preschoolers are able to perform simple operations of division, subtraction, and addition in
their play. Of course, these actions are not automatic for the
child; he must improvise. If a child does not possess the techniques of abstract counting, what does he use in their stead?

What stages does counting pass through before it becomes abstract and automatic?

Experiments designed by E. Kuchurin in our laboratory have enabled us to describe the development of counting in the child more precisely.

In his play a 4-5-year-old subject had to divide a number of objects among 3 or 4 of his playmates. We gave our subjects complete freedom to deal with the problem in any way they wished and recorded only those techniques the child employed for division. We soon found that the children accommodated to this problem in a variety of ways. The younger ones and the most retarded tried to divide up the pile of blocks or tokens directly, without using any auxiliary techniques. They would assemble the items on the table and then would apportion them "by sight" with their hands, shoving some to each of their playmates. This was the very first, simple stage of accommodation to a division problem. It involves a simple and direct operation; the process is not yet differentiated into a series of successive techniques to facilitate division and render it more accurate. The result of the division, of course, is inaccurate and totally dependent on what the child embraces in his field of vision. We may imagine that a primitive adult would develop quite accurate distribution skills for dividing up his prey (by virtue of a splendidly developed direct perception of quantity); but a child, who does not have such a finely developed capacity as primitive man, will never be able to achieve anywhere near such accurate results with this technique.

The process of division is shaped very differently in somewhat older children (5-5 $\frac{1}{2}$ years old). In this group we first notice that the process of direct accommodation becomes differentiated into a number of successive operations, that the child acquires a number of synthetic techniques to aid division, and that he first invents some cultural form for dealing with this complicated task.

We note a peculiar phenomenon in a child of this age: he does not proceed directly to divide up the elements among his playmates, but first performs a series of operations to help him make the division more accurately. Without any prompting from us, the children would begin to make arrangements of the blocks (or tokens) and then distribute these to their playmates.

In our experiments the children made "sofas," "tractors," and "mausolea" (Figure 8), and each of their playmates got one of them.

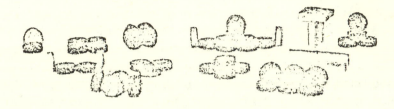

Figure 8

Not yet able to count abstractly or to deal with the concept of number, the child works out little helpful techniques that enable him to solve a problem that without them would have been insoluble.

By giving each playmate a tractor or mausoleum, a child made the division correctly. The way devised was intelligible to him and fit his purposes; he operated with concrete objects with which he was familiar instead of quantities that were difficult and strange to him.

But does this ingenious invention not resemble, to some extent, the device used by a primitive adult in his calculations? Has not the child, in his way, come spontaneously upon the same method of counting as that used by primitive peoples?

We shall put this question aside for the time being, noting only that at this point the child has definitely entered a second stage in the development of his counting abilities. This stage of primitive arithmetic is marked by the fact that the process of division is now mediated: it takes place with the aid of a series of auxiliary operations; and for abstract notions of quantity, which are still lacking, the functional utilization of a number of concrete shapes is substituted.

But the development of counting in the child does not stop with this. Clearly, though this elementary device (sofas, tables, mausolea) helped the child count, it also limited counting and constituted an obstacle to its further development. The most important limitation a shape used as a device for division places on counting is that it does not allow for any quantitative operations; it only enables the division to be made in one fell swoop, that is all. If a "sofa" a child uses for his division consists of six pieces, these pieces will always figure as a single whole; no other element can be added to them, just as no element can be subtracted. This makes the process of division extremely constricted; and if a child uses such shapes for comparing and checking to see if the apportionment he has made is correct, he will have each time to invent new shapes in suitable quantity in terms of the number of elements going to each playmate.

Indeed, because of the primitiveness of this form of counting, using objects and shapes, the child is obliged to take the next step toward developing counting by numbers and to make the transition from objects to spatial figures. In this stage, a peculiar change takes place in the devices a child uses in counting: instead of building figures out of the blocks and then distributing them to his playmates, the child puts the blocks in some spatial order (column, row, etc.) and then distributes the number of such figures required to each of his playmates. These spatial forms give the child considerably more freedom with regard to quantitative operations. They are no longer specific sofas or tractors to which nothing can be added or from which nothing can be taken away. The columns and rows are distinguished by the fact that any number of elements can be added to or subtracted from them. They are therefore no longer simple models of concrete figures, but represent a transition to the spatial symbolization of quantity in general. A child who has constructed such shapes can move elements from one figure to another to even them out and in this way divide as accurately as possible.

This use of spatial, serial shapes, which we find among 5-6-year-olds, not only is a further step toward achieving ultimate mastery over arithmetic but also marks a transition from con-

crete, object-bound notions to abstract notions of quantity, which
makes arithmetic operations freer and less primitive.

The overall evolution of arithmetic skills is elegantly illus-
trated by the different attitudes, appearing at different stages,
of children toward the remainder in a division problem.

In the first stage we distinguished, namely, the phase of primitive, direct division, no remainder exists. The child makes a
crude sight division, and as yet has no sense of a remainder.
As a product of division, a remainder occurs in the second stage,
in which it plays a rather important role. The most striking feature of a remainder in this phase is its indivisibility. If a child
builds four mausolea out of six pieces each, distributes them
to four playmates, and still has enough blocks left to build another mausoleum, he will not be able to distribute them. He may
build another mausoleum, but will then disregard it as belonging
to no one, or take it himself, but he will not try to distribute it.
The shape that enabled him to effect the division is itself whole
and indivisible, and at this stage the rules of division are quite
different from the rules of ordinary mathematics. At this stage
a remainder may be larger than the divisor, but still be indivisible. The child is able to cope with a remainder only in the next
stage, when he begins to employ spatial figures; but it is only
when abstract counting is fully developed, during the school-age
period, that he will have fully mastered the problem of a remainder.

In our experiments we tried to shed light on the basic devices
used by a child who is not yet able to count. By observing in
what order these devices appeared we were able to obtain some
understanding of the steps involved as a child develops cultural
counting abilities, and once again found telling evidence of the
tremendous and unique effort this little creature must make before he is able easily and automatically to perform numerical
operations that seem to us so simple and easy.

Development of Writing

An adult writes down something if he wants to remember it
or transmit it to others.

Group attitudes develop rather late in the child (6), so that this second function of writing does not figure in when writing is still in its embryonic stages. As a means of remembering and recording material, writing passes through a series of specific stages before it achieves an adequate level of development.

Writing is one of the typical cultural functions of human behavior. In the first place, it presupposes the functional use of certain objects and devices as signs and symbols. Instead of directly storing some idea in his memory, a person writes it down, records it, by making a mark that when observed will bring the recorded idea to mind. Direct accommodation to the task is replaced by a complex, mediated technique.

This ability to use an object or sign, mark or symbol, functionally develops rather late in the child, and in the preschool period we still are able to observe children whose way of coping with certain problems is clearly primitive and unmediated, children for whom the functional use of a sign is still a stage beyond their reach.

For example, we may ask a 3-4-year-old in the course of play to note down in some way some material he has to remember. In most cases we find that even the mere thought of using some object or action to record, or not to forget, some item is still wholly alien to the child. Without making any attempt on his own to record anything, the child will confidently assure us that he "can remember better that way." The ability to mediate his memory, to use some notation or mark, some "mnemonotechnical" device, as it is called, in place of direct memorization is lacking in a child at this level of development....*

In our laboratory we have observed how a child devises primitive mnemonotechnical and differentiated descriptive forms of notation. Once symbolic writing has been invented, the situation becomes much more complex; and we are not yet able to say with certainty whether a child would be able to invent such a complex system on his own without outside influences. But all

---

*The material that follows here in the original is described in detail in the paper on writing. — Ed.

the forms of conventional symbolic language and writing in children, the codes and cryptography that flourish during the school-
age period, are, of course, not a spontaneous invention, but an
imitation of the systems invented in the history of civilization
and handed down to children in school. Whatever earlier and
more spontaneous symbolic systems of writing may have existed
are for the time being unknown to us.

It is especially characteristic that once a child has learned
symbolic writing and has passed into this fourth stage, in our
count, the stage of symbolic cultural writing, he loses or discards all the earlier, more primitive forms and immerses himself completely in this new cultural technique. We can now put
the child in any situation at all, and whatever the circumstances,
he will try to use this maximally economical system; any reversion to his earlier, spontaneously devised systems will be unnecessary and often even impossible for him.

Let us return briefly to the example of our experiments. We
gave school-age children the task of remembering a series of
digits. As an aid we gave them a piece of paper (but no pencil),
a string, a bunch of straws, etc. In all cases the school-age
children would try to fashion something resembling a particular
digit out of the paper, but in almost no case tried to note the
figure by means of the quantity of elements.

Figure 9 shows a notation from a school-age child (8 years
old) made with the aid of paper
and straws.

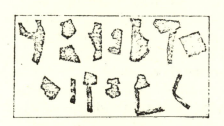

We see that the child made
his notes by tearing from the
paper marks that crudely reproduced the outward shape of
the figures. When there was
no paper left, he used the straws
lying on the floor and made up
his own numerical shorthand,
with simplified, although recognizable, figures.

Figure 9

Under the influence of this task demand, which was made possible by learning new cultural techniques, the child's attitude

toward the devices he had mostly used during the preschool period changed radically. When we gave a preschooler grains or pellets and asked him to use them to note numbers, he would do this quite easily, setting off the required number of grains, etc., in a separate pile. But a school-age child would solve this same problem in a completely different way. From the grains or pellets he would construct a symbolic representation of the digits; and when the process was made more difficult (e.g., if the pellets did not keep together, sliding over the smooth glass surface provided), the child would be more inclined to give up completely than revert back to old discarded forms once he had used a quantitative form of notation.

The development of the cultural skills of counting and writing involves a series of stages in which one technique is continually discarded for another. Each subsequent stage supersedes and supplants the previous one; and only after he has gone through the stages of inventing his own devices and has learned the cultural systems evolved over the centuries does a child arrive at the stage of development that is characteristic of advanced, civilized man.

But a child does not develop at the same pace in all respects. He may learn and invent cultural forms of coping in one area, but remain at previous, more primitive levels in other areas of activity. His cultural development is often uneven, and experiments indicate that traces of primitive thinking often show up even in quite developed children.

But for those involved in the practical tasks of child-rearing and education, the detection of these peculiar remnants of earlier stages of cultural development is a matter of primary importance.

When he enters school, a child is not a tabula rasa the teacher may fashion any way he wishes. This tablet already contains the marks of those techniques the child has used in learning to cope with the complex problems of his environment. When a child enters school he is already equipped, he already has his own cultural skills. But this equipment is primitive and archaic; it has been forged not by the systematic influence of a pedagogical environment, but by the child's own primitive attempts to cope with cultural tasks on his own.

Psychologically, a child is not an adult in miniature. He fashions his own primitive culture; though he does not possess the art of writing, he still writes; and though he cannot count, he nevertheless does so. Empirical study of these primitive forms of acculturation will not only help us attain a better understanding of the child but will also enable us to trace the genesis of the most important forms of culturally acquired skills, which are such important tools in the life of the civilized, adult, human being.

Notes

1) Rorschach, Psychodiagnostik. 1923.

2) All the experiments we shall be discussing later on were carried out at the Laboratory of Psychology of the Academy of Communist Education by laboratory workers and students.

3) The experiments were first set up, at our instigation, by the student Fedorova.

4) In saying this we of course have in mind primarily the child's responses to purely visual, mainly geometric structures. It is beyond question that a child recognizes his mother, father, and others familiar to him before the age of $1\frac{1}{2}$ years and that in this regard the world assumes a structure of sorts already much earlier. In these cases, however, the discrimination of familiar figures and faces does not take place in conformity with the laws of a visual structure. This phenomenon is much more complex; and living, social contact with these people and things and a number of educative, conditioned responses acquired in the course of this contact here play a much more important role than visual structure. Hence, we may still regard our experiments on elementary discrimination of geometric structures as symptomatic of the general trend of development.

5) Major, First steps in mental growth. New York, 1906.

6) Piaget mentions that in the preschool period he only very rarely encountered in children a desire to share with one another, to engage in group dialogue, etc.

A. R. Luria

PATHS OF DEVELOPMENT OF
THOUGHT IN THE CHILD (<u>1</u>)

If with regard to epistemology dialectics is a general method
of inquiry, for psychology the process of dialectical thinking is
itself a subject of inquiry.

For the psychologist, dialectical thinking is a product of long
development and the most complex of the higher forms of intelligence. Hence, it is quite natural for the psychologist to try to
trace the development of thought and to determine the sources
of dialectical thinking.

If dialectical thinking is the most advanced form of thinking,
possible only at the higher stages of evolution, it is natural for
scientists to want to study the phases that preceded it in the
evolution of thought, and perhaps to shed light even on the dialectic of development of thought processes, by contrasting and
comparing complex forms of dialectical thinking with other,
more primitive forms.

Such a historical analysis should show us what forms of
thought distinguish primitive thinking, what categories and
methods are typical of it, and, on the other hand, what categories and methods of thinking did not emerge until later, becoming fully developed only in the dialectical thinking of the civilized, adult, human being.

There are several ways one can approach the study of the de-

From <u>Estestvoznanie i Marksizm</u>, 1929, No. 2, pp. 97-130.

velopment of thinking: one may trace the primitive forms of thinking among peoples at a low level of civilization; one may stop with animal behavior; or one may study the development of thinking ontogenetically, that is, by focusing on the first stages of intelligent activity in the child.

In all these cases our findings would be qualitatively unique, yet undoubtedly relatively primitive, forms of thought. An analysis of each of these forms should reveal some of the unique aspects of primitive thought processes.

We shall be concentrating here on a child's thought, because it is closer and more accessible to us and we are able not only to observe but also to verify certain of its aspects experimentally, and also because intelligence plays a quite specific role in a child's behavior and hence gives it a number of unique features of its own.

Furthermore, in studies on children we are best able to observe directly how the thought of this creature, who has not yet become a part of complex social life, is being molded and what stages it passes through before it achieves the full-fledged status of the thought of a civilized, adult, human being.

The purpose of this study is to investigate the thought of children in the hope of finding in it some clues to the prehistory of dialectical thinking and tracing the antithesis, but also the roots, of dialectical thinking in the primitive aspects of infantile intelligence.

We set out along two paths in our pursuit of this objective:

1. We studied child behavior, the techniques and devices the child employs to cope with the complex problems he must face in his environment.

2. We studied the child's verbal thought, the concepts he uses, his logic.

The first path leads us into the realm of intelligent behavior, which Thorndike described as characterized by a hierarchy of skills aimed at the accomplishment of new tasks. The second path leads us directly into those questions bearing on thought in the most ordinary sense of the term, i.e., a child's judgments, his views of the world, and his logic.

No psychologist who thinks dialectically, however, would dream of isolating one aspect of the question from the other. If we want to study a child's thinking, we must divide our attention equally between the primitive features of his behavior and those of the actual mental operations he performs in solving the most complicated problems posed by his environment.

If the young child displays shortcomings and inconsistencies in his logic and in the structure of his judgments, this must be reflected in his behavior: if certain primitive features are typical of a child's intellectual behavior, this should be reflected in the most complex levels of how the child's outlook on the world is structured.

Let us first look at children's behavior, therefore, and then examine how they actually think (i.e., we shall first examine practical intelligence, and then cognitive intelligence), to see if we can shed any light on what interests us.

Primitive Behavior

The Child's Natural Behavior and Its Inherent Conservatism

What traits have we become accustomed to seeing in behavior guided by dialectical thinking?

A keen regard for the real, the ability to take into account all sorts of changing conditions, so as to be able not only to adapt to the real world but also to predict its dynamics and to adapt it to oneself; a considerable plasticity and flexibility of behavior that enable one to make use of different devices and different means, depending on the situation; and, finally, the definitive rejection of all pat, ossified forms of behavior — these are the traits of behavior that best reflect a dialectical method of thinking.

It is just these traits that we do not observe in the behavior of the small child, however; they develop, we find, at a much later stage. Indeed, we can even observe the very opposite traits; and it is these that constitute the groundwork for the development of a child's more complex forms of behavior.

The younger the child (or more precisely, the more primitive his level of intelligence), the more unvaried, inflexible, and static is his behavior. Once a child has found a particular way of dealing with a certain problem, he is unable to refrain from using it under other conditions and to replace it with another technique; he tries to employ the same tactic everywhere; and the more primitive it is, the more resistant and difficult it is to suppress.

This has led a number of authors to claim that a child's behavior is conservative (Werner, Sully, Skupin). Habits developed in early childhood are fixed and inert, and to gain control over them requires considerable pedagogical effort. This inert, resistant nature of responses is manifested especially clearly by the small child when he tries to cope with complex problems that are new for him; the small child's behavior is distinguished by the fact that he always tries to approach new and complicated problems with the most primitive and habitual methods, which he has solidly learned.

The small child's behavior does not extend over a very wide range: he has a few instinctive responses, which are innate and modified in specific ways by influences from the environment, and an assortment of habits, which have been inculcated in him directly on the basis of these instinctive processes — this is really all we have on the positive side of the ledger for a young child in the first years of life. On the negative side, however, is the need to accommodate to dozens, even hundreds, of new situations with which life confronts him at every turn.

It is perfectly natural that a child should tend first to rely on the repertory of instinctive responses and primitive habits he already possesses to deal with these complex new problems. This confrontation with new problems and the child's attempts to cope with them directly produce a general conflict that, if conditions are favorable, gives rise to new, more complicated forms of behavior in the child as he develops. Let us look at some of the findings.

The following examples are taken from experiments with retarded children conducted by O. Lipmann. (2) They provide us with a lucid model of the primitive, rigid behavior of the small

child under complex condtions and give us some idea of the basic factors determining that behavior.

Lipmann actually only repeated with children Köhler's experiments on primate intelligence, with certain modifications. The
simplest of these experiments went as follows: The experimenter
placed a toy on the upper edge of a blackboard, and the child was
supposed to get it. The edge of the blackboard was too high for the
child to reach with his hand. A stick lay near the blackboard, however, and with it the child could easily knock the toy down and get it.

Lipmann observed the behavior of children of different levels
of mental retardation in this experiment. He was thus able to
define the most primitive forms of child behavior, behavior that,
as we shall see, displayed distinctly conservative features, an
obstinate resistance to routine ways of resolving a complex
problem, and an inability to discard immediately methods that
were unsuitable in the particular situation and replace them
with others that were more appropriate.

Here are two protocols describing the behavior of two children of different levels of development in this situation:

Subject A - 8 years, 6 months old; severely retarded.
  Subject stands in front of the blackboard and begins to
jump up and down, stretching out his hand toward the toy.
He was evidently unable to see that he could not get the
toy in this way.
  Experimenter: You won't get anything that way.
  Subject continues to jump.
  Experimenter: Look, you'll accomplish nothing like
that; try some other way.
  Subject stands on the desk, 0.75 m from the blackboard,
and tries to get the toy with his hands.
  Experimenter: Well, what are you going to use to get
the toy?
  Subject looks confusedly at the experimenter, not know-
ing what to use to help.
  Experimenter casually takes the stick and places it
near the blackboard.

Subject looks at him but does not do anything.

Experimenter: You can use anything you find in the room to help you get the toy.

Subject: I don't know...I can't get it.

Subject B — 8 years, 2 months old; slightly retarded.

Subject: I can't get it.

Experimenter: Think how you can get it.

Subject: I'll have to climb up on the desk. (He tries but fails, since he is too small to reach from the desk to the top of the blackboard.)

Experimenter: Can't you get it in another way?

Subject: I could use a ladder.

Experimenter: We don't have a ladder.

Subject climbs up on the desk again and tries again, but fails.

Experimenter: Can't you do it another way? Try, look around.

Subject: Here, I can do it with the stick. (Takes the stick, climbs up on the desk, and gets the toy.)

We see here two types of behavior differing sharply from one another yet, in many respects, representing two rungs on the same ladder.

One child, in protocol A, wanted to deal with the complicated problem directly. He used the natural responses he had at his disposal. He reached toward the toy, jumped at it, and then stood up on the desk and again jumped. The total senselessness and uselessness of this response did not deter him, and he continued in stereotypical fashion; even the experimenter's promptings did not divert him from these persistent, stereotyped efforts.

The distinguishing feature of the retarded child's behavior was his inability to check a cycle of responses once it had begun and, within a reasonable time, to replace an inappropriate although familiar tactic with a new, more adequate one (this is a phenomenon very typical of each of the most primitive stages of behavior).

These responses, which are semi-instinctive, are repeated conservatively, compulsively, without any regard for the particular situation; the child repeats the simplest actions without trying any more complicated ones (e.g., using the stick to get the toy), which would require curbing direct impulses and switching to more complex, no longer instinctive, but cultural actions, which are possible only for more developed children (protocol B).

The most primitive forms of behavior in young children and in retarded children are, at first glance, quite simple and stereotyped. We might say that this persistent attempt to perform a complex task by means of conservative repetition of the same natural responses, regardless of changing conditions, is very typical of a young child's behavior. This stage predominates until the age of 3, but frequently lasts even considerably longer.

We may observe a number of similar examples in the behavior of animals, and they all show that this instinctive way of coping with a problem is extremely mechanical and very rigid and unvarying in its choice of means, quite independent of the changing conditions.

Köhler performed similar experiments with a chicken. He placed it behind a partition consisting of three screens (Figure 1) and scattered grain on the ground outside. The chicken was unable to suppress his immediate impulses and go around the partition to get the grain; instead, he battered his head against the screen in attempts to get directly at the grain and though, of course,

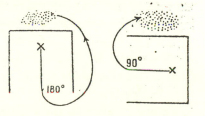

Figure 1

failing completely, persisted in this primitive blind behavior. The chicken was incapable of checking these impulsive attempts and going in the opposite direction, 180 degrees from the goal, in order thus to reach it.

It is interesting that the resistance and strength of these chicken impulses could be measured, and Köhler managed to curb the direct impulses and lead the chicken into the detour by turning the partition so that the bird would have to make only a 90-degree rather than a 180-degree turn to get the grain; this meant that the chicken could make the detour without losing sight of the grain.

The stability of primitive impulses, their resistance to inhibition, their total dependence on stimuli entering the visual field, and the impossibility of replacing direct, impulsive efforts with other, more adequate means are all typical behavioral features of this species; the rigidity and inertness of instinctive responses are not overcome until the higher species, in which new, more flexible means of coping with complex problems are developed. For example, a dog is quite able to overcome a direct impulse and make the 180-degree detour to reach a goal. For our purposes it is important only to note that invariable, blind, and rigid behavior in which only instinctive mechanisms are used to cope with a problem is indeed the most primitive form of behavior, and that it is in this pre-intelligent form of behavior that the features most in contrast to the higher forms of flexible, intelligent behavior are most prominently displayed.

This conservatism in instinctive behavior in primitive species is rather striking. Fabre gives the following surprisingly clear example, showing the extraordinary conservatism of instinctive behavior. He observed a species of wasp that made rather deep holes in the sand. An insect would ordinarily fly up to the hole with its food and leave it at the entrance, fly into the hole, and if it noted that nothing had been altered, would then drag the food in. Fabre tried to move the food left at the entrance a certain distance away with the following result: not finding its food at the entrance, the wasp would crawl out, fetch it, drag it back to the entrance, once again leave it there, and crawl back into the hole again, repeating the same cycle many times in succession (Fabre found that a wasp would repeat its inspection of the hole as many as forty times in succession, following the same accustomed pattern of actions). (3)

The invariance and rigidity of instinctive reactions and the complete inadequacy of the animal's behavioral equipment when faced with new conditions are clearly shown in this example; there is no need to adduce further examples to demonstrate the extreme uniformity of instinctive behavior, which is unable to take sufficiently into account the situation in which the individual must react. (4)

Intelligent Behavior and Its Primitive Forms

Clearly, the conservatism of natural behavior makes for situations that are plainly inadequate for coping with complex circumstances. New and difficult situations require much more flexible forms of behavior, which can be effectuated only if the animal (or child) employs new means appropriate to the given situation. These means must be devised anew each time, in the light of the changing conditions, and must accommodate to the rapid pace of these changes. Instinctive and habitual behavior must be supplemented by a qualitatively new form that is more flexible and has more dynamic means at its disposal. Köhler's primate provides an example of this type of behavior, which involves the suppression of direct, primitive impulses and recourse to implements when the natural functions of organs are inadequate.

The switch to the use of tools marks an extremely important turning point in the history of behavior; it gives behavior a wide range of flexibility and opens up new means for dynamic adaptation to complex situations. An animal or child does not learn to use implements properly all at once, however. In the animal (and at an even higher stage in the child) their employment remains primitive for a long time; and though this quite complex stage of adaptation has been reached, it is still marked by the deficiencies and shortcomings that are typical of thought at this particular stage and that have their roots in the characteristics of primitive behavior.

The primitive features of a child's thinking show up particularly prominently in the way the child handles things in the external world — things he wants to use in dealing with complex tasks.

The ability to employ a particular implement or tool, i.e., to use certain things as means or instruments for achieving some end, is unquestionably a spur to the further development of the child's intelligence and raises his behavior to a new level, at which his relationship to things undergoes a substantial change: it becomes incomparably more flexible and dynamic than it had been before; and depending on the specific conditions of the task,

an object acquires new functions in the child's behavior, and
the child begins to relate to it differently.

In Köhler's primate experiments we already notice the beginnings of this dynamic, functional relationship to things that depends on the situation in which an object is found; a stick that a
monkey had earlier tossed about in a play situation assumes the
role of a pole on which the animal can climb, and in another situation may serve as an implement for getting a banana lying
some distance away. A hat with a wide brim as shield against
the sun in another situation becomes an object for rolling a fruit
toward the animal, for getting at a stick, etc.

In short, a dynamic, functional relationship to an object as a
tool takes the place of an unvarying, absolute relationship; and
behavior becomes incomparably more flexible than at the lower
levels of the historical ladder.

But even these dialectical aspects of behavior take time to develop; the individual begins to use some things functionally, but
by no means always with complete success.

This is because the functional use of things usually develops
much earlier than an understanding of the actual mechanism of
dealing with them, i.e., of the situation in which things really
may be rationally used as implements. The use of wood to make
a fire by rubbing was known to man at the dawn of civilization;
however, an understanding of the process taking place in this,
the conditions under which it would take place most effectively
and those in which it would be impossible — all occurred much
later; and the ultimate view of this process required scientific
development. (5) Clearly, when a device or technique is used
without understanding it, failures will occur that are rooted in
ignorance of the laws of their operation and in inadequate assessment of the conditions under which they operate. Behavioral devices are not always used with success; and often if they
are employed primitively, their use is awkward and ineffective.
A dialectical command of things and of one's own behavior requires time, and an analysis of the deficiencies and mistakes
made by a primitive creature in performing operations with
things provides a very illuminating picture of this phase in the

development of thought. An analysis of some findings may serve
as concrete examples of such instances.

We have already mentioned Köhler's observations on how a
chimpanzee used primitive implements. If a fruit the animal
wanted lay out of reach, the animal would use a stick to get it.
If the fruit hung too high, he would also take a stick, shove it
into the ground, and climb up it to get the fruit. There are instances, however, that reveal to us the primitive nature of this
action. For example, in some cases an animal would take a long
straw instead of the stick, set it upright, and try to climb up it
to get the fruit. This outwardly expedient operation was in this
case employed inappropriately, not all the necessary conditions
were taken into account, and still the animal did not forgo the
operation. Clearly, the entire operation here bore the primitive
features of a stereotyped use of a technique; a closer analysis
reveals that the maneuver was not the consequence of an act of
intelligence of some order of complexity, but derived solely
from the external visual similarity between the piece of straw
and the stick. For the animal, the mere filling of a particular
spot in the visual field was sufficient to get the fruit; the conditions under which the device would function were not sufficiently
taken into account.

We can observe this same insufficient regard for the particular conditions in children's operations with implements. It is
especially obvious in them, because this naïve physics is com-
pounded by what we may call a naïve psychology, a naïve relationship to one's own psychological operation, and a far from
complete understanding of the means used in such operations.
All this rests on the fact that a child learns to use certain devices empirically long before he understands all the conditions
and mechanisms of such operations. When he has mastered the
various complex behavioral devices, he will have taken a tremendous step toward developing maximal flexibility in his adaptation to the world. Unable as yet to use these devices, he often
displays primitive traits in his thinking.

An observation by L. S. Vygotsky (6) is a brilliant example of
a child's insufficient understanding of the conditions under which

his own psychological processes operate. A little girl who was often sent into another room on minor errands noted that she would perform an errand well when her mother repeated it to her several times. Once when her mother sent her on an errand, the child said: "Mother, tell me three times what I must do"; and without actually waiting for her mother to do so, she ran into the next room to do the errand. Thus, although the child had made an accurate observation, she interpreted it incorrectly. Not correctly discerning how repetition actually functioned, she thought that the act of repetition had force in itself and that the words needed simply to be repeated to ensure that the errand would be performed properly. The child's attitude here was absolute: knowing that repetition would help, but not yet being capable of analyzing the relevant conditions, the child began to believe in the independent efficacy of the instructions, and her relationship to her mother's words assumed the nature of magic, to use the expression of some authors.

One of our experiments will show graphically these deficiencies in a child's thought, which we might describe as an absolute relation to an object based on incomplete appreciation of the conditions under which the object will help the child to perform some task. (7)

We gave a child a toy piano (Figure 2) with the instruction to

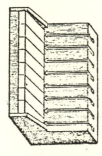

hit some key for every picture presented (complex choice response). To facilitate the operation we allowed the child to place a mark on top of the piano over each key (the marks referred to the picture cues) to help him in his choice. So that the child could determine as quickly as possible which mark referred to which key, red paper arrows (see the figure) were pasted on the front of the piano, leading from each mark on the top to the proper key.

Figure 2

The experiments yielded some extremely interesting results. Despite the considerable difficulty of the task (choice from among 6, sometimes 8, responses), 5-6-year-olds were invariably fully confident that they would be able to perform the task without any helping marks. When asked how they expected to be able to hit the right key at the right moment, the children would point to the arrows, saying, "The arrows will show me."

What does this experiment tell us? The children knew that the arrows were there to show the way. In the initial experiments a child would observe that the arrows did indeed show which key was related to which mark. But the mechanism of this empirically observed fact remained unintelligible to him; and failing completely to take into account all the relevant conditions, the child figured that the arrows in themselves would facilitate his task and show him which key to hit. The empirical experience, the absence of any analysis, and the inability to take all the conditions into account induced the child to ascribe some power to the arrows to show the right way. The fact that several completely identical arrows were pasted on the front of the piano did not confound the child, and to each instruction he would answer confidently that the arrow would help him remember which key to hit and when.

This incomplete appreciation of the conditions involved and belief in the independent action (power) of a sign were not a random occurrence among our 5-7-year-old subjects; we noted it in another situation in the same experiment.

In the first series of experiments the marks we had the children use to remember which keys to hit were pictures easy to associate with the pictures that served as cues for hitting the keys (for example, if the cue was a bell, the hint was a gong; if the cue was an axe, the hint was a little boy cutting wood; if the cue was a chair, the hint was a monkey sitting on a chair, etc.). The children were able to perform the task successfully using these hints.

To test the children's relationship to the reminder pictures, in the second series of experiments we had them choose their own reminders from among several small objects we made available (nails, buttons, feathers, etc.). Once again, among the 5-7-year-olds we found the same peculiar phenomenon confirming their primitive, magical relationship to a sign; the children

believed that any kind of reminding device would help them.
They would take any object from the box indiscriminately, place
it in the required place, and show no further concern about remembering the correct key. The nail would remember said one
of our little subjects. This absolute relationship to a sign, without taking adequate account of the conditions under which it
would operate, often resulted in a situation in which a child distributed reminders (often completely identical) in front of every
key, in the belief that they, in themselves, would ensure that the
task was performed correctly.

On the basis of his empirical experience in the use of signs,
but still not able to understand their mechanisms, a child takes
the more primitive way of ascribing a magical independent power to these signs (a way that, we shall see below, is the simplest
and easiest for the child's thought).

A child's practical thought, having led him to empirical operations with implements, does not go so far as the analysis and
understanding of the psychological mechanism necessary for the
use of these implements, and hence stops halfway along the
route toward the developed thought processes of the adult. We
can do no better than to quote Engels (8) on this point:

> The basic features of the method [of thinking] are the
> same and lead to the same results in man and animals, so
> long as both operate or make shift merely with these ele-
> mentary methods. On the other hand, dialectical thought —
> precisely because it presupposes investigation of the na-
> ture of concepts — [my emphasis — A. L.] — is possible
> only for man, and for him only at a comparatively high
> stage of development....

Operating with basic concepts and methods of thinking, but
still unable to study the nature of these concepts and methods,
a child shows us the primitive level of thinking that is typical
of him at the early stages of his development. These unique
features will become more apparent when we analyze a child's
thought more closely.

The Primitive Thought and Logic of the Child

Let us proceed directly to the problem of a child's thought. We should now inquire into how a child understands the things in the world around him and how he operates with logical categories. Such an analysis should provide us with an insight into some of the characteristic features of his thought, showing us that the dialectical method of regarding things is the product of a complex development the child must pass through and that initially his thought is characterized by a number of predialectical features.

A number of psychologists have already described some of the features of children's thought; most recently, the Swiss psychologist Piaget has devoted a number of interesting monographs (9) to this problem, putting the thought of a child and the various stages through which it passes in sharp relief. (10) The small child thinks concretely and is almost totally incapable of abstract thinking; given the relative primitiveness of his intellectual equipment, he is unable to take into consideration all the conditions under which events occur. He is inclined to think absolutely and nonrelatively, and to replace complex processes in his thinking with naïve, substantive forces without bothering to analyze them more deeply. In short, this thinking still displays primitive traits. To describe these features is all the more interesting since we often observe them in the thinking of many adults. We may best proceed by analyzing in succession a number of typical characteristics of a child's thinking.

The Concreteness of a Child's Thought

Stern once observed that a small child is totally incapable of abstract thinking. Any judgment a child makes is concrete, image-based, emotional, and directly related to his own life, his personal interests, and the situation of which he is a part. A 5-6-year-old is still incapable of complex reasoning; his judgments are concrete and direct. He is unable to pursue a line of reasoning and sees every object solely from his own point of view, recalling directly the role of his own personal experience in it. The small child is still unable to abstract from this personal experience, alter his perspective, or follow a general line of reasoning independent of a situation that is personally familiar to him.

Stern was the first to note this with any clarity. When he asked a small child (age 4 years, 3 months) how many fingers he had, he got the right answer; but when he asked the same child how many fingers his father had, the child answered that he did not know, that he only knew how many he himself had. This narrowness of judgments, their limitation to the sphere of the child's own personal experience, is very characteristic of the small child and is not wholly overcome until quite late.

Piaget demonstrates this very clearly. A child is unable to abstract from his own experience in his judgments or to alter the viewpoint acquired in his own concrete experience. Hence, he is completely unable to reason in abstraction from concrete experience, abstracting logically first one side, and then another, of phenomena. Here is a little conversation with a child to illustrate this:

> The experimenter showed a child a little box tied to a string; when the string was unwound, the box spun and swayed slightly in the air.
> If there were no air, would the box cause a wind?
> Yes.
> Why?
> Because there is always air in the room.
> Yes, but if there were no air at all in the room, would it still be the same?
> Yes.
> Why?
> Because a little air would always be left nonetheless.

The child acted according to premises furnished him by his own experience. To alter it, to abstract from it and reason from the standpoint of another premise was completely impossible for him. The point of view provided him by his personal experience was dominant for him.

We observe a similar situation with regard to the thinking of primitive people. Wertheimer (11), like a number of other au-

thors, describes cases in which a savage, when asked to count
to forty, would ask how he should do this, and understood the
task only when asked to count pigs. After reaching a certain
number, however, he refused to count further, declaring, "One
farmer doesn't have more pigs than that, and it is senseless to
count the pigs of different farmers." The primitive, concrete
nature of thought that does not go beyond the limits of the individual's graphic experience shows up quite clearly here.

A 5- or 6-year-old is totally unable to form an abstract judgment, and attempts to urge him in this direction are often total
failures. (12)

A child may reason about something only if he has seen it or
believes it. An adult reasons thus: "Let's suppose you are
right...let's assume that some condition is altered and that the
result of this would be some change in the process," etc. Reasoning of this sort is completely alien to the child. All a child's
judgments are guided by one point of view: his own. This point
of view is provided him by his own concrete experience, and it
is inconceivable to him to abstract from it and adopt another
viewpoint (an abstract one, or one of another person). Also, a
child's concrete thinking becomes absolute thinking.

Parallels taken from the history of thought only confirm that
the ability to abstract from a concrete initial point of view and
make some abstract assumption the premise of a whole system
is a product of a later period. An enormous amount of time was
necessary before thinkers could abstract from the concrete empirical postulates of Euclid about parallel lines and make the
assumption that two parallel lines intersect under certain conditions into the basis for an entire system of propositions. Non-
Euclidian geometry was possible only when this original concreteness of thought had been surmounted, which was not very
easy, even in mathematics.

The Absolute Character of a Child's Thought

The proposition just discussed, namely, that a child perceives
things concretely from the point of view of his direct experience
and often is almost totally unable to adapt to any other aspect,

leads us to a very important fact: a child tends to perceive the
outside world absolutely rather than relatively. He perceives
it directly, and this means that everything he perceives has one
predominant characteristic at each given moment. If this characteristic changes, it is not because of external conditions, but
because the child's emotional attitude has changed. At any given
moment a child's judgments are absolute; he has tremendous
difficulty learning categories of thought that enable him to see
a thing in the process of development and that are quite common
in developed dialectical thinking. A child's judgments are not
based on consideration of an entire set of conditions: they are
the product of an immediate response to some feature observed
by the child alone.

Piaget (13) asked 5-6-year-old children what a brother or sister
was and received the unhesitating answer: a boy or "It's a girl."
The children gave absolute judgments: that not all boys are brothers, that a boy must have a specific relationship to another boy
to be a brother, that the term brother is above all a relative
term — these things were beyond the children's understanding.

> Z. (5 years) asserted that a brother was a little boy.
> Are all boys brothers?
> Yes.
> Does your father have a brother?
> Yes, and a sister, too.
> Why is your father a brother too?
> Because he is a man.
> F. (6 years, 10 months). A sister is a little girl.
> Are all girls sisters?
> Yes.
> Am I a sister?
> No.
> How do you know?
> I don't know how I know.
> But I have a sister. Am I not her sister?
> Yes.
> But what is a sister?

> A sister is a girl.
> What is necessary to be a sister?
> I don't know.

We see that these judgments are completely unmediated and absolute; an understanding of the relativity of the concept of brother does not develop until much later. Here are some examples of judgments from 8-9-year-olds, in which the element of relativity now figures.

> G. (9 years old). It is when there is a boy and another boy, and there are two of them.
> Is your father a brother?
> Yes.
> Why?
> Because he was born second.
> So what is a brother then?
> It is when a second child is born.
> This means that the first child is not a brother?
> No; it's the second one, the one born later, who is called brother.

Elements of an appreciation of the relativity of this concept are quite clear here, but are not taken to their conclusion. A brother is considered a child who was born second. Obviously, the child was just calling to mind his own direct experience ("Look, now: a little brother has been born for you."), which was quite concrete; and the judgment here is only one step toward the relative. According to Piaget's observations, a correct (relative) notion of this simple concept does not become established until the age of nine.

Although we observe this picture in very simple judgments, the nonrelative, absolute nature of thinking shows up much more clearly in more complex types of judgments.

One of our experiments is a splendid illustration of the inability of a child to take into consideration the dynamic nature of a concept. (14)

We know that if one gives a small child something (nuts, candy, or simply blocks), he will try to grasp as many as possible. This tendency shows up especially clearly when a child is playing in a group and some quantity of something must be divided up among several children. For a child "many" means "good" and always produces an impulsive response. The word "many" may also acquire a negative meaning in a number of cases, however. There are a number of games in which the person who has many extra cards or blocks in his hand loses. Clearly, in these cases taking a lot of the items in the game (blocks, tokens) at the beginning is something negative, and each player tries to avoid doing so. "Many" in this case means "bad"; and a large quantity of things produces an averting response.

We tried to include a situation of "many" in a game with this reverse instruction and found a substantial difference between 4-5-year-olds and 6-7-year-olds. Both groups understood the instructions well. But whereas the older children related to the notion of "many" differently, depending on the rules of the game, the younger children were completely unable to understand that their attitude toward many blocks should change with the changed conditions of the game; and when they began a game in which the first player to go out was the winner (each player would put out one block in turn) and the experimenter asked the children to divide up the blocks that were left among themselves, the younger children reached toward the larger pile or tried to rake as many as possible from the big pile and even quarreled among themselves about who got the largest (and clearly most disadvantageous in the particular game) pile of blocks.

In this case the attitude toward a large quantity was firmly established: "many" always meant good, and a situation that reversed the meaning of this word was totally disregarded by the children. Even the possibility of having a different attitude (under different conditions) toward this phenomenon was simply not understood by the children.

This lack of comprehension of the relativity of any judgment on the part of a child is demonstrated with uncommon clarity in Piaget's classic experiments and observations. . . .

This aspect of children's thought and the gradual development of judgments from absolute to relative are especially clear in their judgment of right and left in one of Piaget's experiments. This test permitted us to distinguish the principal stages in the development of relative judgments in the child.

The same object can be either to the right or to the left, depending on where one stands. But a small child is totally unable to grasp this.

A child's first relationship to right and left (age 5 to 8) is absolute: the child takes his place as the starting point, and "right" and "left" are absolute properties of things in this respect. That an object may be either right or left with regard to some other object — this idea does not even enter the head of the small child. A 5-year-old can readily distinguish between his right and left hands, but almost three-fourths of the children this age are incapable of pointing out the right and left hands of a person facing them. The most difficult, almost insoluble, problem for the small child, however, is to find right and left among three objects placed on a table. If a coin, a button, and a key are placed in a row in front of a child, he is totally unable to understand that an absolute judgment is quite inapplicable to the button, that it is to the right of the coin and to the left of the key. Indeed, the very question is unintelligible to him; and the ability to answer this question, to grasp the relativity of these concepts, does not develop until the age of 11-12 years. (15)

The structure of judgments of this sort is especially clear in one of Burt's tests, in which a child is told: Olya is darker than Katy, but Olya is lighter than Nina. Who is the darkest? This test is soluble only for 11-12-year-olds. Before this age, we usually get results showing that relative thinking is still inadequately developed. On the one hand, the small children often give us direct answers such as since Olya is dark and Nina is dark, both are dark; and others see an insurmountable contradiction in the sentence: Olya is darker ..., and Olya is lighter....

F. (9 years, 4 months): There's no way to know, because you say that Olya is both lighter and darker at the same time. (16)

How can these features of a child's thought be explained psychologically?

There are two crucial factors involved here: on the one hand, the concreteness and image-based nature of children's thinking and, on the other, the relative weakness of their system of abstract operations. A child who hears the above sentence imagines in pictures the situations "Olya is lighter than" and "Olya is darker than" and by the end of the sentence has forgotten the relativity and contingency of these propositions. Of course, the concrete pictures he has formed will become mutually contradictory. The image-based nature of thought makes for concrete and immediate judgments. To go from absolute judgments to relative judgments the child must first overcome this primary, unmediated, image-based kind of thought....

The Naïve Substantivism of a Child's Thought

The properties of a child's thought we have just described go hand in hand with another feature that is even more characteristic: a child will in most cases formulate his thoughts about the most complex dynamic processes with naïve concreteness.

For instance, imagine the conditions necessary to be able to conceive of ice, water, and steam as stages in the same process. In such an operation not a trace is left of the immediacy of naïve thought; and a concrete, eidetic relation to it, such as the child has toward discrete objects that have nothing to do with one another and are complete, independent items, is replaced by a much more complicated process based on considerable empirical experience, in which the focus is on the dynamics of the change involved and on the continuity among these phenomena. How much simpler is a direct relationship to ice, water, and steam as discrete, particular objects, as static things! Of course, the naïve, realistic thinking of the child is much less intricate, and we should not be surprised to find that this naïve, substantive relationship totally dominates the small child's thinking, in which the most dynamic processes and the changes they cause are often seen as independent phenomena.

There is nothing more dynamic than the wind, and perhaps there is nothing simpler than understanding the wind as air in movement that may be evoked by any physical action. We find that for the small child, however, this is not yet the case.

Piaget, whom we have already mentioned many times, conducted some interesting experiments with children that demonstrated this point quite graphically. He took a simple rubber ball, punctured it with a pin, and by squeezing it and letting go, let the air in and out. He then tried to find out how children understood this phenomenon. The results were quite remarkable. Children in the 4-6-year age group did not conceive the "wind" coming out of the ball as air set in motion by squeezing the ball, but as a phenomenon with an independent existence, depending little on the squeezing of the ball; in short, they saw the wind as something with a permanent existence, capable of coming and going, so that the wind coming out of the ball was totally identical with the wind blowing down the street. Here are a few typical experiments (17):

> S. (4 years, 6 months)
>
> Look what I am doing (experimenter squeezes the ball, directing the stream of air to the child's face). What is this?
>
> The wind blows when you move your hand.
>
> Where does it come from?
>
> From the street.
>
> Is it still there (the ball is completely compressed, all the air has been squeezed out of it)?
>
> No.
>
> Where did it go?
>
> It went away.
>
> Where?
>
> Through the window.
>
> How?
>
> When it was open.

But it's not open now, is it?

No.

(The experimenter straightens out the ball as the child looks on.) Where did this air come from?

From the street.

The naïve, substantive nature of this judgment is quite evident. The wind coming out of the ball came from the street. For the child there is nothing unexpected in this. But what is important here is that this is the same wind the child has been used to observing in the street; and when the ball again inflates, it is the same wind that goes into it. This primitive judgment precedes an understanding of wind as the result of mechanical movement, and the child relates to wind naïvely as a substantive entity....

The process we have observed, the child's transformation of a dynamic function into a static situation, is especially evident in children's drawings.

Let us imagine that a child must depict some movement, e.g., the movement of a rolling ball or the movement of a person over some period of time. An adult has a number of ways of doing this, developed in the process of acquiring cultural experience: he can draw a figure and put a sign indicating movement before it (an arrow, a line, etc.), or he can portray this in some schematic way. But the small child does not yet have these means, and he will most often employ a device the French psychologist Luquet (18) has called the device of repetition. If a child is called upon to describe some action graphically, he will simply draw an acting

Figure 3

figure several times in one picture, as if breaking down the action into individual components.

Here is a little example from Luquet's book. Using the picture in Figure 3, a 5-year-old little girl wanted to tell the story about a woman who bought a doll. The child depicted the inside of a store, showing the woman entering it (A_1) and the sales clerk inside (B_1). Then the salesclerk went to the window where the doll was lying. To show this the child drew the clerk again (B_2). The clerk took the doll and went to the cashier to pay the money (B_3) and then gave the woman the package (B_4), after which the woman left the store and went home (A_2).

This primitive repetition of a figure in motion describes an entire complex action. The Swiss psychologist Eng points out, along with others, that this type of repetition was often used in early Italian and Flemish paintings. (19) This method of repeating a sequence of static figures to depict a complex action is still not such an illuminating example, however. We are grateful to I. D. Sapiro for an extremely interesting case description,

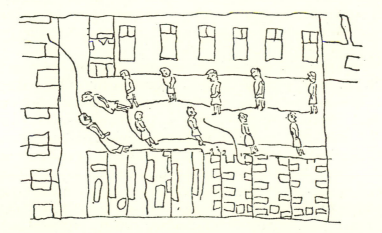

Figure 4

an analogue of which may, we think, be found in early childhood.
The patient he observed was suffering from aphasia and the associated impairment of intellectual functions. When the patient
had to portray on paper (the patient was an enginner, and in the
past had been an excellent draftsman) that he was strolling in
the hall, he showed his stroll by the drawing in Figure 4, in
which we see the walk depicted as a series of repeated figures
of a walking man. With some of the most intricate intellectual
functions no longer operative, this patient resorted to primitive
repetition of static figures to illustrate walking....

The Syncretism of a Child's Thought

The examples we have given demonstrate the child's unre-
strained tendency to generalize about things, to perceive them
in a diffuse, global interrelationship. In the perception of the
small child, "everything is connected with everything else";
but it would be wrong to think that this universal interrelatedness has anything in common with the interrelationships in dialectical thinking.

For a child it is sufficient to perceive two phenomena at the
same time to draw a connection between them. The elementary
logical fallacy of post hoc — ergo propter hoc is replaced in the
child's thinking by an even more primitive form of cum hoc —
ergo propter hoc.

How can we explain this syncretism of a child's thought?
Contemporary psychological literature points out a number of
factors that doubtless play a very crucial role in this. For example, the fact that the child's ability to use logic is not yet
fully developed, the specific function thinking performs in a
child's behavior, which we shall discuss further on, the immediacy, the uninhibitedness of a child's responses, and a number
of other factors all have a part in the child's syncretic judgments. Of all the factors mentioned, we should like to dwell on
one that is especially interesting for us in the present context:
the narrowness of a child's attention. Not possessing complex
schemata with which to mediate the intellectual process (20), a

child's attention is highly variable and susceptible to outside influences. As a rule, it is usually able to focus on no more than
one attribute of an object at a time, and this is generally the
most conspicuous, not the most essential, one. There is nothing
extraordinary about the fact that primitive generalizations made
on the basis of incidental attributes and insufficient appreciation
of all the conditions operative in a given case should be directly
derivable from such a structure in a child's attention. (21)

We shall just mention two characteristic features of syncretic
thinking that flow directly from what we have just discussed.
First, there is the immediacy of a child's judgments. Having
observed one attribute, the child, with extraordinary facility,
makes it serve as the explanation for the general phenomenon
of which it is a part, with total unconcern for the significance
this attribute may have relative to all the other attributes or for
the conditions on which it itself is contingent. Instead of from
prolonged observations or the perception of regular patterns, a
child's thought will draw a conclusion immediately from his
knowledge of one attribute — a kind of short circuit in his
thought processes that the child is unable to restrain. If we tell
a child a story (as in Vygotsky's experiments) about two boats,
one red with a number seven on it and the other white bearing
the number four and say that the first one sank, a child will,
when asked the reason, refer with extremely facility to one of
the attributes of the boats (color, number, etc.). The attributes
within the child's ken are very easily transformed in his thought
processes into a factor with independent causal force; and when
Vygotsky asked his 7-8-year-olds what would have happened to
the boats if their numbers had been reversed beforehand, he in
most cases got the answer: "Then the other boat would have sunk."

These observations bring us closer to the concept of causality
in children and caution us to deal very circumspectly with a
child's causal judgments. What superficially may seem to us to
be a causal judgment may in fact be the mere use of an incidental attribute in place of an explanatory factor. We find an unusual enlargement of the concept of causality that makes this category lose all significance. The child's thought apparatus must

still undergo considerable growth and development in terms of its complexity before this "short-circuit" type of thinking is replaced by genuine logical thinking.

Let us suppose, however, that in his judgment a child is still guided by such immediate conclusions on the basis of one attribute, although the grounds for drawing such a conclusion are very few (often even nonexistent). The child's perception of these attributes is quite variable; and although a judgment yesterday may have been based on attribute A (The sun does not fall because it is hot), today we might get an explanation based on attribute B (The sun does not fall because it is yellow). A child's judgments, defined as they are by the very narrow and variable field of phenomena that attract his attention, are just as variable as their data base and demonstrate the child's total ignorance of contradiction.

When Piaget demonstrated for his subjects the dissolving of a green pellet in water, they explained it as follows (6-8-years-old): "The pellet dissolves because it is green." But when they were shown a green pellet that was insoluble in water, the explanation was: "It does not dissolve because it is green." The children were not at all bothered by the fact that their judgments were mutually exclusive.

Judgments of this short-circuit type, made on the basis of a single attribute, cannot avoid logical contradictions; but the contradictions may escape notice because the judgments are outside any notion of lawfulness. . . .

Paths of Development of a Child's Thought

We have shed some light on the basic features of a child's thought and may now ask: How can the presence of such primitive characteristics be explained?

Of course, the most obvious answer is that the child is still inexperienced; he does not have very much knowledge; he does not yet possess correct and adequate ideas about a whole order of things that to us are commonplace. What, really, can we expect from the thought of a creature who is just taking his first timid steps along the road of knowledge?

But this answer is satisfying only at first glance. Is it really sufficient to postulate merely deficient knowledge in a person to obtain those specific kinds of judgments, that peculiar kind of logic, which we see in children? Imagine initiating a conversation with an educated, civilized adult on a subject he knows very little about, e.g., discussing mathematics with a historian or mechanical engineering with a doctor. Will the switch to these unfamiliar topics be sufficient to produce in these people the same primitive ways of thinking we find in children? To be sure, the form of their arguments will change, and may exhibit some features that seem primitive to us; but we can be certain that we will not see a complete reversion to infantile thought patterns. Instead, our partner will probably simply not continue the conversation; he will profess his ignorance and listen attentively to what we say, only occasionally interjecting his own comments, which will actually be logical conclusions from what we have told him or from his own experience.

A child placed in the same situation, on the other hand, behaves in a way that is in sharp contrast to what we have just described. As a rule, every question will produce an answer. His thinking, which is at the opposite pole from scientific thinking, is not restricted by the constraints of method.

A child begins to set up hypotheses of the rawest and most arbitrary nature with extreme facility. His thinking is an immediate generation of hypotheses; he does not reason in accordance with set, accepted patterns, but throws himself directly into the problem, not at all concerned that he may perhaps not yet have the adequate means to deal with it. Most difficult of all for a child is to check the steady flow of responses that pop into his head, and in this his thinking basically differs from an adult's. A child does not know much, but he is still unaware of his ignorance. To achieve such an awareness requires at least an initial ability to examine the nature of one's own concepts, and it is just this examination that is still lacking in the child. A child who is able to say "I don't know" has already achieved a considerable level of development in his thought processes;

indeed, we should measure intellectual development not in terms of the quantity of knowledge the child has been able to amass, but in terms of the number of "I don't know's" we get in response.

Of course, the peculiar logic of a child's thought is by no means explained simply by his ignorance. Clearly this logic is the window dressing for some more fundamental characteristics. In fact, a child's logic is very likely based on the specificity of the functions intelligence is called upon to perform in a child's behavior, on the one hand, and, on the other, on the relatively small extent to which the child has examined the nature of his own concepts.

Changes in the functions of thought and in the role of thought in a child's behavior, the accumulation of experience and the development of new, previously nonexistent methods of thinking, and, finally, the development of the rudiments of operations aimed at clarifying for the child the structure of his own thought processes are all stages in the development of a child's thinking. Let us examine each of them briefly in turn.

The Structure of a Child's Behavior and the Function of His Thought

By intelligent behavior we mean the behavior displayed when a person called upon to deal with some problem or perform some task restrains the first impulses toward resolving it, works out a tentative plan in his mind (or even draws up a draft plan), checks it against the real situation, and having satisfied himself that it is in order, sets to work. In short, we may define intelligent behavior as any mediated behavior in which between the task and action there is some intermediate system that helps to solve the problem. To use Marx's famous example, we can call an architect's behavior intelligent, but not the activity of a bee.

Which kind of activity does a child's behavior most closely resemble? Everything that we know indicates that its most characteristic feature is its completely unmediated nature: a child does not set up his actions after prolonged deliberation and preliminary planning: his actions do not follow from his thoughts. On the contrary, it would be more correct to say that his thoughts are born of his actions. A child first acts and then begins to reason. For a child, thought is not so much the regulator of his actions as it is either a justification of something he has already done (rationalization) or — and this is more usual — merely the direct result of the impulse evoked by an action.

Not only does thinking play a secondary role in a child's behavior but its role is completely different and performs a completely different function than for an adult. Clearly, however, this different role of thought is possible only if the structure of all of a child's behavior is also completely different. The child must not be given complicated tasks with which to cope and which require complex intellectual operations. Only if these conditions are observed will the absence of the normal regulating function of thought not have a harmful influence on the child's overall behavior.

If we examine a child's behavior, we see that these really are the conditions in which it unfolds. The child has much less need to foresee and test his actions, to assess and plan them, than an adult. The child is not yet actively involved in work relations. He plays; he does not yet work. And this is the basic, decisive influence on the structure of his behavior. (22)

Indeed, play to a considerable extent eliminates from a child's situation the category of necessity, with its associated tasks of verification, weighing, and planning. These are traits of the kind of thinking that is part of a system of work relations in the real world. If there is something a child lacks in the course of his play, he does not have to mobilize all existing forces to get what is needed: he need only alter the course of his imagination a bit. In play, which lies beyond the category of necessity, what is real and what is illusory are blended; reality is modified by the imagination, and there is no need to alter the real situation by introducing some devised expedients.

The behavior of the small child is governed very little by the constraints of the real world, and this circumstance molds all of his thinking. Here is an example from one of Stern's diaries:

Gilda, age 2 years, 2 months. Gilda has a flat, rectan-
gular piece of wood in her hands, which she is playing with
as if it were a ball. Suddenly she puts it on her head and
shows me her "nice little hat." A short time later it becomes a plate.

A thing changes its function in a child's imagination from one
play situation to another: to come up with a pretend situation
to cope with a task is the easiest of all. Of course, the value of
such a solution measured in real terms is nil; but in play this
is not important: what matters most is that it enables the child
to cope with complex situations without requiring complex (and
still undeveloped) intellectual equipment.

Primitive Logic. Transduction

Clearly, this sort of play behavior, in which the category of
necessity is still but vaguely operative, must have its own system of thought, its own logic.
And in fact we find that it does, and that many of the primitive
features we have outlined are merely the product of this pre-
labor (and to a considerable extent primitively social) stage in
a child's behavior. One negative feature was pointed to above:
thinking does not have a regulatory role in this behavior; instead
it is born of the act and does not feature a system of logical operations aimed at accomplishing some task. It is rather a chain
of discrete associations, images, which arise under the influence
of an accomplished action. Images, judgments, and conclusions
are not viewed by the child as a means of resolving some task,
but are simply a reaction to the task. As such, once they have
occurred, they go their own way, unconnected with the task, neither returning to it nor helping to accomplish it. Piaget characterizes this aspect of a child's thinking as "immediacy and
irreversibility" and regards it as a fundamental aspect of the
mind of a child.
In the play stage a child does not employ thinking as an organized tool he can use to solve a problem. A thought conveyed

to him does not serve as material for deduction. In his behavior he does not use his thoughts for drawing conclusions. He prefers to form his judgments directly, without a system of logical constructs.

But a child learns; he acquires experience and makes judgments. If this is not logical thought, what is the basis of this cognitive activity? What is the logic corresponding to this stage in his behavior?

A child learns from case to case; his judgments go from fact to fact. Whereas an adult's judgments are necessary conclusions from particular premises, the judgments of a child are direct responses to obvious stimuli. The role played by logical premises in an adult's reasoning is secondary to that of external stimuli in the thought of the child. Instead of a logical process of reasoning, in the child we find a direct reaction to an object. (23)

This kind of thinking creates its own logic, a logic that is ignorant of the common laws of necessity; in fact — if one may use such an expression — it is a prelogical logic. Claparède and Piaget called this logic transductive logic, borrowing a term from Stern.

Whereas inductive logic involves drawing conclusions from the particular to the general and deductive logic goes from the general to the particular, transductive logic dispenses with this middle stage entirely. Transductive logic draws a conclusion directly from the perceived event; it is a logic that is ignorant of the category of "rules" as a means of logical reasoning. A child's reasoning is only outwardly such: actually, it is composed of a series of direct reactions to conspicuous objects, with no elements of reasoning present at all and, as we have seen, with total disregard of the binding nature of facts that are taken as premises....

Transductive logic is a logic of direct relations to an object, not the logic of reasoning; it is a logic of particular conclusions that does not yet employ the derivation of general laws from a knowledge of particular cases as a method of thinking; and, finally, it is a logic that does not require verification, because it is untroubled by and oblivious of contradictions. Indeed, if the category of general laws is completely lacking in a child's logic, if his judgments are simple, unverified responses to particular cases, how easy it will be for him to fall into contradictions and how difficult it will be to notice them if he does not even possess the category! In fact, a child who has just finished saying that boats float because they are light goes right on to say that steamers float because they are heavy. His primitive mind has not yet acquired an awareness of formal contradiction, because he does not yet know general laws. A dialectical mind has outgrown general laws because it knows these laws in their dynamic state. A formal mind is in the middle of this dialectical triad.

Transduction is the first stage of primitive logical thinking, and is born of the direct reactions of the child to things without any accompanying awareness of these reactions, without reduction of particular cases to general laws, and without the use of logical operations as the tools of correct thoughts.

Factors in the Development of Logic.
Socialization of Thinking

Transductive logic lacks two factors: its judgments are devoid of any element of logical consistency (they are determined by incidental impressions) and, viewed formally, they have none of the characteristics of reasoning (they are given as direct reactions to an external stimulus). As a result, transductive logic, the logic of the play stage in a child's behavior, is not an adequate tool for real coping with complicated tasks.

What are the factors that cause the child to move on to the next stage of thought? How does this incidental, unsystematic logic of reactive thinking become the logic of reasoning thought?

Two factors seem to be principally involved here: the child is inducted into work conditions, and his thought becomes socialized.

Obviously, given his emotional, playful relation to life, the child does not yet perceive the need for discursive, rational thinking that tries to substantiate every judgment. This will become clearer if we consider the relatively minor role still played by social conditions in a child's thought.

Stern (24) observed that children do not begin to engage in

games of a complex social nature until quite late. During the
first 3 or 4 years, a child usually does not go beyond primitive
social games. In experiments conducted in our laboratory (25)
we obtained graphic examples of how 5- and 6-year-olds were
still incapable of spontaneous division of labor. A group of children of this age is in the best of cases constituted on the basis
of primitive imitation and almost never on the basis of differentiated interactions and complex contacts.

This view was developed in an interesting (although in some
places questionable) manner in Piaget's observations of children's speech. Observing children's conversation, he found that
it by no means always had a communicative function. Much
more often children talk to themselves; and their speech, like
all their behavior, is egocentric. Even the liveliness exhibited
by a group of children at play Piaget saw merely as a phenomenon of group monologue, in which no child tried to establish
even the simplest form of verbal contact with the other children.
The number of such egocentric utterances is very high: for a
3-4-year-old, 60% of all utterances are egocentric; for 6-year-
olds, it is still 43-47%, and for 7-year-olds, it falls to 27-30%.
This egocentrism characterizes the thought of a child, and Piaget noted that up even to the age of 10-11, a child still reasoned
only from his concrete point of view and in a conversation was
unable to assume the viewpoint of his interlocutor by substituting it for his own habitual egocentric attitudes.

Even leaving aside questionable statements about the "asocial
nature" of primitive childhood thinking, one cannot doubt that
primitive forms of thought can be overcome only when the child
is placed in a system of more complicated social conditions.

Clearly, such egocentric behavior does not require thinking
in forms that are intelligible to others, that is, forms that start
with commonly accepted facts (or facts that are accepted at
least by one's partner in the discussion) and that presume that
judgments are subject to verification and generalization. It is
understandable that egocentric thought is restricted to isolated
declarations and exclamations in the course of emotional reactions to objects — short-circuit reactions, as it were, based on

the child's immediate experience.

The transition to the logic of reasoning, the logic of binding forms and mutual understanding, presupposes social contact. Objective thought, which requires that judgments and the arguments on which they are based be tested, is engendered by the collision of one's own thought with the thoughts of others; it derives from contact, from disagreement. Logic is born of dialectics. As a child enters into social contacts, little by little egocentric speech gives way to socialized speech, and the categories we see in fully developed form in the logic of an adult first appear in his thinking. Subjective and casual reactions to objects are replaced by a system of reasoning, and immediate utterances are replaced by a tendency to substantiate and test a judgment; the child begins to show concern that his utterances be intelligible to others, thought begins to take note of contradictions, and transductive, direct logic is replaced by judgments based on conclusions drawn from general concepts; in short, the primitive thinking of a child becomes logical thinking when it becomes socialized.

The child's entry into complex and active social contacts transforms his thinking in another indirect way as well. Communicative speech develops, and new and much more complex forms and turns of speech are created. Expressions such as "because," "although," "besides," etc., become more than just the external appurtenances of speech and serve to introduce new categories into thinking, to introduce some order into thought processes by furnishing them with the categories of relation, lawfulness, and consistency. Acquired externally, from encounters with others, these forms are first learned through imitation, but later, imperceptibly, reorganize the entire mind; they infiltrate it, as it were; and from the external devices they originally were, they become internal forms of thought. Observations of children convince us that this is actually what takes place. During the period following the first active social contact, we see not only a reduction in the number of egocentric utterances and an increase in the percentage of "socialized judgments" but also the appearance, for the first time, of interludes of silence, pauses, which are the first signs that the child is reasoning to himself. Direct judgments, "short-circuits," begin to be restrained, held back; judgments begin to be separated from stimuli by short intervals during which internal reasoning takes place, and thought begins to precede action. Verbal thinking, engendered by dialectics, assumes certain essential organizing functions in the child's behavior, and he begins his metamorphosis from a bee to an architect.

Factors in the Development of Logic.
The Verbal Implements of Thinking

In singling out the place in a child's behavior that begins to be filled by speech, we have arrived at an analysis of the major transformation speech induces in the entire thought and behavior of the child.

We regard speech as a powerful cultural tool that transforms primitive, natural forms of behavior into complex, cultural forms. One example will suffice to show that this tool, acquired through social contact, transforms the entire sequence of acts of primitive behavior and creates the first forms of planning and regulative behavior. (26). Let us try to shed some light on the mechanism of solving some intellectual problem with nonverbal and with verbal operations. The experiments of Jaensch (27), in which he performed Köhler's experiments in an eidetic situation, appear to us to be crucial for an analysis of nonverbal, primitive problem-solving. Projecting a fruit and stick with a hook attached to it onto a screen for test subjects, he asked them to concentrate on this situation; he then took away these objects and operated only with the vivid images the subjects now had of them. When he then asked the subjects to imagine how they could get the fruit, changes took place in the eidetic image; the stick moved toward the fruit and the hook grasped it.... What we have here is a primitive form of adaptation to a visually presented problem. The changes the hand would accomplish through action, these subjects, who were known to form eidetic images, performed in the perceived image. Instead of motor

activation, sensory activation took place; and the problem was
solved by shifting the trace excitations in the visual field. We
can see, however, that illusory problem-solving of this type
still plays a considerable role in the adaptation of behavior to
complex situations; it is conceivable that at primitive stages in
the development of the mind, this preliminary assimilation of
trace images in the visual field was the first means by which a
person learned to cope with complex problems; very probably,
this sort of sensory circuit was the origin of the first imagic
thinking.

Despite all the interest this sensory accommodation incites
in us, we are obliged to comment on one essential flaw. It can
play a role only in cases in which the problem is presented visually and, moreover, when it is presented in one visual field.
If we move the fruit and stick into different visual fields, the
problem becomes insoluble by such a primitive method. The
limitations of this eidetic accommodation are very narrow; it
is restricted to reactions to an immediately given visual field,
and there is no possibility of an active search for ways to solve
a problem.

But what an advance is made in the next stage of development,
when the individual acquires another form of trace excitations,
namely, speech, and when the comparison of eidetic images is
replaced by the comparison and combination of words. And how
much greater do the possible combinations of different conditions become once they are freed from what is visually given in
tangible conditions! A child who has a good vocabulary plus the
ability to use it is able to call on his experience by making active combinations of all his previous experience; he is no longer
limited to the mere eidetic recall of some situation. The passive comparison of objects is replaced by a new ability — the
ability to select objects actively after first solving a problem
at the verbal level.

Lipmann carried out a series of experiments that compare
well with those of Jaensch we have just described. Lipmann had
his child subjects solve some practical problem like the ones
Köhler's primates had to solve. We have already described

similar experiments in which the child subjects had to get a toy with the aid of a stick. From his observations of how the children tackled the task by proceeding directly to the act, Lipmann concluded that a child would be able to arrive at a solution to the problem only after an object that could serve as an implement was placed in his visual field along with (or right after) the object the child was supposed to get. The operation would then flow directly from the perceived situation; the situation determined the action directly.

To determine the role speech could play in problem solving, Lipmann introduced one modification into these experiments. Sometimes he would stop a child who had begun to act and suggest that he first solve the problem verbally, that is, that he tell in words how he was going to get the object. This radically transformed the child's behavior. Instead of proceeding gropingly, by directly reacting to the situation, the child would first work out the necessary combinations in words, devise a verbal plan for solving the problem, and then put it into action in an organized fashion. By working out a plan of action verbally the child was freed from the random encumbering influences of the situation; he was no longer restricted to what was directly placed before him. He took the stick (needed to get the toy), but this time did not have to wait until it caught his eye, but actively began to look for it since he had already decided to use it as a tool. Verbal planning does indeed help to alter the function of thought in a child's behavior; it transforms it from a reactive mechanism, bound to the situation, to a mechanism that plans behavior.

Some interesting experiments by Vygotsky illustrate this organizing role of speech quite well. Six-year-olds were placed in a similar situation (the subjects had to get an orange with the aid of certain tools), and 3-year-olds had to observe the entire process. The older children first tried to get the orange with their hands, reached for it, stood on a chair, and made a number of unsuccessful movements. After some time they would finally get the stick and roll the orange toward them.

When a $3\frac{1}{2}$-year-old was given the same task, he did not pro-

ceed immediately to act according to a plan, but first began to
reproduce in succession all the movements of the older child;
he did not just select those that served his purpose, but repeated
them all mechanically, imitating everything he had observed.
Without the planning function of speech, the child was not able
to solve the problem verbally first and then implement it in action. His thinking was only an imitative reaction to the situation;
it did not command it.

There can be no doubt that by restructuring the entire process
of thinking, the acquisition of speech as a tool also gives birth
to new logical categories that radically distinguish this stage
of thinking from the preceding primitive, syncretic stage. We
should like to demonstrate that above all it establishes the category of causality in the logic of a child.

A child who has learned to cope with particular situations by
reacting directly to them, acting first and speaking later, would
not have a sufficiently complete command of either the concept
of causality or the concept of succession. Simple experiments
will demonstrate this, and we personally have observed the truth
of this proposition many times.

For example, let us place before a child several containers
and in one of them place a nut. We do this in such a way that the
position or color of the nut will attract the child's attention. He
chooses this container, gets the nut, and when asked what im-
pelled him to make his choice, he answers that he took that container because there was a nut in it (Vygotsky's experiments).
The effect — the final stage in the process — is here given as
the cause; the result of the action is regarded as one of its conditions. The child, in throwing himself directly into the situation, displays a logic in which the category of causality is completely absent.

The results we obtain are completely different in the case of
a child with whom we introduce speech as a stage in the problem-solving process, as an aid for solving the given problem.
In reasoning what he must do, a child no longer makes mistakes
like the one just described. For the first time, cause and effect
begin to occupy definite and meaningful places in his reasoning.

By spelling out beforehand in words the condition that will later help him to solve his task, the child for the first time begins to conceive of it as a condition or cause and the result achieved with its aid as an effect. . . .

Verbal operations introduce another important change in a child's thought: with them the child is for the first time able to isolate, one at a time, the different features of a perceived situation; verbal operations carry a child beyond the elementary diffuseness, the totalness of his perceptions, and enable him for the first time to make the transition to an analytical approach to learning about the world.

When a mother for the first time points out an object to a child and names it ("This is a rabbit") she, as Vygotsky quite correctly observes (28), is isolating that object from its surroundings and creating for the child a totally new structural focal point in those surroundings. The initial, undifferentiated wholeness of a child's perceptions is replaced by organized, structured perception, coordinated around this isolated element. The new denotation, the naming of a new object ("This is a dish") creates a new, temporary dominant in the child's perceptual field. In place of an undifferentiated, holistic perception (broken only by permanent biological dominants — biological structures, to use Koffka's term), the child for the first time perceives a situation as a dynamic, changing structure or, more precisely, as a structure with a dynamic, changing focal point. But when, after dealing with a problem first on the verbal plane, with different combinations, a child begins to liken and compare the most varied words (and hence ideas as well), which have not even occurred directly in his experience, when he begins to draw connections between them under different conditions and in different structures, his perception of the world becomes extremely dynamic. The child becomes aware that a particular object may play a different role in different situations; and his perception, refracted through this prism, acquires a more dynamic nature and he begins not only to perceive the world from a passive perspective but also, in perceiving it, to analyze it in order to act upon it.

The appearance of analytic thought frees the child from his direct perception of a situation and from all its chance attributes; hence we would say that the stage in which a child describes a picture, called by Stern the first and most primitive, the stage in which the child names individual figures, is already a very high stage; in any case, it is not the first stage in the development of analytic thought. In singling out a particular object from its general background, the child replaces his global perception with an analytic, discriminating perception, and this prepares him for acting in the situation in an organized way.

Finally, and this is perhaps the most important point, with the development of the forms of verbal thinking, the child acquires a powerful set of tools with which he can fashion a series of logical concepts to aid him in abstracting from the concrete diversity of his perception of the world and to understand phenomena in their mutual relationship, in terms of an ordered system.

When Stern's $3\frac{1}{2}$-year-old asked, "Is today tomorrow? Is now today?" we can see that she was trying with the aid of verbal terms she knew to get a grasp on complicated time relationships that still seemed chaotic to her. The child did not accomplish this all at once. At the age of 4 years, 3 months, Stern's daughter was still confusing the term yesterday with the term today; she grasped what they had in common (one day away from today), but could not yet see the differences: "Today we'll pack, and yesterday we'll leave." She did not have a complete grasp of these concepts until the age of $5\frac{1}{2}$, when she expressed them in a specific combination: "After the day after tomorrow is the tomorrow of the day after tomorrow." (29) These logical experiments are possible only after quite distinct and rich forms of speech have appeared, and by mastering speech the child is able also to gain command of his thought processes. . . .

The acquisition of certain tools of thought — we have discussed only speech here — transforms a child's thought processes; thought and action now shift places, and the very functions of thought are altered. A child's behavior in complex situations for the first time is mediated by certain preceding processes coming in between. Involvement in a verbal field takes the place of direct actions and prepares the child for coping with complex situations in a planned way. A child's life experience and logical experimentation cause primitive syncretic and trans- ductive logic to fade from the picture, since they have no means of dealing with the lawful, causal arrangement of things. Inner speech is the next stage following egocentric and socialized speech; and once it is acquired, the child, for the first time, is able to organize his thinking in the ways learned in his verbal contact with other people (dialectic) and in coping with problems (logical experimentation). Thinking acquires ordered, organized features.

Factors in the Development of Logic.
Clarification of the Nature of Terms

A child's play behavior, his primitive contact with a social en- vironment, and defects in speech development do not completely explain those primitive features of a child's thought that distin- guish it from the complex, mature thinking of an adult. To use Engels's expression, the "low level of examination of the nature of concepts themselves" is the last factor responsible for the primitiveness of a child's thought; as this defect is gradually eliminated, the child accumulates the foundations for organized, practically correct, and logically structured thought.

All that we know of children in the very early stages of life indicates they are quite incapable of understanding the mech- anisms of mental activity. . . .

What is the reason for this late appearance of the ability to examine the nature of his own concepts in the child, and by what means does he arrive at an understanding of the mechanisms underlying his own psychological processes? This question is truly one of the most complicated of modern psychology, and we cannot presume to give a sufficient and complete answer to it here.

Indeed, the assertion that oneself and the laws governing one's own activity (which would appear to be the most familiar to the child) are learned latest may seem strange at first glance: nev- ertheless, the most recent findings demonstrate that this is really the case, and that Engels was unquestionably right when he placed the examination of the nature of one's own concepts among the later stages of development of thinking. (30)

There are a number of reasons why an awareness of one's own psychological processes should develop so late.

Claparède (31) studied these processes in the small child and made a number of observations that led him to speak of general laws governing the difficulty experienced by the child in acquiring awareness of some phenomena (la loi de prise de conscience). According to his observations, a child becomes conscious of a process when in the course of carrying out some action he encounters an obstacle. Processes that do not encounter any obstacles along the way may take place without the child's acquiring full awareness of them, and an analysis of automatic actions confirms this. We may ask in exactly what cases the child encounters such obstacles. Everything we know about the behavior of the young child indicates that he reacts directly to each situation and that preliminary reflection does not play the same role for him as for adults, that he acts first and reasons afterward. Of course, all the difficulties and obstacles occur on the level of direct action, not in thought, and his awareness is directed toward them. The child begins to be aware of and to evaluate the mechanisms of the external world much earlier than the mechanisms of his own psychological processes. . . .

The possibility of becoming conscious of one's own psychological processes initially arises when a child's actions begin to be preceded by some preliminary activity or work, when the child begins to resolve difficulties and obstacles at the verbal and conceptual levels rather than by direct action.

But the first definitive turn toward an examination of the nature of one's own concepts is not possible until external speech, which arises from the child's encounter with operations and in contact with other people, begins to "grow inward," i.e., when it begins to be replaced by "internal speech."

A number of studies by American psychologists have shown that the process of gaining awareness is very closely connected with the process of speech, and that the unconscious element in our behavior may quite accurately be called "the unverbalized" element. (32) This is surely why we cannot expect any really effective efforts from the child to examine the nature of his own concepts. We know that inner speech appears quite late in the child; the role of egocentric speech in his behavior begins to decrease, and reflective pauses begin to appear only by the 7th or 8th years. (33) Until this process reaches completion, the child simply does not have sufficient equipment to be able to acquire an awareness of the mechanisms of his thinking with any degree of success.

One more consideration will help us determine when to expect this extremely important process, i.e., the child's advance from a simple action to an understanding of the mechanism by which this action occurs.

A number of experiments, described elsewhere (34), persuaded us that in learning the various devices and modes of behavior, the child starts with the external aspects, which are finally internalized. He begins to approach the world about him through culturally acquired forms by learning, first, the outward manifestations of behavior. Such, for example, are the processes Köhler observed in higher primates; and such, too, is the first use of tools by a child, or the phase we observed (Leont'ev and Vygotsky) of using external devices to develop mnemonotechnical memory or to develop attention. It is not until much later, when the child begins to internalize these externally acquired devices, that he begins to rely on internal behavioral means; at that point a profound transformation takes place in his entire behavior on the basis of these sociocultural influences. This transformation is further accompanied by the acquisition of a thorough understanding of the mechanisms of psychological processes and a tremendous broadening of the ability to examine the nature of one's own concepts. Internal operations are supplemented by new means and acquire a new significance in the child's behavior; they are put to the test more frequently and more thoroughly, and at the same time the child moves on to more refined forms of coping with the real world, as the primitive forms of thinking are replaced by more complicated cultural forms.

We should be quite eager to follow the further course of development of a child's thought, his rejection of the primitive prelogical phase, the next formal logic phase of development, and, finally, the emergence of genuinely dialectical forms of thinking.

Unfortunately, however, we do not yet have sufficient material to deal fully with this problem.

We do feel that it is proven beyond question that a child's thought begins with a phase marked by a number of primitive features. This phase is the most primitive in the child's development and is fully explainable in the light of the specific conditions in which a child's behavior unfolds (the child's primitive social contacts, his disposition toward play), and from the specific function fulfilled by thought in the system of his behavior as a whole. But the child grows out of this phase as he gets older; and under the influence of being involved in practical work situations, more complicated, active social contact, the use of new techniques of thinking, and, finally, the child's increasing awareness of the "nature of his own concepts," he develops a logic that, discarding its primitive features, becomes much more vital and practical.

Further research should tell us how these primitive forms of intelligence break down and how the extremely complex, dynamic forms of thinking observed at the highest stages of development of human intelligence evolve in the process of man's active, practical engagement in the world around him.

Notes

1) Talk given before the Society for Materialist Neuropsychologists. Discussion paper.

2) See O. Lipmann & H. Bogen, Naive Physik. Leipzig, 1923. P. 109.

3) Cited in H. Werner, Einführung in die Entwicklungspsychologie. 1926. P. 74.

4) See data presented by V. A. Wagner, for example: [Comparative psychology]. Vol. II, pp. 141-57.

5) Engels gives this example — [Dialectics of nature].
P. 181.

6) [The history of the cultural development of the child].
In press.

7) This study, done by us together with N. G. Morozova,
will be published in its entirety in Tr. Psikhol. Lab. Akad.
Komm. Vosp.

8) [Dialectics of nature]. P. 59.

9) J. Piaget, Le langage et la pensée de l'enfant. 1923; Le
jugement et la raisonnement de l'enfant. 1924; La représenta-
tion du monde chez l'enfant. 1926; La causalité physique chez
l'enfant. 1927.

10) We shall reserve our criticism of the methodological
flaws in Piaget's constructs for presentation elsewhere; because
of them, we are forced to interpret some of his conclusions
somewhat differently.

11) M. Wertheimer, Drei Abhandlungen über Gestalttheorie.
1925.

12) We were able to obtain some vivid examples of concrete
and practical thinking in our analysis of the intelligence of vag-
abond children: [Speech and intelligence in the child]. Tr.
Psikhol. Lab. Akad. Komm. Vosp.

13) Le jugement et le raisonnement de l'enfant. P. 136. The
examples are taken from this work (pp. 138-39).

14) These experiments, like the others, were conducted in
our laboratory at the Academy of Communist Upbringing.

15) Piaget, Le jugement et la raisonnement.... P. 156.

16) Piaget, Une forme verbale de la comparaison chez
l'enfant. J. Psychol. (Paris), 18, 141-72.

17) Piaget, La causalité physique chez l'enfant. Pp. 18-19.

18) Luquet, La narration graphique chez l'enfant. J. Psychol.
(Paris), 21.

19) H. Eng, Kinderzeichnen. 1927. P. 153.

20) See Revault d'Allones, L'attention indirecte. Rev. Philo-
soph. 1914.

21) We shall not undertake here an analysis of the specific
physiological mechanisms responsible for the variability and

instability of attitudes in the child.

22) When we use the term "child" here, we are referring primarily to preschoolers between the ages of 3 and 5 years; but the features we describe may also often be found in older children.

23) We know that this position has to be accepted with a grain of salt; it is not the characterization of the child's thinking, but the traditional characterization of adult thinking that we question. Does anyone believe that adults always draw logical conclusions from logical assumptions? Emotions and the structure of one's visual and intellectual surroundings make us think that the thought processes of adults are less planned and logical than is usually assumed.

24) [Psychology of early childhood]. St. Petersburg, 1915. P. 194.

25) Experiments were conducted by B. V. Belyaev-Bashkirov.

26) The problem of the transformation of a child's behavior under the influence of behavioral attributes acquired in the process of assimilation of cultural experience is described in great detail by L. S. Vygotsky in [The history of the cultural development of the child].

27) E. Jaensch, Zum Aufbau der Wahrnehmungswelt. (2nd ed.) 1927. P. 195.

28) See [The history of the cultural development of the child].

29) W. Stern, Psychologie der frühen Kindheit. 1928. P. 341.

30) [Dialectics of nature]. P. 59.

31) E. Claparède, La conscience de la ressemblance et de la différence chez l'enfant. Arch. Psychol., XVII.

32) J. B. Watson, The unverbalized in human behavior. Psychol. Rev., 1924.

33) See L. S. Vygotsky, [Genetic roots of thinking and speech]. Estestvoznanie i Marksizm, No. 1.

34) See Vygotsky & Luria, [Studies in the history of behavior]. Giz, 1925. Vygotsky, [Problems in the cultural development of the child]. Zh. Pedol., 1929, No. 6. Luria, The problem of the child's cultural behavior. J. Genet. Psychol., 1928, Dec.

Translated by
Michel Vale

A. R. Luria

THE DEVELOPMENT OF WRITING IN THE CHILD

I

The history of writing in the child begins long before a teacher first puts a pencil in the child's hand and shows him how to form letters.

The moment a child begins to write his first school exercises in his notebook is not actually the first stage in the development of writing. The origins of this process go far back into the prehistory of the development of the higher forms of a child's behavior; we can even say that when a child enters school, he has already acquired a wealth of skills and abilities that will enable him to learn to write within a relatively short time.

If we just stop to think about the surprising rapidity with which the child learns this extremely complex technique, which has thousands of years of culture behind it, it will be evident that this could come about only because during the first years of his development, before reaching school age, a child has already learned and assimilated a number of techniques leading up to writing that have already prepared him and made it immeasurably easier for him to grasp the concept and technique of writing. Moreover, we may reasonably assume that even be-

From Voprosy marksistkoi pedagogikii [Problems of Marxist education]. Moscow: Academy of Communist Education, 1929. Vol. 1, pp. 143-76.

fore reaching school age, during this individual "prehistory," as it were, the child has already developed a number of primitive techniques of his own that are similar to what we call writing and perhaps even fulfill similar functions, but that are lost as soon as the school provides the child with the culturally elaborated, standard and economical system of signs, but that these earlier techniques served as necessary stages along the way. The psychologist is faced with the following important and intriguing problem: to delve deeply into this early period of child development, to ferret out the pathways along which writing developed in its prehistory, to spell out the circumstances that made writing possible for the child and the factors that provided the motive forces of this development, and, finally, to describe the stages through which the development of the child's primitive writing techniques pass.

The developmental psychologist therefore concentrates his attention on the preschool period in the child's life. We begin where we think we shall find the beginnings of writing, and leave off where educational psychologists usually begin: the moment when the child begins to learn to write.

If we are able to unearth this "prehistory" of writing, we shall have acquired a valuable tool for teachers, namely, knowledge of what the child was able to do before entering school, knowledge on which they can draw in teaching their pupils to write.

II

The best way to study this prehistory of writing and the various tendencies and factors involved in it is to describe the stages we observe as a child develops his ability to write and the factors that enable him to pass from one stage to another, higher stage.

In contrast to a number of other psychological functions, writing may be described as a culturally mediated function. The first, most fundamental condition required for a child to be able to "write down" some notion, concept, or phrase is that some particular stimulus or cue, which in itself has nothing to do with this idea, concept, or phrase, is employed as an <u>auxiliary sign</u>

whose perception causes the child to recall the idea, etc., to
which it referred. Writing therefore presupposes the ability to
use some cue (e.g., a line, a spot, a point) as a functional auxiliary sign with no sense or meaning in itself but only as an auxiliary operation. For a child to be able to write or note something, two conditions must be fulfilled. First, the child's relations with the things around him must be differentiated, so that
everything he encounters will fall into two main groups: either
things that represent some interest of the child's, things he
would like to have, or with which he plays, or instrumental objects, things that play only a utilitarian, or instrumental, role
and have sense only as aids for acquiring some object or achieving some goal and therefore have only functional significance
for him. Second, the child must be able to control his own behavior by means of these aids, in which case they already function as cues he himself invokes. Only when the child's relationships with the world around him have become differentiated in
this way, when he has developed this functional relationship with
things, can we say that the complex intellectual forms of human
behavior have begun to develop.

The use of material tools, the rudiments of this complex, mediated adaptation to the external world, is observable in apes.
In his classic experiments Köhler (1) demonstrated that under
certain conditions things may acquire a functional significance
for apes and begin to play an instrumental role. When an ape
takes a long stick to get at a banana, it is quite obvious that the
banana and the stick are psychologically of different orders for
the animal: whereas the banana is a goal, an object toward which
the animal's behavior is directed, the stick has meaning only in
relation to the banana, i.e., throughout the entire operation it
plays only a functional role. The animal begins to adapt to the
given situation not directly, but with the aid of certain tools. The
number of such instrumental objects is still few, and in the ape
their complexity is minimal; but as behavior becomes more complex, this instrumental inventory also becomes richer and more
complex, so that by the time we reach man, the number of such
objects playing an auxiliary functional role in the life of a human

being, who is a cultural animal, is enormous.

At a certain stage in evolution, external acts, handling objects of the external world, and internal acts as well, i.e., the utilization of psychological functions in the strict sense, begin to take shape indirectly. A number of techniques for organizing internal psychological operations are developed to make their performance more efficient and productive. The direct, natural use of such techniques is replaced by a cultural mode, which relies on certain instrumental, auxiliary devices. Instead of trying to size up quantity visually, man learns to use an auxiliary system of counting; and instead of mechanically committing things to, and retaining them in, memory, he writes them down. In each case these acts presuppose that some object or device will be used as an aid in these behavioral processes, that is, that this object or device will play a functional auxiliary role. Such an auxiliary technique used for psychological purposes is writing, which is the functional use of lines, dots, and other signs to remember and transmit ideas and concepts. Samples of florid, embellished, pictographic writing show how varied the items enlisted as aids to retaining and transmitting ideas, concepts, and relations may be.

Experiments have shown that the development of such functional devices serving psychological ends takes place much later than the acquisition and use of external tools to perform external tasks. Köhler (2) attempted to set up some special experiments with apes to determine whether an ape could use certain signs to express certain meanings, but was unable to find any such rudiments of "record keeping" in apes. He gave the animals paint, and they learned how to paint the walls, but they never once tried to use the lines they drew as signs to express something. These lines were a game for the animals; as objects they were ends, never means. Thus, devices of this sort develop at a much later stage of evolution.

In what follows we shall describe our efforts to trace the development of the first signs of the emergence of a functional relation to lines and scribbles in the child and his first use of such lines, etc., to express meanings; in doing so we shall hopefully be able to shed some light on the prehistory of human writing.

III

The prehistory of writing can be studied in the child only ex-perimentally, and to do this the skill must first be brought into being. The subject must be a child who has not yet learned to write; he must be put into a situation that will require him to use certain external manual operations similar to writing to de-pict or remember an object. In such a situation we should be able to determine whether he has acquired the ability to relate to some device that has been given to him as a sign or whether his relation to it still remains "absolute," i.e., unmediated, in which case he will be unable to discover and use its functional, auxiliary aspect.

In the ideal case the psychologist might hope to force a child to "invent" signs by placing him in some difficult situation. If his efforts are more modest, he can give the child some task that is easier for the child to cope with and watch the successive stages the child goes through in assimilating the technique of writing.

In our preliminary experiments we followed this second course. Our method was actually very simple: we took a child who did not know how to write and gave him the task of remembering a certain number of sentences presented to him. Usually this num-ber exceeded the child's mechanical capacity to remember. Once the child realized that he was unable to remember the number of words given him in the task, we gave him a sheet of paper and told him to jot down or "write" the words we presented. Of course, in most cases the child was bewildered by our sugges-tion. He would tell us that he did not know how to write, that he could not do it. We would point out to him that adults wrote things down when they had to remember something and then, ex-ploiting the child's natural tendency toward purely external im-itation, we suggested that he try to contrive something himself and write down what we would tell him. Our experiment usually began after this, and we would present the child with several (four or five) series of six or eight sentences that were quite simple, short, and unrelated to one another.

Thus, we ourselves gave the child a device whose intrinsic technique was unfamiliar to him and observed to what extent he was able to handle it and to what extent the piece of paper, the pencil, and the scribbles the child made on the paper ceased being simple objects that appealed to him, playthings, as it were, and became a tool, a means for achieving some end, which in this case was remembering a number of ideas presented to him. We think our approach here was correct and productive. Drawing on the child's penchant for imitation, we gave him a device to use that was familiar to him in its outward aspects but whose internal structure was unknown and strange. This allowed us to observe, in its purest form, how a child adapts spontaneously to some device, how he learns how it works and to use it to master a new goal.

We assumed that we would be able to observe all the stages in a child's relationship to this device, which was still alien to him, from the mechanical, purely external, imitative copying of an adult's hand movements in writing to the intelligent mastery of this technique.

By giving the child merely the external aspects of the technique to work with, we were able to observe a whole series of little inventions and discoveries he made, within the technique itself, that enabled him gradually to learn to use this new cultural tool.

It was our intention to provide a psychological analysis of the development of writing from its origins and, within a short period, to follow the child's transition from the primitive, external forms of behavior to complex, cultural forms. Let us now examine our results. We shall try to describe how children of different ages responded to this complex task and to trace the stages of development of writing in the child from its beginnings.

IV

Not surprisingly, at the outset we encountered a problem that could have presented a considerable obstacle. It turned out that

4-5-year-olds were totally unable to understand our instructions. On closer analysis, however, we found that this "negative" finding actually reflected a very essential and fundamental characteristic of this age group: 3-, 4-, and 5-year-old children (it was impossible to fix a definite dividing line: these age demarcations depend on a multitude of dynamic conditions having to do with the child's level of cultural development, his environment, etc.) were still unable to relate to writing as a tool, or means. They grasped the outward form of writing and saw how adults accomplished it; they were even able to imitate adults; but they themselves were completely unable to learn the specific psychological attributes any act must have if it is to be used as a tool in the service of some end.

If we asked such a child to note (or write) on paper the sentences presented to him, in many instances the child would not even refuse with any special insistence, simply referring to his inability to perform the task.

Little Vova N. (5 years old), for the first time in our laboratory, in response to the request to remember and write down the sentence "Mice have long tails," immediately took a pencil and "wrote" a number of scrawls on the paper (Figure 1). When the experimenter asked him what they were, he said, quite confidently, "That's how you write."

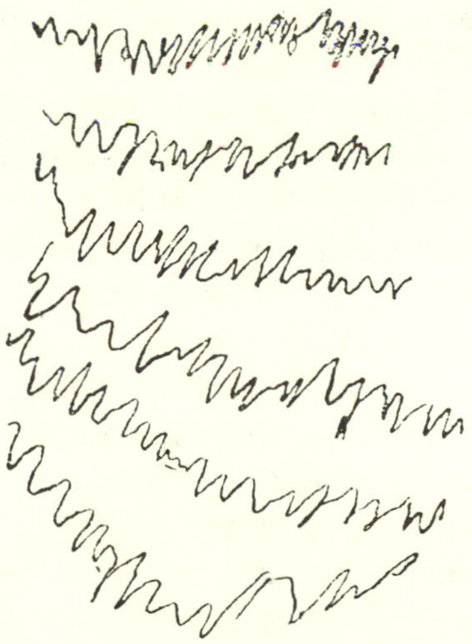

The act of writing is, in this case, only externally associated with the task of noting a specific word; it is purely imitative. The child is interested only in "writing like grownups"; for him the act of writing is not a means of remembering, of representing some meaning, but an act that is sufficient in its own right, an act of play. But such an act is by no means always seen as an aid to helping the child later remember

Figure 1

the sentence. The connection between the child's scrawls and the idea it is meant to represent is purely external. This is especially evident in cases in which the "writing" is sharply and noticeably divorced from the sentence to be written and begins to play a completely independent and self-sufficient role.

We frequently observed one peculiar phenomenon in small children: a child whom we had asked to write down the sentences we gave him would not limit himself to ordinary "writing down," as in the case just described; he would sometimes invert the normal order of writing and begin to write without hearing out what we had to say.

In these cases the function of "writing" had become dissociated from the material to be written; understanding neither its meaning nor its mechanism, the child used writing in a purely external and imitative way, assimilating its outer form, but not employing it in the right way. Here is a graphic example from an experiment with Lena L., 4 years old. Lena was given some sentences and told to remember them, and to do this she had to "write them down." Lena listened to the first three sentences and after each began to write down her scribbles, which were the same in each case, i.e., they were indistinguishable from one another. Before the fourth sentence I said to her: "Listen, this time write...." Lena, without waiting until I finished, began to write. The same thing happened before the fifth sentence.

The results are the undifferentiated scrawls in Figure 2, characteristic of this phase of development. There are two points that stand out especially clearly here: "writing" is dissociated from its immediate objective, and lines are used in a purely external way; the child is unaware of their functional significance as auxiliary signs. That is why the act of writing can be so completely dissociated from the dictated sentence; not understanding the principle underlying writing, the child takes its external form and thinks he is quite able to write before he even knows what he must write. But a second point is also clear from this example: the child's scrawls bear no relationship to the meaningful sentence dictated to him. We have deliberately presented an example with quite explicit features that would be reflected in the mere outward form of writing if only the child understood the actual purpose and mechanism of writing things down, and its necessary connection with the meaning of what is to be written. Neither the number of items (five pencils, two

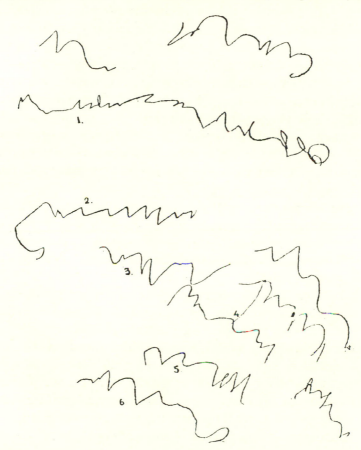

Figure 2. 1. There are five pencils on the table. 2. There are two plates. 3. There are many trees in the forest. 4. There is a column in the yard. 5. There is a large cupboard (written prematurely). 6. The little doll (written prematurely).

tablets), the size factor (large table, small table), nor the shape of the object itself had any influence on the jottings; in each case there were the same zigzag lines. The "writing" had no connec-

tion with the idea evoked by the sentence to be written; it was
not yet instrumental or functionally related to the content of what
was to be written. Actually, this was not writing at all, but simple scribbling.

This self-contained nature of the scrawls is evident in a number of cases: we observed scribbling in children from 3 to 5
years old, and sometimes even as old as 6 (although in these
older children it was not as invariant, as we shall show further
on). In most children in kindergartens, scribbling on paper is
already an accustomed activity, although its functional, auxiliary
significance has not yet been learned. Hence, in most children
of this age, we observed a similar, undifferentiated scrawling,
which had no functional significance and surprisingly easily became simple scribbling on paper merely for fun. We cannot refrain from the pleasure of relating a typical example of this total
dissociation between writing and its primary purpose and its
transformation into the mere fun of scribbling on paper.

Experiment 9/III, series III, Yura, age 6 (middle kindergarten group).

After Yura discovered in the first series that he was
unable to remember by mechanical means all the sentences
dictated to him, we suggested he note them down on paper;
and in the second series we obtained results like those
shown in Figure 2. Despite the undifferentiated nature of
what he wrote down, Yura remembered more words in the
second series than in the first, and was given a piece of
candy as a reward. When we went on to the third series
and again asked him to write down each word, he agreed,
took the pencil, and began (without listening to the end of
one sentence) to scribble. We did not stop him, and he continued to scribble until he had covered the whole page with
scrawls that bore no relation to his initial purpose, which
was to remember the sentences. These scrawls are shown
in Figure 3. Everything on the right side (A) was done before the sentences were presented; not until later, after
we stopped him, did he begin to "write down" the sentences

shown on the left side (Nos. 1-7).

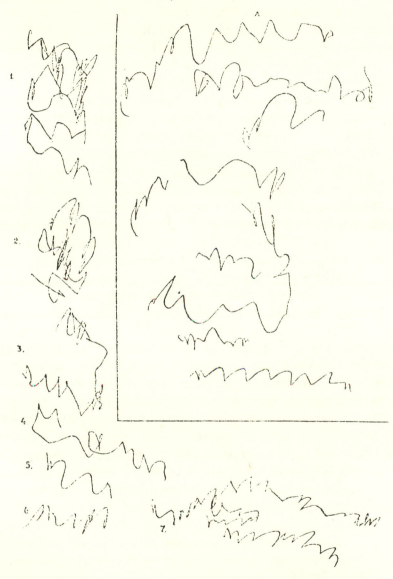

Figure 3. 1. There are many stars in the sky. 2. There
is one moon. 3. I have thirty teeth. 4. Two hands and
two legs. 5. A large tree. 6. The car runs.

Complete lack of comprehension of the mechanism of writing, a purely external relation to it, and a rapid shift from "writing" to self-contained fun bearing no functional relation to writing are characteristic of the first stage in the prehistory of writing in the child. We can call this phase the prewriting phase or, more broadly, the pre-instrumental phase.

One question remains that has a direct bearing on this first phase in the development of writing and has to do with its formal aspects: Why did most of the children we studied choose to write zigzags in more or less straight lines?

There is considerable literature on the first forms of graphic activity in the child. The scrawling stage is explained in terms of physiological factors, the development of coordination, etc. Our approach to the phenomenon was more straightforward. The drawings that interested us were the scribbles. Hence, the most crucial factor here was unquestionably the one that brought these scribbles most closely, albeit only outwardly, to adult writing, namely, the factor of outward imitation.

Although the child at this stage does not yet grasp the sense and function of writing, he does know that adults write; and when given the task of writing down a sentence, he tries to reproduce, if only its outward form, adult writing, with which he is familiar. This is why our samples actually look like writing, arranged in lines, etc., and why Vova immediately said, "This is how you write."

We can persuade ourselves of the crucial role of pure, external imitation in the development of this process by a very simple experiment: if we reproduce the experiment in the presence of a child with another subject (a different one) who is asked to write signs, not words, we shall see how this immediately alters the way the child's "writing" looks.

Lena, 4 years old, who gave us the typical scribbles (see Figure 2), in the break after the session noticed that her friend Lina, age 7, "wrote down" the dictated sentences with a system of "marks" (one mark for each sentence). This was enough to induce her, in the next session, after the break, to produce scrawls that looked completely dif-

ferent. Adopting the manner of her friend, she stopped
writing lines of scribbles and began to note each dictated
sentence with a circle.

The result is shown in Figure 4. ... Monkeys have long tails.

Despite its uniqueness of form, this
specimen is not fundamentally dif-
ferent from those presented above. ... The dark night.
It, too, is undifferentiated, random,
and purely externally associated with
the task of writing; and it, too, is
imitative. Just as in the previous ... There is a tree in the yard.
examples, the child was unable to
link the circles she drew with the
ideas conveyed in the sentence and ... Lyalya has two eyes.
then to use this circle as a function-
al aid. This phase is the first phase
of direct acts, the phase of pre-in- .. A large apple.
strumental, precultural, primitive,
imitative acts.

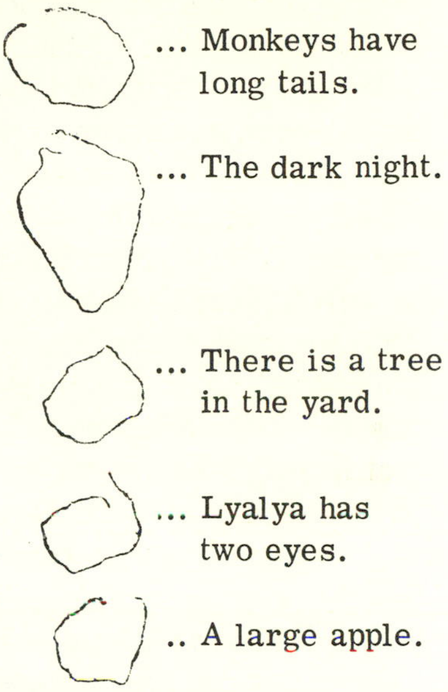

Figure 4

V

Does "writing" help a child, at this stage, to remember the
meaningful message of a dictated sentence? We can answer
"no" in almost all cases, and that is the characteristic feature
of this prewriting stage. The child's writing does not yet serve
a mnemonic function, as will become obvious if we examine the
"sentences" written by the child after dictation. In most cases
the child remembered fewer sentences after "writing" them
down in this way than he did without writing; so writing did not
help, but actually hindered, memory. Indeed, the child made no
effort to remember at all; for in relying on his "writing," he was
quite convinced that it would do his remembering for him. (3)...
Let us, however, take a case in which the child remembered
several sentences even in a writing experiment. If we observe
how these sentences were recalled, we shall see clearly that

"writing" had nothing at all to do with this remembering, that it took place independently of the child's graphic efforts.

The first thing a psychologist studying memory notices is that a child mobilizes all the devices of direct mechanical memory, none of which are found in reading. The child fixes and recalls; he does not record and read: some of his jottings are quite beside the point, and without effect. In our experiments we frequently observed that a child would repeat the sentence after writing it down, to nail it down, as it were; when we asked him to recall what he had written, he did not "read" his jottings from the beginning, but would go right to the last sentences, to catch them while they were fresh in his memory — a procedure very typical of the phenomenon of making a mental note.

Finally, the most instructive observation was how a child would behave in recalling. His behavior was that of someone remembering, not of someone reading. Most of the children we studied reproduced the sentences dictated to them (or rather, some of them) without looking at what they had written, with their gaze directed toward the ceiling questioningly; quite simply, the entire process of recall took place completely apart from the scribbles, which the child did not use at all. We recorded some cases of this sort on film; the child's total disregard of his writing and his purely direct form of remembering are clearly evident from his facial expressions recorded on film.

Thus, the way children in our experiments recalled the dictated sentences (if they did at all) clearly demonstrates that their graphic efforts at this stage of development are actually not yet writing, or even a graphic aid, but merely drawings on paper, quite independent of, and unrelated to, the task of remembering. The child does not yet relate to writing as a tool of memory at this stage of development. This is why in our experiments the children almost always cut a poor figure: of a total of six to eight sentences, most of which they were able to remember by mechanical means, they could remember only two or three at most if asked to write them down, which indicates that if a child has to rely on writing without the ability to use it, the efficiency of memory is considerably reduced.

Nevertheless, our findings also include some cases that at first glance are rather surprising in that they are completely at variance with all we have just described. A child would produce the same undifferentiated nonsense writing as we have described, the same meaningless scribbles and lines, yet he would still be able to recall perfectly all the sentences he had written down. Moreover, as we observed him, we had the impression that he was actually making use of his writing. We checked this and indeed discovered that these scribblings actually were more than just simple scrawls, that they were in some sense real writing. The child would read a sentence, pointing to quite specific scrawls, and was able to show without error and many times in succession which scribble signified which of the dictated sentences. Writing was still undifferentiated in its outward appearance, but the child's relation to it had completely changed: from a self-contained motor activity, it had been transformed into a memory-helping sign. The child had begun to associate the dictated sentence with his undifferentiated scribble, which had begun to serve the auxiliary function of a sign. How did this come about?

In some sessions we noted that the children would arrange their scribblings in some pattern other than straight lines. For instance, they would put one scribble in one corner of the paper and another in another, and in so doing begin to associate the dictated sentences with their notations; this association was further reinforced by the pattern in which the notations were arranged, and the children would declare quite emphatically that the scribble in one corner meant "cow," or that another at the top of the paper meant "chimney sweeps are black." Thus, these children were in the process of creating a system of technical memory aids, similar to the writing of primitive peoples. In itself no scribble meant anything; but its position, situation, and relation to the other scribbles, i.e., all these factors together, imparted to it its function as a technical memory aid. Here is an example:

Brina, age 5 (first time in our laboratory), was asked

to write down a number of sentences dictated to her. She
quickly learned how to proceed and after each word (or
sentence) had been dictated, she would make her scribble.
The results are shown in Figure 5. One might think that
our little subject had made
these marks without any connection with the task of remembering the dictated sentences, just as most of the
children discussed above.
But to our surprise, she not
only recalled all the dictated
sentences (true, there were
not many, only five) but also
correctly located each sentence, pointing to a scribble
and saying: "This is a cow"
or "A cow has four legs and a tail," or "It rained yesterday evening," etc. In other words, she recalled the dictated
sentences by "reading" them. It is clear that Brina understood the task and employed a primitive form of writing,
writing by means of topographical markings. These markings were quite stable; when she was questioned directly,
she did not mix them up, but rigorously distinguished one
from the other, knowing exactly what each one meant.

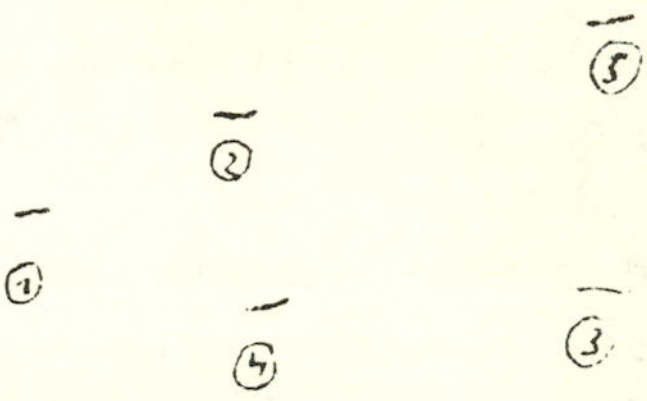

Figure 5. 1. Cow. 2. A cow
has legs and a tail. 3. Yesterday evening it rained.
4. Chimney sweeps are black.
5. Give me three candles.

    This is the first form of "writing," in the proper sense. The
actual inscriptions are still undifferentiated, but the functional
relation to writing is unmistakable. Because the writing is undifferentiated, it is variable. After using it once, a child may
a few days later have forgotten it, and revert back to mechanical scribbling unrelated to the task. But this is the first rudi-
ment of what is later to become writing in the child; in it we see
for the first time the psychological elements from which writing will take shape. The child now recalls the material by associating it with a specific mark rather than just mechanically,
and this mark will remind him of the particular sentence and

help him to recall it. All this and the presence of certain techniques of undifferentiated topographical writing in primitive peoples spurred our interest in this undifferentiated technical aid
to memory, the precursor of real writing.

What role actually is played by the little mark the child makes
on a piece of paper? We saw that it had two main features: it
organized the child's behavior, but did not yet have a content of
its own; it indicated the presence of some meaning, but did not
yet tell us what this meaning was. We could say that this first
sign plays the role of an ostensive sign or, in other words, the
primary sign to "take note." (4) The mark jotted down by the
child creates a certain set and serves as an additional cue that
some sentences have been dictated, but provides no hints as to
how to discover the content of those sentences.

An experiment demonstrated that this interpretation of a primary sign was unquestionably the right one. We can describe a
number of cases to prove this. A child at this stage of development in his relationship to a sign tries to use the marks he has
made to guide him in recalling. Frequently, these "sentences"
have nothing in common with those dictated, but the child will
formally fulfill his assignment and for each cue find the "match-
ing word."

> Here is an example of this relation of the child's to a
> primitive sign (we omit the actual drawing as it is very
> similar in structure to the preceding illustrations). We
> gave a child 4 years, 8 months old a series of words:
> "picture — book — girl — locomotive."
> The child noted each of these words with a mark. When
> she had finished her writing, we asked her to read it.
> Pointing to each mark in succession, the girl "read":
> "girl — doll — bed — trunk."
> We see that the words recalled by the child have nothing
> in common with the words given; only the number of words
> recalled was correct; their content was determined com-
> pletely by the emotional sets and interests of the child
> (R. E. Levin's experiment).

This illustration enables us to get to the psychological structure of such a primary graphic sign. It is clear that a primary, undifferentiated, graphic sign is not a symbolic sign, which discloses the meaning of what has been written down; nor can it yet be called an instrumental sign in the full sense of the word, as it does not lead the child back to the content of what was written down. We should rather say that it is only a simple cue (although one artificially created by the child) that conditionally evokes certain speech impulses. These impulses, however, do not necessarily direct the child back to the situation he has "recorded"; they can only trigger certain processes of association whose content, as we have seen, may be determined by completely different conditions having nothing at all to do with the given cue.

We might best describe the functional role of such a cue as follows:

Let us imagine the process of writing (alphabetic, pictographic, or conventionally agreed on) in an adult. A certain content A is written with the symbol X. When a reader looks at this symbol, he immediately thinks of the content A. The symbol X is an instrumental device to direct the reader's attention to the initial written content. The formula:

(Auxiliary sign)

is the best expression of the structure of such a process.

The situation with respect to a primitive mark such as we have just been discussing is completely different. It only signals that some content written down by means of it exists, but does not lead us to it; it is only a cue evoking some (associative) reaction in the subject. We actually do not have in it the complex instrumental structure of an act, and it may be described by the following formula:

(Given content) A——X

X——N (Recalled association)

(Primitive mark)

where N may not have any relation to the given content A, or, of course, to the mark X.

Instead of an instrumental act, which uses X to revert attention back to A, we have here two direct acts: (1) the mark on the paper, and (2) the response to the mark as a cue. Of course, in psychological terms this is not yet writing, but only the forerunner of it, in which the most rudimentary and necessary conditions for its development are forged. (5)

VI

We have already discussed the insufficient stability of this phase of undifferentiated, memory-helping writing. Having taken the first step along the path of culture with it, and having linked, for the first time, the recalled object with some sign, the child must now go on to the second step: he must differentiate this sign and make it really express a specific content; he must create the rudiments of literacy, in the truest sense of the word. Only then will the child's writing become stable and independent of the number of elements written down; and memory will have gained a powerful tool, capable of broadening its scope enormously. Finally, only under these conditions will any steps forward be taken along the way toward objectivization of writing, i.e., toward transforming it from subjectively coordinated markings into signs having an objective significance that is the same for everyone.

Our experiments warrant the assertion that the development of writing in the child proceeds along a path we can describe as the transformation of an undifferentiated scrawl into a differentiated sign. Lines and scribbles are replaced by figures and pictures, and these give way to signs. In this sequence of events lies the entire path of development of writing in both the history of nations and the development of the child.

We are psychologists, however, and our task is not confined to simple observation and confirmation of the sequence of individual phases: we should like also to describe the conditions that produce this sequence of events and to determine empirically the factors that facilitate for the child the transition from a stage of undifferentiated writing to the level of meaningful signs expressing a content.

Actually, one can say there are two pathways by which differentiation of the primary sign may take place in a child. On the one hand, the child may try to depict the content given him without going beyond the limits of arbitrary, imitative scrawling; on the other hand, he may make the transition to a form of writing that depicts content, to the recording of an idea, i.e., to pictograms. Both paths presuppose some jump that must be made by the child as he replaces the primary, undifferentiated sign with another, differentiated one. This jump presupposes a little invention, whose psychological significance is interesting in that it alters the very psychological function of the sign by transforming the primary sign, which merely establishes ostensively the existence of a thing, into another kind of a sign that reveals a particular content. If this differentiation is accomplished successfully, it transforms a sign-stimulus into a sign-symbol, and a qualitative leap is thereby effected in the development of complex forms of cultural behavior.

We were able to follow the elementary inventions of a child along both these paths. Let us examine each of them separately.

The first signs of differentiation we were able to observe in the small child occurred after several repetitions of our experiment. By the third or fourth session, a child of 4 or 5 years would begin to link the word (or phrase) given him and the nature of the mark with which he distinguished the word. This meant that he did not mark all the words in the same way: the first differentiation, as far as we could judge, involved reflection of the rhythm of the phrase uttered in the rhythm of the graphic sign.

The child quite early begins to show a tendency to write down short words or phrases with short lines and long words or phrases with a large number of scribbles. It is difficult to say whether this is a conscious act, the child's own invention, as it were. We are inclined to see other, more primitive mechanisms at work in this. Indeed, this rhythmic differentiation is by no means always stable. A child who has written a series of sentences given him in a "differentiated" manner in the next session (or for that matter even in the same session) will revert to primitive, undifferentiated writing. This suggests that in this rhythmically reproductive writing some more primitive mechanisms, not an organized and conscious device, are at work.

But what are these mechanisms? Are we not dealing here with simple coincidence, which leads us to see a pattern where there is only the play of chance?

An example drawn from one of our experiments may serve as material for a concrete analysis of this problem.

> Lyuse N., age 4 years, 8 months. We gave her a number of words: mama, cat, dog, doll. She wrote them all down with the same scrawls, which in no way differed from one another. The situation changed considerably, however, when we also gave her long sentences along with individual words: (1) girl; (2) cat; (3) Zhorzhik is skating; (4) Two dogs are chasing the cat; (5) There are many books in the room, and the lamp is burning; (6) bottle; (7) ball; (8) The cat is sleeping; (9) We play all day, then we eat dinner, and then we go out to play again.
>
> In the writing the child now produced, the individual words were represented by little lines, but the long sentences were written as complicated squiggles; and the longer the sentence, the longer was the squiggle written to express it.

Thus, the process of writing, which began with an undifferentiated, purely imitative, graphic accompaniment to the presented words, after a period of time was transformed into a process that on the surface indicated that a connection had been made between the graphic production and the cue presented. The child's graphic production ceased being a simple accompaniment to a cue and became its reflection — albeit in very primitive form. It began to reflect merely the rhythm of the presented phrase:

single words began to be written as single lines, and sentences
as long, complicated scribbles, sometimes reflecting the rhythm
of the presented sentence.

The variable nature of this writing suggests, however, that
perhaps this is no more than a simple <u>rhythmic</u> reflection of the
cue presented to the subject. Psychologically, it is quite com-
prehensible that every stimulus perceived by a subject has its
own rhythm and through it exerts a certain effect on the activity
of the subject, especially if the aim of that activity is linked to
the presented stimulus and must reflect and record it. The primary effect of this rhythm also produces that first rhythmic differentiation in the child's writing that we were able to note in
our experiments.

Below we shall discuss the very intimate relationship that we
believe exists between graphic production and mimicry. Functionally, graphic activity is a rather complex system of cultural
behavior, and in terms of its genesis may be regarded as ex-
pressiveness materialized in fixed form. It is just this sort of
reflection of mimicry we see in the example given above. The
rhythm of a sentence is reflected in the child's graphic activity,
and we quite frequently encounter further rudiments of such
rhythmically depictive writing of complex speech clusters. It
was not invention, but the primary effect of the rhythm of the
cue or stimulus that was at the source of the first meaningful
use of a graphic sign.

VII

This first step along the way of differentiation of primitive,
imitative, graphic activity is still very weak and impoverished,
however. Although a child may be able to reflect the rhythm of
a sentence, he is still unable to mark the content of a term presented to him graphically. We must await the next step, when
his graphic activity begins to reflect not only the external rhythm
of the words presented to him but also their content; we await
the moment when a sign acquires meaning. It is then that we
shall doubtless be dealing with inventiveness.

Actually, when undifferentiated, imitative, graphic activity first acquires expressive content, is this not a tremendous step forward in the child's cultural behavior? But even here, again, it is not enough merely to show invention. Our task must be to ascertain what factors are responsible for the shift to a meaningful, depictive sign; and to show what they are means to discover the internal factors determining the process of invention of expressive signs in the child.

The task of the experimenter in this case is consequently to test certain inputs into an experiment and determine which of them produces the primary transition from the diffuse phase to the meaningful use of signs.

In our experiments there was one serious factor that could influence the development of writing in the child: this was the content of what was presented to him; and in varying this, we might ask, What changes in the content we presented were conditions for inducing a primary transition to differentiated, depictive writing?

Two primary factors can take the child from an undifferentiated phase of graphic activity to a stage of differentiated graphic activity. These factors are number and form.

We observed that number, or quantity, was perhaps the first factor to break up that purely imitative, unexpressive character of graphic activity in which different ideas and notions were expressed by exactly the same sort of lines and scribbles. By introducing the factor of number into the material, we could readily produce differentiated graphic activity in 4-5-year-old children by causing them to use signs to reflect this number. It is possible that the actual origins of writing are to be found in the need to record number, or quantity.

Perhaps the best thing to do is to reproduce a protocol showing the process of differentiation of writing as it took place under the influence of the factor of quantity.

Lena L., 4 years old, in her first attempt to write sentences produced an undifferentiated scrawl for each sentence, with completely identical scribbles (see Figure 2). Of course, since these scribbles were totally unrelated to

the ideas, they did not even give the effect of writing, and
we concluded that this kind of mechanical graphic production hindered rather than helped memory.

We then introduced the factor of quantity into a number
of experiments to determine how the altered conditions
would affect the development of graphic activity. We were
immediately able to note the beginnings of differentiation.

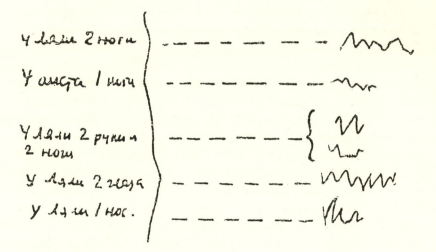

Indeed, graphic production changed sharply under the
influence of this factor (especially if one compares it with
the sample in Figure 2). We now see a clear differentiation, linked to the particular task. For the first time each
scrawl reflects a particular content. Of course, the differentiation is still primitive: what differentiates "one
nose" from "two eyes" is that the scribbles representing
the former are much smaller. Quantity is still not clearly expressed, but relations are. The sentence "Lilya has
two hands and two legs" was perceived and recorded in a
differentiated fashion: "two hands" and "two legs" each
had their own scribble. But most important, this differentiation appeared in a child who had just produced some totally undifferentiated scribblings, not betraying even the

least indication that they might have anything at all to do with the sentences dictated.

This example brings us to the following observation: quantity was the factor that broke up the elementary, mechanical, undifferentiated, graphic production and for the first time opened the way toward its use as an auxiliary device, hence raising it from the level of merely mechanical imitation to the status of a functionally employed tool.

Of course, the graphic production itself is still muddled; and the technique has not yet assumed precise, constant contours: if we again dictated material having no reference to quantity, we would again obtain an undifferentiated scribbling by the same child, with no attempt on her part to represent a particular content with a particular mark. But now that the first step had been taken, the child was, for the first time, able really to "write" and, what is most important, to "read" what she had written. With the transition to this primitive but differentiated graphic activity, her entire behavior changed: the same child who had been unable to recall two or three sentences was now able to recall all of them confidently and, what is more, for the first time was able to read her own writing.

Thanks to the quantity factor, this differentiation was achieved in children 4-5 years old. The influence of the factor of quantity was especially strong in cases in which the factor of contrast was added — when, for example, the sentence "There are two trees in the yard" was followed by the sentence "There are many trees in the forest," the child tried to reproduce the same contrast, and hence could not write both sentences with the same markings and instead was forced to produce differentiated writing.

Having noted this, let us go on immediately to the second factor defining and accelerating the transition from undifferentiated play writing to real, differentiated, expressive, graphic activity.

In our experiments we observed that differentiation of writing could be considerably accelerated if one of the sentences dictated concerned an object that was quite conspicuous because of its color, clear-cut shape, or size. We combined these three fac-

tors into a second group of conditions that would promote the
child's learning to put a specific content into his writing and
make it expressive and differentiated. In such cases we saw
how graphic production suddenly began to acquire definite contours as the child attempted to express color, shape, and size;
indeed, it began to have a rough resemblance to primitive pictography. Quantity and conspicuous shape lead the child to pictography. Through these factors the child initially gets the idea
of using drawing (which he is already quite good at in play) as
a means of remembering, and for the first time drawing begins
to converge with a complex intellectual activity. Drawing changes
from simple representation to a means, and the intellect acquires a new and powerful tool in the form of the first differentiated writing.

Here is a protocol illustrating the guiding role played by the
factor of form in the child's discovery of the mechanism of writing; this protocol also shows clearly the process of differentiation as it progresses.

Vova N., 5 years old, first time in our laboratory. The
subject was asked to write sentences dictated to him in
order to remember them. He began immediately to produce scribbles, saying, "This is how you write" (see Figure 1). Obviously, for him the act of writing was purely
an external imitation of the writing of an adult without any
connection with the content of the particular idea, since
the scribbles differed from one another in no essential
way. Here is the record:

1. The mouse with a long   Subject (writes:) This is how
   tail.   you write.
2. There is a high column.   Subject (writes:) Column...
                               This is how you write.
3. There are chimneys on   Subject (writes:) Chimneys
   the roof.   on the roof... This is how
                               you write....

Now we give the subject a picture in bright colors, and
the reaction immediately changes.

4. Very black smoke is coming out of the chimney.

Subject: Black. Like this! (Points to the pencil and then begins to draw very black scribbles, pressing hard.)

5. In the winter there is white snow.

Subject: (Makes his usual scribbles, but separates them into two parts, apparently unrelated to the idea of "white snow.")

6. Very black coal —

Subject: (Again draws heavy lines.)

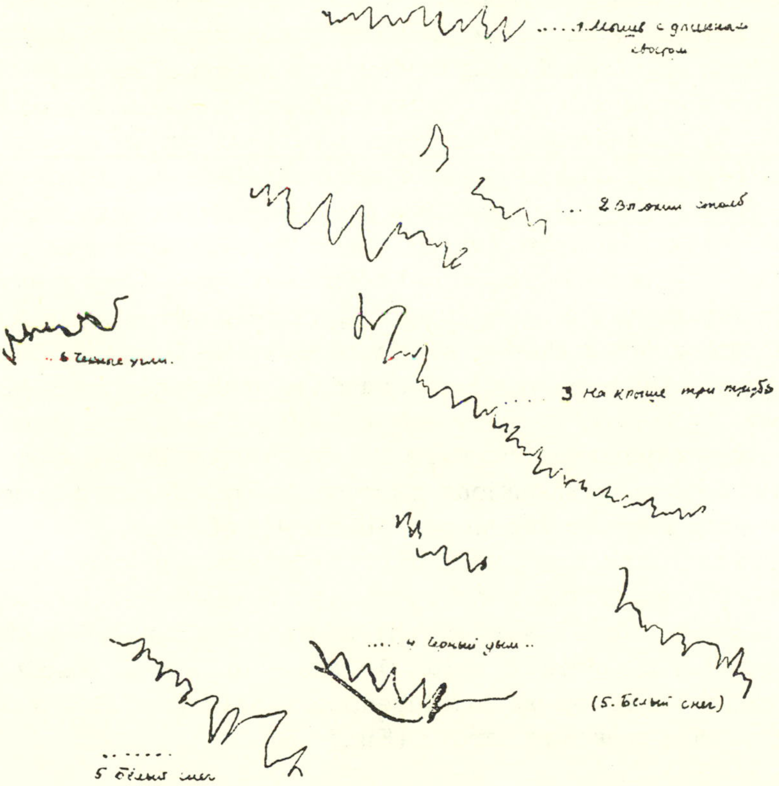

Figure 6

Both the protocol and the writing itself in Figure 6 show that the generally undifferentiated writing acquires an expressive character in only two cases (4 and 6), in which "black smoke" and "black coal" are depicted with heavy black lines. For the first time the scrawls on paper assume some of the features of true writing.

The effect becomes clear when we see how the subject recalls what he has written. When asked to recall what he has written, he refuses to recall anything at all. It seems that he has forgotten everything, and his scribblings tell him nothing. But after examining the scrawls, he suddenly stops at one of them and says, spontaneously: "This is coal." This is the first time such spontaneous reading occurs in this child, and the fact that he had not only produced something differentiated in his graphic activity but also was able to recall what it represented fully confirms that he had taken the first step toward using writing as a means of remembering.

This sort of differentiation was achieved in 4- and 5-year olds, and it is quite possible that in some cases it can occur even much earlier. The most important thing about all this is that the emergence of the conditions necessary for writing, the discovery of pictographic writing, the first use of writing as a means of expression, occurred before our eyes. We can say with assurance that after observing with our own eyes, in our laboratory, how a child gropingly repeated the first primitive steps of culture, many elements and factors in the emergence of writing became incomparably clearer for us. Sometimes, in the same experiment, we were able to observe the sequence of a whole series of inventions carrying the child forward to one new stage after another in the cultural use of signs.

The best thing to do, perhaps, is to present a protocol from one of our experiments in its entirety. We have therefore selected a record for a 5-year-old girl in which we may follow step by step her discovery of cultural signs. We have purposely chosen a subject whose undifferentiated, mnemotechnical writing we have presented earlier (Figure 5).

Brina Z., age 5. The experiment was done in a number of consecutive sessions in each of which five or six sentences were dictated with the instruction to write them down in order to remember them.

1st session. The experimenter dictated five sentences: (1) The bird is flying. (2) The elephant has a long trunk. (3) An automobile goes fast. (4) There are high waves on the sea. (5) The dog barks.

The subject made a line for each sentence and arranged the lines in columns (see Figure 7A, I). The lines were identical. In the recall test, she remembered only three sentences, i.e., the same number she remembered without writing anything down. She recalled spontaneously, i.e., without looking at her scribblings.

2nd session. The experimenter dictated five sentences, which included quantitative elements: (1) A man has two arms and two legs. (2) There are many stars in the sky. (3) Nose. (4) Brina has 20 teeth. (5) The big dog has four little pups.

The subject drew lines arranged in a column. Two hands and two legs were represented by two discrete lines; the other sentences were represented by one line each (Figure 7A, II). In the recall test the subject declared that she had forgotten everything and refused to try to remember.

3rd session. The experimenter repeated the second series "to help her write down and remember what was dictated a little better." He then dictated the second series again with a few changes: (the subject's scribblings are given in Figure 7A, III):

1. Here is a man, and he has two legs. — Subject: Then I'll draw two lines.

2. In the sky there are many stars. — Subject: Then I'll draw many lines.

3. The crane has one leg. — (Makes a mark)... The crane is on one leg... There you are... (Points) The crane is on one leg.

4. Brina has 20 teeth. — (Draws several lines.)

5. The big hen and four little chicks. — (Makes one big line and two small ones; thinks a little, and adds another two.)

In the recall test, she remembered everything correctly
except for sentence No. 2. When the experimenter dictated
this sentence to her and asked, "How can you write this so
as to remember it?" she answered, "Best with circles."

4th session. The experimenter again dictates sentences
and the subject writes them down.

1. The monkey has a long tail.	Subject: The monkey (draws a line) has a long (draws another line) tail (yet another line).
2. The column is high.	Okay, so I'll draw a line. The column came broken.
3. The bottle is on the table.	Now I can draw the table and then the bottle. But I can't do it right.
4. There are two trees.	(Draws two lines.) Now I'll draw the branches.
5. It's cold in winter.	Okay. In the winter (draws line) it's cold (draws line).
6. The little girl wants to eat.	(Draws a mark.) [Experimenter:] Why did you draw it like that? [Subject:] Because I wanted to.

In the recall test she remembered correctly Nos. 2, 3,
5, and 6.(see Figure 7B). About No. 4 she said: "This is
the monkey with the long tail." When the experimenter
pointed out that this sentence was No. 1, she objected:
"No, these two long lines are the monkey with the long tail.
If I hadn't drawn the long lines, I wouldn't have known."

This experiment began with completely undifferentiated writing. The subject would jot down lines without relating to them
in any way as differentiated signs referring to something. In
the recall test she did not use these lines and recalled directly,
as it were. It is understandable that the failure in the first two
experiments depressed her somewhat, and she tried to refuse
to go on, declaring that she couldn't remember anything and that
she "didn't want to play anymore." At this point, however, a

sudden change occurred, and she began to behave completely differently. She had discovered the instrumental use of writing; she had invented the sign. The lines she had drawn mechanically became a differentiated, expressive tool, and the entire process of recall for the first time began to be mediated. This invention was the result of a confluence of two factors: the interjection of the factor of quantity into the task, and the experimenter's insistent requirement that she "write so that it could be understood." Perhaps even without this last condition the subject would have discovered the sign, maybe a little later; but we wanted to accelerate the process and restore her interest. This we were able to do; and the subject, after switching to a new technique and finding it successful, continued to cooperate for another hour and a half.

In the third session, which we shall now discuss, she discovered for the first time that a sign, by means of numerical

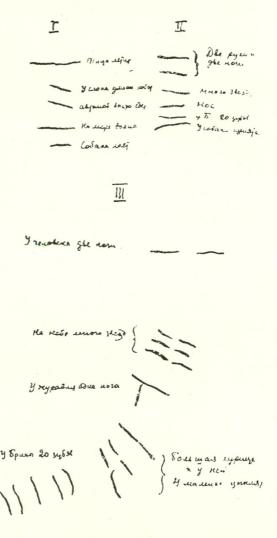

Figure 7A

differentiation, had an expressive function: when asked to write
"The man has two legs" Brina immediately declared, "Then I'll
draw two lines"; and once having discovered this technique, she
continued to use it. She then combined this device with a rough
schematic representation of the object: the crane with one leg
she depicted with a line with another meeting it at right angles;

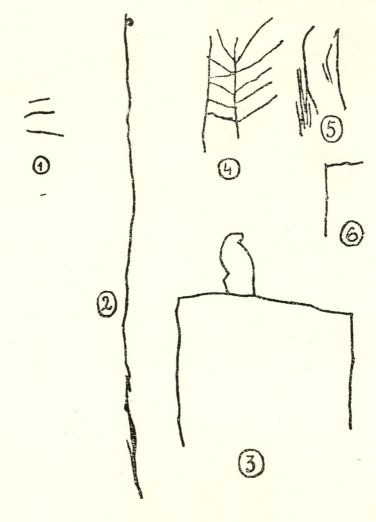

Figure 7B

the large dog with four pups became a large line with four smaller ones. Thus, in the recall test she no longer proceeded completely from memory, but read what she had written, each time pointing to her drawing. The only case of failure was "There are many stars in the sky." In the test session this was replaced with a new drawing in which the stars were represented by circles, not lines.

Differentiation continued in the fourth session, in which the length of the column was represented by a long line and the tree and bottle were drawn directly. Of particular interest is her attempt to differentiate her writing in another direction, mentioned above: when Brina had difficulty expressing a complex formulation, she wrote down the dictated sentence semimechanically, rhythmically breaking it down into words, each of which was represented by a line (monkey — long — tail, winter — cold). She continued to use this technique for some time; we have observed the same technique in 7-8-year-old children. This technique was less successful than the technique of real, differentiated writing, however, and hence is a special case. After writing "It is cold in winter" with two long lines, the subject began to recall them as the "monkey with the long tail," declaring that she had purposely drawn the long line and that without it she would have been unable to remember the monkey's long tail. We see here how a technique that has been used ineffectively is reworked and acquires an attribute corresponding to one of the ideas; the line is then interpreted differently and is transformed into a sign.

After having started with undifferentiated play writing, before our very eyes the subject discovered the instrumental nature of such writing and worked out her own system of expressive marks, by means of which she was able to transform the entire remembering process. Play was transformed into elementary writing, and writing was now able to assimilate the child's representational experience. We have reached the threshold of pictographic writing.

VIII

The period of picture writing is fully developed by the time a

child reaches the age of 5 or 6 years; if it is not fully and clearly developed by that time, it is only because it already begins to
give way to symbolic alphabetic writing, which the child learns
in school — and sometimes long before.

If it were not for this factor, we should have every reason to
.expect that pictography would achieve a flourishing development;
and this is what we actually see everywhere that symbolic writing is not developed or does not exist; pictography flourishes
among primitive peoples (there have been many interesting studies of pictography). The richest development of pictography is
found in retarded children, who are still preliterate; and we
should, without reserve, recognize that their fine and colorful

Figure 8

pictographic writing is one of the positive accomplishments of retarded children. (In Figure 8 we show some drawings by a retarded child that are quite impressive in their vividness and grace.)

The pictographic phase in the development of writing is based
on the rich experience of the child's drawings, which need not in
themselves serve the function of mediating signs, in any intellectual process. Initially drawing is play, a self-contained process
of representation; then the perfected act can be used as a device,
a means, for recording. But because the direct experience of
drawing is so rich, we often do not obtain the pictographic phase
of writing in its pure form in the child. Drawing as a means is
very frequently blended with drawing as a self-contained, unmediated process. Nowhere in such material can one discern any
sign of the difficulties the child experiences in going through the
differentiation of all these processes into means and ends, objects and functionally related techniques, which, as we saw above,
are the necessary condition for the emergence of writing.

We shall not dwell in detail on all the characteristic features
of this pictographic phase in the development of writing in the
child, since this phase has been studied much more than all the
others. We shall merely underscore the distinction between pictographic writing and drawing, and once again draw on an actual
experimental record to illustrate our point.

> Marusya G., 8 years old, is a mentally retarded child.
> She cannot write, and has poor command of speech. Her
> Binet-Bert IQ is 60. Despite this handicap, however, she
> has remarkable representational gifts. Her drawings are
> an excellent example of how drawing may not be an indica-
> tor of intellectual aptitude, but may in compensation devel-
> op in people whose intellectual (especially verbal) aptitudes
> are impaired.
>
> We performed our usual experiment with Marusya. In
> the first natural series, she remembered only one of the
> six words. After noting this, we went directly on to the
> writing experiment. Here is the record:
>
> Experimenter: Now I shall tell you a number of things,

and you should write them down on the paper so you can remember them better. Here is a pencil.

Subject: How should I write it? House and girl, right? (Begins to write "girl"; see Figure 8, 1.)

Experimenter: (1) Listen. Write that a cow has four legs and a tail.

Subject: A little cow, a real little cow. I think I'd better draw the girl instead. I don't know how (draws the girl).

(Experimenter repeats the instructions.)

(2) Chimney sweeps are black.

Black. A little box. I don't know how to draw a chimney (draws a box, then begins to draw a flower). (Figure 8, 2 and 3a ["This is a flower."])

(3) Yesterday evening it rained.

It was wet. I put on my galoshes. There was a little drizzle. Here it is (makes a few light lines on the paper [Figure 8, 3]). I can draw snow, too. Here it is (draws a star, Figure 8, 3a).

(4) We had a tasty soup for lunch.

Soup, tasty (Figure 8, 4); they go together.

(5) The dog is running about the yard.

Dog, little (draws a dog).

(6) The boat is sailing the sea.

Here's the boat (draws).

At this point a bright light was turned on so that we could film the process, and the experimenter called the subject's attention to it: "Look at our little sun." The subject then proceeded to draw a circle and declared: "Here is the sun" (Figure 8, 2a).

In the recall test, the subject named all the figures she had drawn, regardless of whether they depicted what had been dictated or were spontaneous drawings: (1) Girl, (2) Soup, (3) The boat is sailing, (4) The black box, (5) Here is a flower, (6) The dog.... She then took the pencil and drew a road and said, "Here is a road" (Figure 8, 7).

Our record gives a good, detailed description of the development of pictographic writing in the child. What is especially noteworthy is the extraordinary ease with which the child took up this kind of writing yet dissociated the depicted figures from the writing task and turned it into spontaneous, self-contained drawing. It was with this tendency to draw pictures, not to write with the aid of pictures, that our experiment began, when Marusya at our request to pay attention to everything said to her immediately answered: "How should I write? A house, a little girl, right?" The process of the functional use of writing was incomprehensible to her; and if she learned it later, it would remain a shaky acquisition. Several times during the course of the experiment, Marusya reverted to spontaneous drawing, with no function related to remembering the dictated material.

This dual relationship to drawing remained with our subject throughout all the following experiments, and the agility with which she would switch from pictographic writing back to spontaneous drawing was something observed in many preschoolers and, especially, in older retarded children. The more outstanding the pictography, the easier it was for these two principles of picture writing to be mixed.

A child may draw well but not relate to his drawing as an auxiliary device. This distinguishes writing from drawing and sets a limit to the full development of pictographic literacy in the narrow meaning of the term. The more retarded the child, the more marked is his inability to relate to drawing other than as a kind of play and to develop and understand the instrumental use of a picture as a device or symbol, though his drawing skills may be well developed.

But now we have come to the problem of the development of the symbolic phase of writing; and in order not to lose the connection with what has been said, we should pause for a moment on a very important factor at the borderline between pictography and symbolic writing in the child.

IX

Let us imagine a case in which a child who can write picto-graphically must put down something that is difficult (or even impossible) to express in a picture. What does the child then do?

This situation, of course, forces the child to find ways around the problem, if he does not simply refuse to perform the task. Two such detours, very similar to each other, are possible. On the one hand, the child instructed to record something difficult to depict may instead of object A put down object B, which is re-lated in some way to A. Or, he may simply put down some ar-bitrary mark instead of the object he finds difficult to depict.

Either way leads from pictographic writing to symbolic writ-ing, except that the first still operates with the same means of pictographic representation whereas the second makes use of other qualitatively new devices.

In experiments with mentally retarded children we often observe the development of indirect means of the first type; school and school instruction provide ample opportunities for the second type.

Let us imagine that a small child or a retarded child is able to draw well, and we suggest to him some picture that, for some rea-son, he finds difficult to draw. How does he proceed in this case?

We can analyze the indirect means a child devises in such a case in their purest form on the basis of one of our experiments. Let us first take a subject whom we have already discussed ear-lier — Marusya G.

In a fourth session we again gave her a series of sentences that were not all equally easy to write down. Here is an extract from the record (see Figure 9).

1. Two dogs on the street.

Subject: Two dogs (draws) ...and a cat (draws a cat). Two big dogs.

2. There are many stars in the sky.

What stars ... here is the sky (draws a line). Here is some grass below (draws)... I see them from the window (draws a window).

What does this extract tell us ? The subject has difficulty in
representing pictographically the sentence "There are many
stars in the sky," and she creates her own unique way to get
around the problem: she does not draw the image given her, but
instead portrays an entire situation in which she saw stars. She
depicts the sky, the window through which she saw the stars,
etc. Instead of the part, she reproduces the entire situation,
and in this way solves the problem.

Figure 9

A similar situation was encountered with another subject,
Petya U., $6\frac{1}{2}$ years old. Here is an extract from the record.

Session III, (2) There
are 1,000 stars in the sky.

Subject: I can't draw 1,000
stars. If you want, I'll draw
an airplane. This is the sky
(draws a horizontal line)...
Oh, I can't....

We see here the difficulty of an image that does not lend itself well to graphic representation, so that the subject tries to
get around the problem by depicting other, related objects.

These children had insufficient ability to use drawing as a
sign or a means, and this was complicated by their attitude toward drawing as a self-contained game. Hence, the representation is extended from a single image to a whole situation in which
this image was perceived; it is given new roots. In this situation, however, the indirect path is purely of the most primitive
sort. The whole instead of the part is the first indirect device
used in early childhood; we shall be able to understand it if we
take into account the diffuse, holistic, poorly differentiated nature of a child's perceptions. (6) At the very last stages, these
indirect means acquire another, more differentiated and more
highly developed nature.

It is hardly necessary to present all the instances in which a
child chooses an indirect means and, instead of a whole that he
finds difficult to depict, draws some part of it, which is easier.
These features of all infantile drawing that is already at a more
differentiated stage have been described many times, and are
well known to all. Two tendencies are characteristic of the pictographic writing of a child at a relatively advanced stage: the
object to be depicted may be replaced either by some part of it
or by its general contours or outline. In either case the child
has already gone beyond the aforementioned tendency to depict
an object in its entirety, in all its details, and is in the process
of acquiring the psychological skills on whose basis the last
form, symbolic writing, will develop. Let us give just one more
example of the first appearance of this kind of representational
drawing in a child. This is the "part instead of the whole" device we observed in the experiments involving writing a number.

Shura N., $7\frac{1}{2}$ years old. The child is instructed to write
the sentence we presented above: "There are 1,000 stars
in the sky." The subject first draws a horizontal line ("the
sky"), then carefully draws two stars, and stops. Experimenter: "How many do you still have to draw?" Subject:

"Only two. I'll remember there are 1,000."

Clearly, the two stars here were a sign for a large quantity. It would be wrong, however, to assume that such a small child was capable of using the "part for the whole" device. We had occasion to observe a number of children who wrote the sentence about 1,000 stars with so many "stars," i.e., marks, that after demurring several minutes, we finally had simply to stop this procedure, which looked as though it were going to end with a thousand stars. A considerable degree of intellectual development and abstraction are necessary to be able to depict a whole group by one or two representatives; a child who is capable of this is already at the verge of symbolic writing.

> Let us consider briefly some experiments we ran in this regard on adults. An adult audience was asked to represent concrete or abstract concepts graphically; these adults invariably depicted one attribute of the whole (e.g., "stupidity" was represented as donkey ears, "intelligence" by a high forehead, "fear" by raised hair or big eyes, etc.). Graphic representation by means of a particular attribute, however, is not at all easy for a child, whose discriminating and abstracting powers are not very well developed.

We have arrived at the question of a child's symbolic writing, and with this will have reached the end of our essay on the prehistory of a child's writing. Strictly speaking, this primitive period of infantile literacy, which is so interesting to the psychologist, comes to an end when the teacher gives a child a pencil. But we should not be completely correct in saying such a thing. From the time a child first begins to learn to write until he has finally mastered this skill is a very long period, which is of particular interest for psychological research. It is right at the borderline between the primitive forms of inscription we have seen above, which have a prehistoric, spontaneous character, and the new cultural forms introduced in an organized fashion from outside the individual. It is during this transitional

period, when the child has not completely mastered the new
skills but also has not completely outgrown the old, that a number of psychological patterns of particular interest emerge.

How does a child write who, although he is still unable to
write, knows some of the elements of the alphabet? How does
he relate to these letters, and how does he (psychologically) try
to use them in his primitive practice? These are the questions
that interest us.

Let us first describe some extremely interesting patterns we
observed in our material. Writing by no means develops along
a straight line, with continuous growth and improvement. Like
any other cultural psychological function, the development of writing depends to a considerable extent on the writing techniques
used and amounts essentially to the replacement of one such
technique by another. Development in this case may be described
as a gradual improvement in the process of writing, within the
means of each technique, and sharp turning points marking a
transition from one such technique to another. But the profoundly dialectical uniqueness of this process means that the transition to a new technique initially sets the process of writing back
considerably, after which it then develops further at the new and
higher level. Let us try to see what this interesting pattern
means, since without it, in our opinion, it would be impossible
for such cultural psychological functions to develop.

We saw that the prehistory of infantile writing traces a path
of gradual differentiation of the symbols used. At first the child
relates to writing things without understanding the significance
of writing; in the first stage, writing is for him not a means of
recording some specific content, but a self-contained process
involving imitation of an adult activity but having no functional
significance in itself. This phase is characterized by undifferentiated scribblings; the child records any idea with exactly the
same scrawls. Later — and we saw how this develops — differentiation begins: the symbols acquire a functional significance and
begin graphically to reflect the content the child is to write down.

At this stage the child begins to learn how to read: he knows
individual letters, and he knows that these letters record some

content; finally, he learns their outward forms and how to make particular marks. But does this mean that he now understands the full mechanics of their use? Not at all. Moreover, we are convinced that an understanding of the mechanisms of writing takes place much later than the outward mastery of writing, and that in the first stages of acquiring this mastery the child's relation to writing is purely external. He understands that he can use signs to write everything, but he does not yet understand how to do this; he thus becomes fully confident in this writing yet is still totally unable to use it. Believing completely in this new technique, in the first stage of development of symbolic alphabetic writing the child begins with a stage of undifferentiated writing he had already passed through long before.

Here are some examples from our records for different subjects obtained under different conditions.

Little Vasya G., a village boy 6 years old, could not yet write, but knew the individual letters A and I. When we asked him to remember and write down some sentences we dictated, he easily did so. In his movements he showed total confidence that he would be able to write down and remember the dictated sentences. The results are shown in the following record.

1. A cow has four legs and a tail.   Subject: I know he has four legs, and this (writes) is "I."

2. Chimney sweeps are black.   (Writes) and this is "A."

3. Yesterday evening it rained.   Here's rain. Here's "I" (writes).

4. There are many trees in the woods.   Subject: (writes) Here is "u."

5. The steamer is sailing down the river.   The steam goes like this (makes a mark). Here's "I."

The result was a column of alternate I's and A's having nothing to do with the dictated sentences. Obviously, the subject had not yet learned how to make such a connection, so that in the task in which he was to read what he wrote, he read the letters (I and A) without relating them at all to the text.

In this case the letters were completely non-functional; the child was at a stage fully analogous with the stage studied earlier.

But one may object: the child had obviously not yet learned the function of writing, and psychologically the letters were totally analogous to the earlier scribbles. He had not yet gone beyond the stage of primary, undifferentiated, graphic activity. This observation is quite true, but it does not vitiate the law we wished to demonstrate. We can present data showing that this inability to use letters, this lack of understanding of the actual mechanism of alphabetic writing, persists for a long time. To study the psychological underpinnings of automatized writing skills rather than these skills themselves we selected a somewhat different approach; the children were instructed not to write each word in a sentence completely. The results of this test gave us a deeper insight into a child's attitude toward writing. Here is an example:

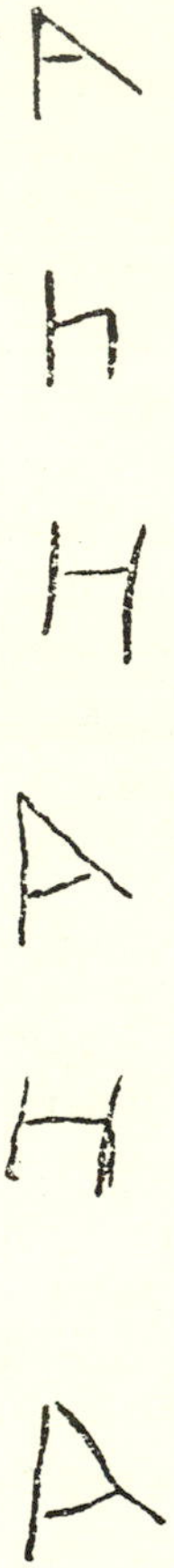

Figure 10

Vanya Z., 9 years old, a village boy, wrote the letters well, and willingly participated in our experiment. The results, however, showed a very unique attitude toward his writing. Here is the record:

1. Monkeys have long tails.	Subject writes first "n" and then crosses it out and writes "i" (saying to himself: u obezyan-i).
2. There is a tall tree.	"v"
3. It's dark in the cellar.	"v"
4. The balloon soars.	"v"
5. The big dog gave birth to four pups.	"u"

6. The boy is hungry.   "m"

[Translator's note: Each of the Russian sentences begins
with the letter the boy wrote down.]

Of course, the subject was able to recall very
little of the written words on the basis of what
was written here. The way he wrote three different sentences (2, 3, and 4) induced us to do
the following test.

In a second session we gave the boy six sentences beginning with the preposition "u." All
six sentences were written down as six completely identical letters "u" (see Figure 11).

These data show that the ability to write does not
necessarily mean that the child understands the process of writing and that a child who can write may,
under certain conditions, display a totally undifferentiated attitude toward writing and a lack of comprehension of the basic premises of it, namely, the
need for specific distinctions to record different
contents.

Figure 11

We obtained even clearer results when we asked
a schoolchild who had recently learned how to write to write
some idea with any marks (or graphic designs); he was forbidden only to use letters. The most conspicuous result of these
experiments was the surprising difficulty the child had in re-
verting to the phase of pictorial, representational writing
through which he had already passed. Our expectation, which
seemed quite reasonable, that given the conditions of our experiment, the child would immediately revert to simple drawings proved wrong. The child whom we had forbidden to use
letters did not revert to the picture stage, but remained at the
level of symbolic writing. He worked out his own signs and,
using them, tried to do the assignment. Finally, what was most
interesting of all was that in using these signs he started with
the same undifferentiated phase with which he began the development of writing in general, only now he gradually developed

differentiated techniques for this higher level of development.

Here is a record of an experiment done with Shura I.,
a city schoolboy $8\frac{1}{2}$ years old. We asked him to note each
sentence we dictated with marks to remember it. The
subject quickly consented to the experiment, and in the
first session used a very simple system. He marked each
sentence with crosses, each element of the sentence being
noted by one cross. Here is what he produced:
Session I:

1. A cow has four legs and a tail.   XXX
                              (Cow — four legs — tail.)
2. Negroes are black.   XXX
                              (Negroes — are — black.)
3. It rained yesterday evening.   XXX
                              (It rained — yesterday — evening.)
4. There are many wolves in the forest.   XXX
                     (There are — many wolves — in the forest.)
5. House.   X
6. Two dogs, a large one and a small one.   XXX
                     (Two dogs — large one and — small one.)

The completely undifferentiated nature of this writing shows
with graphic clarity that the subject had not yet grasped the mechanism of symbolic writing and used it only externally, thinking
that these marks in themselves would be of assistance to him.

The effect of such writing was quite expected; the subject remembered only three of the six sentences, and moreover was
completely unable to indicate which of his markings represented
which sentence.

To follow the process in its purest form, we forbade our subject to make crosses. The result was a transition to a new form,
marks that were not as undifferentiated but that he continued to use
in a purely mechanical fashion. In this second trial, however, we
were already able to achieve some differentiation; the subject discovered pictographic writing and resorted to it after a number
of failures with his marks. Here is the record (see Figure 12).

Session II:

1. Monkeys have long tails.   (Makes two marks.)

2. There is a high column on the street.   (Two marks.)

3. The night is dark.   (Two marks.)

4. There is one bottle and two glasses.   (I'll write down a bottle.)

5. One big dog and one small dog.   (Makes two marks.)

6. Wood is thick.   (I'll write down wood.)

We see that at first this writing was undifferentiated; but then, in cases that were especially conducive to pictography, the subject went over to a graphic depiction of the objects. He was not consistent in this, however, and at even the slightest difficulty in depicting something would again revert to undifferentiated use of signs.

But in this case, we were able to advance one step in our inquiry into the most difficult problem of our study, namely, the mechanisms by which this arbitrary con-

Figure 12

ventional sign is created. Session III shows this mechanism.

We gave the subject a number of concrete images with a word between them identifying the situation. Figure 13 shows the interesting process of generation of a sign to identify an abstract term.

Session III:
1. There is a column.   (The subject draws something.)
2. The night is dark.   I'll put a circle for the night
                              (draws a filled-in circle).
3. The bird is flying.   (The subject draws something.)
4. Smoke is coming from   I'll draw a house with smoke
    the chimney.   (draws).
5. The fish is swimming.   Fish...fish.... I'll draw a fish.
6. The girl wants to eat.   I'll draw a girl.... She wants to
                              eat (makes a mark) — there it is
                              — she wants to eat (Figure 13,6,7).

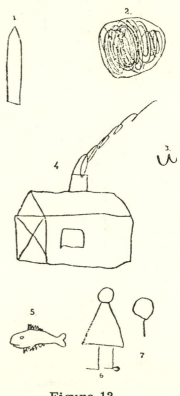

Figure 13

The last is very characteristic. The subject, unable to draw "hunger," reverted to his system of signs and, next to the figure of the little girl, placed a mark meant to signify that the girl wanted to eat. Pictography here is combined with arbitrary symbolic writing, and a sign is used where pictographic means are not sufficient.

Our example clearly shows that a child initially assimilates school experience purely externally, without yet understanding the sense and mechanism of using symbolic marks In the course of our experiment, however, a positive aspect of this assimilated experience emerged; when conditions were restricted, the child reverted to a new, more complicated form of pictographic writing, in which the pictographic elements were combined with symbolic marks used as technical means for remembering.

The further development of literacy involves the assimilation of the mechanisms of culturally elaborated symbolic writing and the use of symbolic devices to simplify and expedite the act of recording. This takes us beyond our topic, and we shall explore the psychological fate of writing further in another study of adults who are already cultural beings. We have come to the end of our essay, and may sum up our conclusions as follows.

One thing seems clear from our analysis of the use of signs and its origins in the child: it is not understanding that generates the act, but far more the act that gives birth to understanding — indeed, the act often far precedes understanding. Before a child has understood the sense and mechanism of writing, he has already made many attempts to elaborate primitive methods; and these, for him, are the prehistory of his writing. But even these methods are not developed all at once: they pass through a number of trials and inventions, constituting a series of stages with which it is very useful for an educator working with school-age children and preschoolers to be acquainted.

The 3- or 4-year-old first discovers that his scribblings on paper can be used as a functional aid to remembering. At this point (sometimes much later) writing assumes an auxiliary instrumental function, and drawing becomes sign writing.

At the same time as this transformation takes place, a fundamental reorganization occurs in the most basic mechanisms of the child's behavior; on top of the primitive forms of direct adaptation to the problems imposed by his environment, the child now builds up new, complex, cultural forms; the major psychological functions no longer operate through primitive natural forms and begin to employ complex cultural devices. These devices are tried in succession, and perfected, and in the process transform the child as well. We have observed the engrossing process of the dialectical development of complex, essentially social forms of behavior that after traversing a long path, have brought us finally to the mastery of what is perhaps the most priceless tool of culture.

October-December 1928

Notes

1) W. Köhler, <u>Intelligenzprüfungen an Menschenaffen</u>. 1917.

2) W. Köhler, ibid.

3) This is yet another example of a purely external relation to writing that does not take into account its sense. We could say that the child's relation to writing assumes a primitive, magical character. We shall take up this point in more detail elsewhere.

4) See L. S. Vygotsky, "Development of higher forms of attention," in this book.

5) It is difficult to enumerate on the spur of the moment all the factors that allow the child to enter this phase of primary utilization of some undifferentiated sign. The topography and integral perception of the entire surface of the paper and the relationships among the signs on it probably play an essential role here. Werner (<u>Einführung in die Entwicklungspsychologie</u>) gives the example of the graphic production of primitive peoples, some of which signifies nothing whatever and acquires meaning only through its topographical position.

6) See H. Werner for details on this point in <u>Einführung in die Entwicklungspsychologie</u>, 1926.

A. R. Luria

THE DEVELOPMENT OF CONSTRUCTIVE
ACTIVITY IN THE PRESCHOOL CHILD

Psychological analysis of the development of play, so important for the preschool child, still suffers from relative neglect
in modern educational science.

Montessori's theory of educative games was based on concepts
of associationistic psychology that have long since been discarded. With its premise that educational play should develop
each of the child's senses in isolation and form in him the necessary associations, this theory attempted to defend the pedagogical significance of nonmeaningful activities in the cultivation
of the elementary sensations of play. Instead of meaningful play
activity, this theory proposed exercises to train the senses of
hearing, vision, and touch and regarded such exercises as particularly essential in pedagogy, in contrast to the development
of the complex thinking activity of the child, with which the
theory was not directly concerned.

This theory was long ago demonstrated to be false by our increasing knowledge of the structure of psychological processes
and by pedagogical practice.

The development of a child's mental processes cannot be reduced to mere progressive improvement in the functioning of

From Voprosy psikhologii rebenka doschkol'novo vozrasta
[Problems in the psychology of the preschool child]. Moscow-
Leningrad: APN RSFSR, 1948. Pp. 34-64.

the sense organs or to the formation of associations. Three decades of research in Soviet psychology have demonstrated without question that a child's mental development is marked by a succession of different kinds of concrete activity, a steadily growing complexity in the structure of this activity, and the enrichment of the psychological processes developing as part of this activity. For this reason alone, the attempt to reduce the role of educative play to the training of specific senses and the formation of specific associations must be regarded as scientifically unsound. Reflecting the state of bourgeois psychology at the end of the 19th century, this theory sent educators off in the wrong direction and interfered with the genuine development of the diverse forms of mental activity typical of childhood.

A need has arisen to analyze the kinds of play activity employed in children's institutions in the light of modern ideas about children's mental development. There is also a need to devise psychologically sound kinds of educative play that could be put to good use in preschool education.

In the present article we shall describe studies begun several years ago by Professor V. N. Kolbanovskii and A. N. Mirenova, and later continued by Mirenova and me.

Games designed to develop constructive activity in the child often consist of a set of blocks of various shapes with which the child must build different kinds of structures. These games are intended to develop the child's creative imagination and promote the development of his constructive activity. They are entertaining, in that a variety of things can be built; yet they should, at the same time, according to educators, develop the child's elementary mental processes (his ability to estimate things visually; to discriminate shapes, etc.).

Usually two types of such constructive games are used in preschool teaching. In the one, the child must build some sort of structure with blocks (see Figure 1) on the basis of a model given to him beforehand. These models are usually drawings of the structures that can be built with the blocks; all the outlines of the elements from which these structures are made are shown in the drawing distinctly enough so that a child, after scrutinizing it carefully, can then step by step proceed to put the elements depicted in it together correctly. People who work with pre-schoolers say that play of this sort teaches the child to pursue

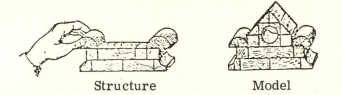

Structure   Model

Figure 1. An example of building from an elementary figure.

a definite goal, to keep his mind on a specific task, to analyze the pattern before him, to find its component parts, and, finally, to select the required construction elements in the correct shape, color, and size.

This kind of constructive game, however, very rarely lasts in preschool institutions. The patterns, drawn on paper, are usually quickly lost; and the task of putting the blocks into place according to patterns is usually so boring and so unappealing that it does not catch on with the child as an activity in its own right but remains among the group activities led by the educator.

Hence, it is usually a second kind of constructive game that is used: "free building." In this the child is given a large set of blocks and begins to build with them freely, making houses, a railroad, a tractor — whatever he wishes. When constructive play is used in this way, it is especially conducive to the development of the child's creative imagination. Constructive games of this "free" type are ordinarily very widely used.

Yet do these different uses of constructive games correspond to the purposes play should serve, namely, to develop genuinely constructive activity in the child? Psychological analysis shows that both of these uses of constructive games have a number of essential shortcomings, and that if they are going to be continued to be widely used, they must be substantially modified. A constructive game that is designed correctly from the psychological point of view must meet certain requirements.

First, the constructive task with which it confronts the child must be fully defined. He must have a definite goal before him. This goal may be stated verbally (given by someone else, or formulated by the child himself) or may be in the form of a model to which the child must refer in building the required structure. In either case the child must observe certain conditions as he builds; he must learn to analyze the problem, find ways to solve it, select the blocks that match the elements of the model, and find the distinctive features in how they are constructed, rejecting blocks that are unsuitable, and selecting combinations that will enable him to complete his building exercise. Only if these conditions are met, only if the child maintains a clear idea of what he is doing and is obliged to find the right ways to solve it, will the game be really constructive and capable of developing his creative activity and visual analytical acuity. Only under such conditions will play remain constructive for a child.

Obviously, neither of the two above-described kinds of constructive play used in children's institutions meet these requirements.

Building on the basis of a pattern, for example, as depicted in Figure 1, gives the child a completely defined goal, namely, to reproduce the figure from blocks. But it does not meet the second condition: it does not spur the child to find the means needed to carry out the constructive exercise. What is distinctive about the drawing is that all its component parts are clearly visible in outline. Hence, there is really no longer a truly constructive exercise. All the child must do is select one by one the blocks he notes one by one in the drawing. It is not hard to see that there is no longer anything constructive about this task: the child proceeds step by step, selecting the blocks, until finally the whole picture is completed of itself, as it were. With this kind of play activity there is little possibility of developing the child's creative imagination or active intelligence. Since there is nothing in this task that requires reasoning, in the best of cases it will provide only objective practice for functions involved in the selection of like elements — i.e., visual assessment of size, discrimination of color and shape, etc. Objectively, such play does no more than train the child's elementary perceptions, and for all practical purposes goes no farther than the Montessori games. Indeed, because such a game does not involve a really constructive task, it becomes boring for the child; and the attentive observer will note that children will complete such constructive activity, copying the models in the drawing in all their details, only in rare cases.

The second kind [of play] — free building — meets our conditions as inadequately as the first. Psychologically, free constructive play is completely different from building from a pattern. What most distinguishes it is that it gives the child a tangible and appealing task to perform. The goal, formulated by either the child or the teacher — to build a castle, tractor, train, etc. — allows the child to form an image of the end product in his mind, although it does not tell him how to achieve it. The child must find the way himself; he must himself select those construction elements suited for completing the task and the procedures for accomplishing it. As he builds, both the task itself and the ways he finds to do it are flexible; the task becomes more subtle, more refined; new details are added, and new and better means are found as he goes along. Because of this psychological structure, free building activity is always interesting to the child and holds his attention for a relatively long time.

However, although it may meet this requirement, this type of activity has a number of defects that considerably detract from its pedagogical value.

In formulating his task, the child is not at all concerned with whether he can accomplish it or whether the material at hand has objective building properties that make it suitable for completing the task. The reason for this lies in certain specific features of the preschool child's mental makeup, particularly in the psychology of children's play. A child's free play activity unfolds along a plane of ad hoc meanings; for this reason play can to some extent get along without an analysis of the objective properties of the material with which the child is playing. In creative play a child quite readily will give some element an ad hoc designation to suit the purpose of his play. He puts down

a block and says, "Let this be a tree"; another block may be a
cow, and a third, smaller block, a dog. Using the blocks the
child, especially the younger preschooler, will give free rein to
his creative play, which will remain entertaining, but have none
of the features of constructive activity. Once he has decided
what the blocks stand for, the child is no longer concerned with
whether the objective properties of the things wholly fit the task.
Constructive play is essentially transformed into an ad hoc labeling game. The child is no longer required to select elements
suited to putting together a whole structure; and whereas it was
originally a means of developing observational skills, thinking,
and constructive activity, such play has now been transformed
into a means for developing the child's speech and imagination.

This potential for drifting from a truly constructive activity
into ad hoc creative play presents a considerable obstacle to the
child's free constructive building. In cases in which building
does not take place in accordance with the direct instructions of
the teacher and becomes the child's own free activity, this drift
is especially likely to occur; and the value of this type of play
for the development of the child's constructive thinking becomes
negligible. Even a child who has been immersed in such constructive activity for a long time may not develop the ability to
analyze which constructive elements are suited for accomplishing particular tasks and which typical combinations are best
suited for other cases. The conditions necessary for developing
the child's own ability to think constructively do not exist.

A new type of constructive play is needed, one that would provide the child with the required goals, would still be appealing,
and would guarantee that his play would not exceed the bounds of
truly constructive activity. A. N. Mirenova once proposed such
a play activity, which involved building from solid models. This
method, which meets all the above enumerated requirements,
takes the following forms.

The child is presented with a solid model that he must reproduce from the blocks he has at hand. This model differs from
those normally used in preschool institutions in that the contours
of the individual elements from which it is made are hidden from

the child. This is accomplished by giving the child only the outline of the model he must construct, or else — and this is even
better — a model made by the teacher is covered with thick
white paper that conceals its individual components (Figure 2).

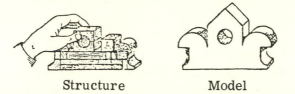

Structure   Model

Figure 2. An example of building from a model figure.

As is evident from the figure, the model gives the child a specific task, but does not tell him how to accomplish it. Any part
of the model (wall, roof) may be made from different elements,
and to accomplish the task the child must find different alternatives of the required solution. Psychologically this kind of constructive play differs sharply from both of the forms described
above.

The model gives the child a completely defined task to perform. Because the model does not also offer a ready-made solution to the task and the child must himself find the required
solutions, the task is interesting and often holds the child's attention for a long time. However, in seeking the right solution
the child is always obliged to remain within the framework of
constructive activity. He must find the required constructive
solutions and exercise his analytical reason to determine which
elements can be used to construct a straight wall, for example.
With the model at hand he is continually able to measure his solution against it and to assess whether it is correct. Even slight
discrepancies in dimensions or shape will always be noticeable
to the child when he compares the model and the structure he
has built from it. Thus, in performing this task a child always
remains within the framework of genuinely constructive thinking
and runs no risk of drifting into a merely nominal labeling of the
elements (window, roof) of which the structure is composed, in
which his constructive activity would degenerate into simple

spur-of-the-moment play.

Play of this sort, designed to develop visual thinking, analysis, and constructive synthesis, must necessarily develop complex forms of perception in the child, and will not degenerate into the simple play of free creative imagination.

Our purpose in the present paper is to determine what sort of psychological influence can be exerted on play structured in this manner, what aspects of visual thinking and perception are cultivated by such play, and whether the psychological and intellectual changes it achieves persist for some time. (1)

To obtain sufficiently unambiguous data on the psychological changes produced by the described type of constructive play, we were obliged to compare it with some of the other forms of constructive play and games in common use. For this comparison we chose ordinary model building, in which the elements from which the object is to be constructed are clearly designated on an accompanying diagram.

The experiment was reduced to the following: one group of children was allowed to practice building for an extended period, using only the methods indicated to them. (We shall call this method "building by elements," or method E for short.) Another group of children was allowed to do its building with Mirenova's models for the same amount of time (this method we shall call "building by models," or method M for short). The two groups of children were engaged in both these kinds of play for the same amount of time. Of course, the children practicing with method E built a considerably greater number of structures (since each of them was easier and took less time). The children practicing with method M accomplished considerably fewer tasks in the same amount of time.

The groups of children occupied with these constructive games had, of course, to forgo any other forms of play for the time being. Only if that were the case would we be able to observe the effect of prolonged use of each of these kinds of play activity in sufficiently pure form.

To ensure that the results of our study would be on as firm foundations as possible, each kind of play activity had to be in-

vestigated in a sufficiently large number of children relatively
similar in development.

It was only rarely that this last requirement could be fully
met. Usually the composition of the groups of children was
quite varied, and it could easily happen that one of the groups
we intended to compare quite by chance had a disproportionate
number of more developed children.

This, of course, would inevitably influence the results. To
eliminate this problem without at the same time being forced
to observe large groups of children (random variation within
groups can be eliminated in such cases only by using a large
number of subjects), we took a completely different course. We
carried out our study by means of a comparative analysis of two
very small groups of monozygotic twins.

Monozygotic twins (i.e., from the same egg) (2) have identical
natural endowments, so that only in rare cases — for example,
if one of them has suffered prolonged illness or been reared in
a different environment — will they display any notable differences in abilities. We designed our experiment with this in
mind and carried it out in the kindergarten for identical twins
at the Institute for Medical Genetics. For our purposes we selected five pairs of monozygotic twins between the ages of $5\frac{1}{2}$
and 6 years. They were divided into two groups so that each
twin of a pair was in a different group, lived in a different room,
had a different room for doing his work, and met his sibling only
on walks. Each of these groups, consisting of five children each,
was given constructive tasks to do daily for $2\frac{1}{2}$ months, one
group using method E and the other, method M. Altogether,
each twin performed a total of 50 experimental tasks. Before
beginning the experiments we gave each pair of twins a psychological examination to determine specific features of their perception and their visual constructive thinking. After the examinations, a test was also run in which the two groups were given
control tasks to perform, involving building from diagrams
showing individual elements, building from models, and free
constructive activity. This control enabled us to determine differences introduced into the children's constructive activity by

what they had learned in school.

In order to be better able to study the changes produced in perception and visual thinking as a result of prolonged practice in constructive play, the two groups were given a series of special psychological tests in which we studied the specific characteristics of these processes. The results showed that the constructive play techniques we used really did result in considerable psychological changes and that the visual thinking processes of our two groups of twins did indeed begin to show substantial differences.

The constructive activity of our twin groups was subjected to a psychological analysis just before the exercises described above were begun.

Both groups had considerable difficulties in constructive activity: for example, the children would often select blocks of the wrong dimensions and sometimes of the wrong shape, and hence ended up with structures that often diverged flagrantly from the example they had been given. The main building problem for both groups was that they very often would simply announce that some particular block represented such and such a feature on their model rather than build from the blocks the actual shapes required. For instance, if the model had a pitched roof, they would often use a pyramid or simply lean two elongated blocks against one another and call this a "pointed roof." If the model had a window, they would take a wooden cylinder and call it a window, showing no concern at all for whether it conformed in all details to the model. Doors or windows were also often represented by wooden blocks. The result would be a figure which bore no resemblance at all to the proposed example or diagram and in which all the details in the example were merely nominally represented (B, C, D, E, in Figure 3).

Because of this principal psychological feature, the child's constructive activity became a peculiar form of labeling or naming. One might say that instead of constructing the model, the child gave a visual account of it. As a rule the children were satisfied with the results of their efforts and were not aware that what they had produced left something to be desired.

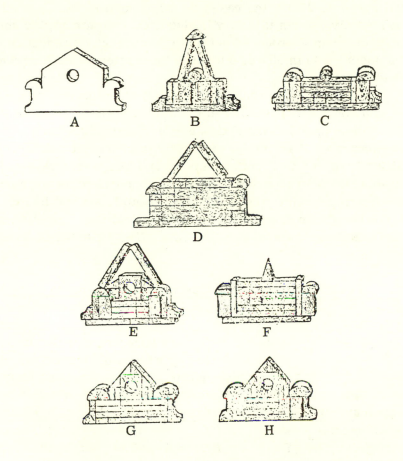

Figure 3. Types of model structures used with groups M and E.

After $2\frac{1}{2}$ months of practice in constructive activity, the two twin groups were given a control task. They were given three each of the two different kinds of examples (E and M) and had to build them from the blocks they had at hand. The results of this control were very illuminating.

After the long period of practice with one or the other of the methods, the two groups of twins now began to show substantial differences in their constructive activity. Group M built a correct reproduction of the proposed model of the figure in 74% of the cases; in 20% of the cases the reproduction was imprecise, and in only 6% was it totally inadequate. In contrast, the children in group E produced not a single correct reproduction of the model, and in 80% of the cases their attempt was flagrantly inadequate.

This result, of course, could mean that children in group E lagged considerably behind in the kind of activity in which they had had no practice and that our control experiment merely demonstrated the effect of the recent practice. It was reasonable to expect that if both groups of children were presented an "elemental figure" in which all the component parts were quite evident and in which the children of group E had had long practice, then group E would make a better showing. However, as Table 1 shows, this was not the case. The difference between

Table 1

Control Construction Tasks for Groups E and M

Experiment	Group	Figure reproduced incorrectly (%)	Figure reproduced adequately but not precisely (%)	Figure reproduced completely adequately (%)
A. Elemental	M	0.0	13.3	86.7
figure	E	6.6	66.6	26.8
B. Model	M	6.0	20.0	74.0
figure	E	80.0	20.0	0.0

the two groups of twins remained, and children in group E made a much poorer showing even in the type of building that they had practiced for $2\frac{1}{2}$ months. The children in group M reproduced the example completely correctly in 86.7% of the cases, whereas the children in group E did so in only 26.8% of the cases, and in most cases (66.6%) the building was rather crude, with the wrong dimensions, windows and doors in the wrong places, the wrong shapes, etc.

A psychological analysis of the mistakes made by the children shows that the two groups approached the construction task in quite different ways. As a rule, children in group M had already learned during the practice period how to proceed systematically, as is required in building: they examined the model carefully, analyzed it into its component parts in their minds, and tried to reproduce the structural relationships they perceived in it. In contrast, the children in group E usually did not go any farther than the simplistic labeling kind of construction we have described above. In many cases they did not reproduce the necessary proportions of the model, but simply labeled its various parts without regard for whether the necessary constructive relationships were retained. As a result, there was a gross discrepancy between the example and the end product for group E. Figure 3 illustrates this discrepancy.

It is understandable that such discrepancies occurred mainly in reproducing the solid model (in which the relationships among the elements were hidden). In reproduction of the elemental example, there was almost no instance of the simplistic kind of building by labeling; the children in group E, on the other hand, very often did not get the dimensions right, did not observe the right proportions and relations, etc.

These findings show that group-M children had learned how to analyze the model visually into its component parts and had achieved a much greater precision in their perception of the relationships in which these elements stood with regard to one another in the figure, in their perception of the size and shape of these elements, etc.

Sharp differences between the two groups of children appeared not only in how the figures looked after being built but also in the actual process of building. Table 2 shows this quite clearly.

We see that usually the children in group M did their building according to some sort of plan. Before they built their model, the children examined the example carefully, tried out different alternatives, and only then set about methodically achieving their objective. Most of the children in group M worked in this planned manner. In contrast, the children in group E were almost totally unsystematic, having no sort of plan. They usually set right to work: without any preliminary analysis or deliberation, they took the blocks that seemed to them to be the right ones and began to build the various parts of the model with them. This impulsiveness, which was almost completely absent in the children in group M, was found in most of the children in group E. It is especially interesting that it occurred in both kinds of construction: with detailed diagrams, and with solid models. This indicates that the habits of systematic analysis and visual thinking in doing constructive activity were highly developed in children in group M, but remained undeveloped in the group-E children.

Table 2
Control Building Test for Groups E and M

Experiment	Group	Direct, impulsive building (%)	Methodical, planlike building (%)
A. Figure composed	M	13.3	86.7
of elements	E	73.4	26.6
B. Solid model figure	M	6.6	93.4
	E	66.7	33.3

The last characteristic in regard to which the two groups diverged was also extremely instructive. It was typical of children in group M that they almost always noticed the mistakes they made (shown in Table 3); and if the teacher expressed any doubt that they had reproduced the figure correctly, the children would easily find the mistake and in many cases would correct it. In contrast, the children in group E were usually completely satisfied with their results and did not notice their mistakes. As Table 3 shows, this inability to uncover their own mistakes or the inability to single them out and correct them was characteristic of most of the children in group E regardless of the approach to building used.

Table 3
Analysis of the Mistakes Made in
Building by Groups E and M

Experiment	Group	Did not notice mistakes (%)	Noticed mistakes, but could not correct them (%)	Noticed and corrected mistakes (%)
Building from	M	11.2	0	88.8
elements	E	85.6	0	14.4
Building solid	M	0	26.6	73.4
models	E	46.0	40.0	13.4

Sometimes this inability to notice and analyze the mistakes they made in building was quite pronounced. The child who had constructed item D in Figure 3, in which nothing matched the example, the round window being represented by a simple cylinder, and the roof being in the form of two boards placed together, continued stubbornly to insist that he had built everything quite correctly and, commenting on his own work, declared, "Here is a window, and there is a window; here is a roof, and there is a roof; everything is okay." This paradox becomes intelligible if we assume that in trying to analyze their building and compare it with the example, what the children compared was what the various parts were construed to represent, not the fidelity of the outward design. Hence, for this child the mere fact that he construed the example correctly (quite irrespective of how his building was put together) was enough to make him conclude that the object he had built coincided completely with the model and not notice all the disparities. The control experiments showed that children in group M had really developed constructive thinking by practice with the solid model, whereas the activity of the children in group E remained at the same level as before.

In the experiments just described, we placed the children in clearly unequal situations: we presented the solid model to the children in group E, who had never had any previous prac-

tice in building these types. As might be expected, in this kind
of constructive activity there was a considerable disparity between the two groups of twins. The advantage of the children in
group M also showed up in the control experiments (with detailed
diagrams): the children in group M did these piece-by-piece
tasks much better than the children in group E, who had had special practice in them for $2\frac{1}{2}$ months. However, in order to demonstrate this advantage obtained by the group M children better,
it was necessary to place the two groups of children in more
equal conditions.

This we did in a special series of control tasks called "building from missing parts." Both groups of children were given
an example that outwardly differed in no way from the detailed
diagram; there was a substantial difference, however; this model was built from elements some of which were missing in the
material available. The children had to picture this model in
their minds, fill in the missing parts with some new combination, and reproduce the latter from elements that did not figure
in the presented example. Thus, the task, which outwardly was
a piece-by-piece one, required the same analytical abilities
needed in building from a solid model.

In these control tasks the children in group M displayed incomparably greater building aptitude than their partners who
had been taught by method E. Figures 4 and 5 give examples of
the differences between the two groups in these tasks. As a rule,
the children in group M easily overcame the obstacles that arose
as the particular task was being carried out. They readily varied the relationships among the elements, replaced the missing
elements with new ones, and built the model with completely new
combinations of blocks. In contrast, their partners in group E
were quite unable to cope with this task.

As a rule, they simplistically reproduced the same relationships among elements they found in the example, despite the fact
that they did not have the blocks they needed. As a result the
structures they built were completely inadequate (see Figure
4B). They would begin their building with one block that was
either larger or smaller than the one required, so that the end

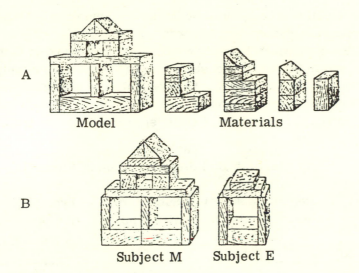

A   Model   Materials

B   Subject M Subject E

Figure 4. Examples of structures built by children
in groups E and M in "missing element" experiments.

result was either too large or too small. This fixation on their
immediate perceptions and total inability to modify them occurred
with most of the children in group E, but with none of those

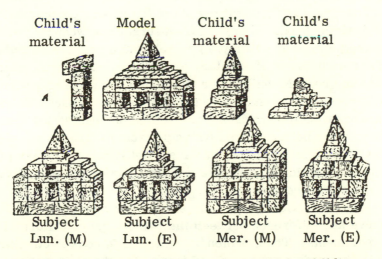

Child's Model Child's   Child's
material   material   material

Subject Subject Subject Subject
Lun. (M) Lun. (E) Mer. (M) Mer. (E)

Figure 5. Examples of structures built by children
in groups E and M in "missing element" experiments.

in group M, of whom, on the contrary, a certain free-thinking in their constructive activity was typical.

Table 4 shows that the free substitution of missing elements observed in 86.6% of the cases in group M was done by only 13.4% of the children in group E. Consequently, by stressing practice in method M, we were able to achieve a substantial change in the analytical perception of children trained by this method.

Table 4
Experiments in Building with Missing Elements

Group	Refusal to substitute the missing elements (%)	Substitution with similar elements (%)	Free substitution of missing elements (%)
M	0.0	13.4	86.6
E	33.3	53.3	13.4

In subsequent experiments we made a more detailed analysis of the structure of perception in the two groups of children.

The first question that occurred to us was to ascertain whether training produced any clear difference between the two groups in the perception of simple geometric figures, i.e., whether the discrimination of elementary geometric figures was more precise in group-M children or whether there were no noticeable differences between the two groups in this respect. To answer this question the children were shown successively a series of simple geometric figures (triangle, square, trapezoid, etc.), each figure being displayed for a brief time; after each presentation the children were to draw the figure from memory. Table 5 gives our results.

An examination of the table shows that we were unable to observe any difference between the two groups of children in these experiments. Thus, prolonged practice in constructive activity with the model method helped to develop the elementary acts of perception of geometric figures equally for both groups.

Table 5
Reproduction of Simple Geometric
Figures by Groups E and M

	Incorrect reproduction (%)		Inaccurate reproduction (%)		Correct reproduction (%)	
	M	E	M	E	M	E
Average per-centage correct	14.3	11.4	14.3	14.3	71.4	74.3

Analogous results were obtained in another series of experiments designed to analyze how long the children were able to maintain visual concentration on differences among elementary geometric figures. The children were given a large number of geometric figures cut out of plywood (five- and six-pointed stars, triangles, trapezoids, etc.) and asked to analyze them, concentrating on this task for an extended period. The results of this test were almost the same for the two groups.

The experiments just described suggested the hypothesis that the differences we noted in the constructive activity of the two groups of children were due not so much to differences in their perception of elements, but to differences in their ability to analyze more complex components of the visually perceived structures and, especially, in their ability to perceive geometric relations. To test this hypothesis we presented the series of figures shown in Figure 6A to both groups of children. The distinguishing feature of these figures lay in the fact that although they had a

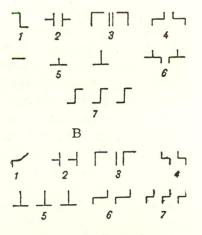

Figure 6. Experiment in discrimination of geometric relations.

distinct geometric shape, they also embodied complex geometric
relations; their component parts were arranged spatially with
respect to one another in such a way that a regular figure could
be reproduced by irregularly arranging its parts in space. These
figures were also presented to the children for a brief period,
and then they were asked to draw them from memory.

Usually the children in group M correctly reproduced both the
basic shape of each drawing and the relationship of its parts to
one another. In contrast, the children in group E in most cases
reproduced the shape of the parts of the figures correctly, as
Figure 6B shows, but very often arranged them incorrectly in
space, being unable to preserve the necessary relationships
among the parts. The test showed that although there was no
notable difference between the two groups so far as the correct
reproduction of the figures was concerned, there was a distinct
difference in the reproduction of the geometric relations. The
children in group M correctly reproduced these relations in 80%
of the cases, whereas the children in group E did so in only 51%.

These results induced us to analyze a little more closely to
what extent the children in the two groups were able to perceive
and reproduce geometric relations.

To do this we gave the two groups the task of copying a drawing resembling a honeycomb. To copy this drawing correctly it
was not enough simply to perceive it: it was necessary to analyze the features of its construction, to note in what relation each
element in the drawing stood to another, and to understand that
the side of each element was at the same time a part of another
element occupying another position. (3)

Figure 7 shows that this task, which is very difficult for pre-
school-age children, was accomplished successfully by both
groups of children. It is evident from Figure 7 that group-M
children usually tried to understand the logic of the construction
of what they had to draw and often partly solved the problem by
finding the relations of the elements to one another. In contrast,
the children in group E usually did not go beyond perception of
the individual elements in isolation; and only one of the most
gifted children from this group was able at least partly to cope

with the problem, although he was still unable to find the necessary relationships.

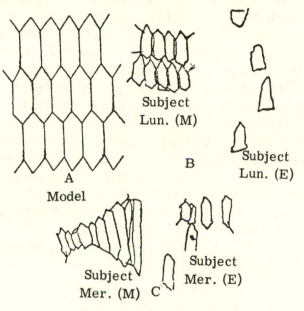

Figure 7. Reproduction of a drawing by
children in groups E and M.

The results in Table 6 show the tremendous difference between the two groups.

Table 6
Percentage of Correct Solutions by Groups M
and E of a Problem Involving Copying a Drawing

	From memory (%)		With object present (%)	
	M	E	M	E
Average percentage of correct solutions	80	20	80	20

These findings convincingly demonstrate that the exercises

these children had done with constructive play using models really had given them the ability not only to perceive elementary geometric shapes but also to analyze geometric relations that were not immediately accessible to perception and that they therefore had to analyze further in order to make the proper discriminations.

In addition, the experiments described above give rise to the following question. The transformation of a simple perception into a complex act of visual analysis makes perception more voluntary. A child who has learned how to analyze visual material presented to him learns how to distinguish at will the required elements in that material; his perception thus loses its passive nature and becomes increasingly active and voluntary.

But did the series of exercises we conducted with the children really have an effect on the development of voluntary perception? To answer this question we carried out a series of special experiments designed by A. N. Mirenova.

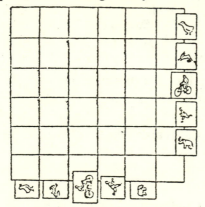

Children in both groups were presented a checkerboard-type grid (Figure 8). A number of small figures were arranged along its sides. The child had to find where the figures would intersect. He was asked questions of this type: "Where will one bicycle meet the other bicycle?"; "Where will one rabbit meet the other rabbit?"; "Where will the bicycle meet the rabbit?"; etc. He then had to show the point where the lines, extended in his mind, intersected, isolating it from a uniform field.

Figure 8. Board for isolating arbitrary elements from a uniform field.

As Table 7 shows, the children in the two groups differed sharply in their solution of this problem. The children in group M in 100% of the cases easily solved the problem, whereas those in group E were able to find the point in the uniform field in only 34% of the cases. Analogous results were obtained in other,

more complicated experiments on voluntary discrimination of
complex figures in a uniform field.

Table 7
Pinpointing a Specific Point in a Uniform Field
by Children in Groups M and E

	M		E	
	Unable to discriminate (%)	Voluntary discrimination (%)	Unable to discriminate (%)	Voluntary discrimination (%)
Average by group	0	100	66	34

The children were shown the
complex grid (consisting of separate triangles) in Figure 9 and
were asked to find one of the figures shown and then isolate it
either by removing the other
elements in the grid or by tracing
around it with a finger. This task
doubtless requires considerable
voluntary perception and is very
difficult for preschool children.
However, as Table 8 shows,
group-M children were able to
carry it out with relative ease,
whereas it was almost completely beyond the children in group E.

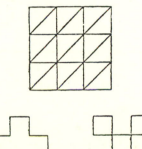

Figure 9. Isolating a figure
from a uniform field.

Table 8
Isolation of a Figure from a Uniform
Field by Groups M and E

Figures	1		2		3	
Subjects	M	E	M	E	M	E
Correctly done (%)	100	40	80	20	60	20

This experiment is graphic demonstration that the practice the children in group M had in constructive activity did indeed help to develop their ability to discriminate voluntarily a figure in a uniform field, an ability which, quite understandably, is an essential prerequisite for constructive thinking. To demonstrate this point conclusively, we conducted another series of experiments that were especially difficult for the children. They were shown the complex grid in Figure 10. In it they had visually to

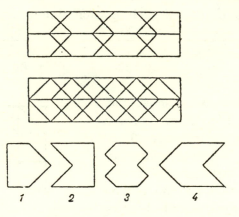

Figure 10. Discrimination of shapes
against a uniform background.

discriminate ten complex figures by circling them with a pencil. Because of the difficulty of the task, they were given an unlimited amount of time. As is evident from Table 9, the two groups differed significantly.

Table 9
Discrimination of Complex Shapes
by Children in Groups M and E

	M	E
Average percentage of correct solutions	82.5	53.0

The children in group M were usually able to deal with this task successfully, whereas half of the children in group E were simply unable to discriminate the required shape. These differences between partners in groups E and M were negligible in only one case, a particularly gifted twin pair; for another pair, somewhat retarded in their development, this task was almost as difficult for the one as for the other.

From everything we have said, it may be assumed that in the process of constructive activity in which they practiced model-building, children not only acquired the ability to use perception for voluntary analysis but they also learned how to maneuver voluntarily with the visual structures they had discriminated, i.e., their perception acquired the needed mobility.

To check this hypothesis two more series of experiments were run on the two groups. First they were shown the series of geometric figures in Figure 11. They were asked to examine these figures attentively and turn them around in their minds, drawing them so the right side was on the left and the left side on the right. This experiment required the child not only to analyze the geometric relationships in a particular figure but also to fix consciously on these relationships while turning the figure in his mind. This ability to move the figure mentally is a psychologically complex and highly developed form of activity.

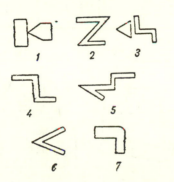

Figure 11. Geometric figures used in the rearrangement task.

Once again we noted considerable differences between the two groups of children in this task. The children in group M coped with this task with relative ease. On the other hand, the children in group E usually found that it presented insuperable difficulties; they simply copied the drawing, and were totally unable to reverse it mentally. Their perception had simply not acquired the needed mobility.

Table 10
Movement of Geometric Shapes
by Children in Groups M and E

	M	E
Average percentage of correct solutions	82.8	25.4

Table 10 sums up the results of this series of experiments. It shows that the children in group M were able mentally to shift the position of the figure correctly in 82.8% of the cases, whereas those in group E did so in only 25.4% of the cases. Indeed, some of the children were completely unable to cope with the task.

Analogous results were obtained in another, easier experiment. The children were presented a model of a house with a small wing attached on the right. The model was built of blocks. The doors and windows in the house (see Figure 12) were situated at the ends of a diagonal running from top to bottom and right to left. The children were asked to draw the mirror image of this house. A child was shown visually what he was supposed to do, although no drawings were shown to illustrate the desired result.

Usually the two groups of

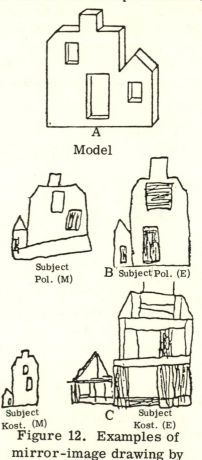

A
Model

Subject
Pol. (M)   B Subject Pol. (E)

Subject
Kost. (M)   C   Subject
Kost. (E)

Figure 12. Examples of mirror-image drawing by twins in groups M and E.

children produced quite different results. The children in group M in most cases carried out the task correctly, depicting the house with the wing on the left and the windows and doors along a diagonal running from upper left to bottom right. The children in group E put the wing on the left, but drew the windows and doors in the same geometric relationship as perceived in the visual model, being incapable of abstracting from their visual perception. Figure 12 shows examples of how children in both groups performed the task.

Table 11 shows the figures, from which we see that not one of the twins in group E was able to complete this task, whereas 60% of those in group M were able to do so.

Table 11

Experiment with Transposition
of Relationships in Figures (%)

Group	Incomplete transposition	Partial transposition	Full transposition
M	0	40	60
E	40	60	0

If the children in group M had really acquired the ability to abstract from their visual perception of an object and transpose it in their minds, i.e., if their perception had acquired the necessary mobility, then this had to show up in other forms of activity as well, even activity that was quite different from the content of the exercises they carried out in their constructive play. To test this hypothesis we gave the children the following task. The experimenter and the subject stood facing one another, and the subject had to reproduce the experimenter's actions exactly, raising first one and then the other arm to his eye, nose, and ear as the experimenter did so. In order to do this a subject would have to abstract from his immediate perception to raise his hand on the side contralateral to the experimenter's.

This test, which is so difficult for preschool children, was quite within the abilities of the children in group M, who did it correctly in 87.4% of the cases; children in group E performed much more poorly (except for one case), doing the task correctly in only 44.0% of the cases.

This experiment, which we repeated many times, gave the same results each time. It thus provided a quite clear indication that constructive activity with model-building really does develop very complex forms of visual analysis, with sufficient mobility.

The conclusion to be drawn from all this is that prolonged practice in constructive activity with model-building does indeed develop a child's ability to set up a building problem and work out an active analysis of the visual material. We see that play of this sort transforms constructive building into a purposeful activity, to which the child applies his mind correctly. We also see that as a result of this activity, the child's perception acquires voluntariness and mobility; and he learns to form distinct mental images, which are readily susceptible to his control.

Another question arises, however: Are all these achievements restricted wholly to passive constructive activity (building from ready-made models), or do they also foster the development of active creativity?

The fact alone that these exercises made the child's perception more active and more mobile and that constructive activity became more methodical under their influence is a strong indication that free creativity also benefits considerably. To answer this question we gave the two groups of children a new control task in which they were to build anything they pleased from the materials available to them. They were given a whole set of building materials and told to build what they wished. These experiments were done with the children individually, so that they could not influence one another.

The results showed that, as a rule, children who previously had not differed notably from one another now displayed completely different abilities in free constructive activity.

Usually all the children in group M went about their task quite methodically. They first mapped out the problem for themselves, selected the elements they would need to build what they had decided on, and then built it in such a way that if one followed what

they were doing step by step, one would say that they were operating according to a definite plan. The initial design became
more detailed as they went along, and it was only at the very end
of the building that a completed whole emerged.

The children in group E went about their building activity in a
totally different way. Usually they did not have a clear idea of
what they wanted to build at the very outset. There was nothing
distinctly purposeful or goal-directed about their constructive
activity. One part was set up and other pieces added to it, and
it was difficult to discern the unfolding of any clear plan in the
relatively complex pile of elements they had put together. Sometimes the building ended up as nothing but a complex repetition
of individual parts, and the initial intention was formulated in
words rather than embodied in any tangible construction.

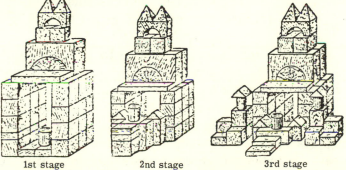

1st stage   2nd stage   3rd stage
Subject Lun. (M)

Figure 13. Stages in the
constructive activity of
a twin from group M.

4th stage

Figures 13 and 14 indicate this
quite clearly. They show four successive stages in free constructive
activity of two twins, the first of
whom was in group M and the second, in group E. If we examine
these figures carefully, we see how
methodically the free constructive
building progressed for the group-

M twin, and how randomly and unsystematically the group-E twin piled together all the pieces without any clearly defined goal or plan. Thus, there were distinct psychological differences in the creative activity of the two twins.

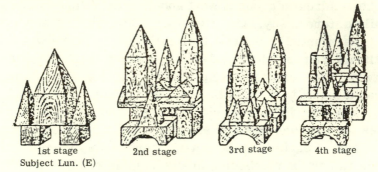

1st stage   2nd stage   3rd stage   4th stage
Subject Lun. (E)

Figure 14. Stages in the constructive
activity of a twin from group E.

These experiments thus confirm that <u>by giving a child a good deal of practice with constructive tasks over a prolonged period we were able to develop his creative constructive abilities.</u>

Our study would be incomplete without one final, very important question: How lasting were the results we obtained in developing this constructive activity? Do the psychological differences between these two groups persist for some time, or do they disappear quite quickly, being limited to the temporary acquisition of the skill learned during the activity?

To answer this question we stopped any further special practice exercises in constructive activity and checked the differences we observed in the two groups $1\frac{1}{2}$ years later. This time only three sets of twins from the original study were compared. At the time of this control experiment the children were from 7 years to 7 years and 8 months old.

Two twin groups that earlier had had practice from a model and building from elements were asked to reproduce three control models. We distinguished among a primitive approach to the task (1 point), an inadequate approach (2 points), and, finally, a correct approach (3 points). As Figure 15 shows, the results varied. In one, the most gifted pair of twins, the differences observed previously had diminished, although the child who had been in group E continued to build his building with a number of defects, while his partner from group M was perfectly able to cope with the task. In a second pair, the earlier differences were still as pronounced as they had been originally. The child who had been in group M continued to carry out the tasks correctly, whereas his partner from group E, who had completely forgotten the skills he had learned, came up with some totally inadequate construction. The third pair produced no distinctive results.

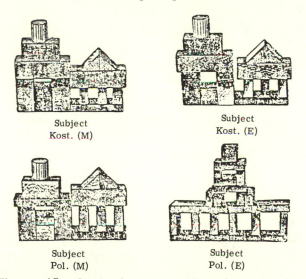

Subject
Kost. (M)

Subject
Kost. (E)

Subject
Pol. (M)

Subject
Pol. (E)

Figure 15. Control constructions by twins in
groups M and E 1½ years after practice.

Similar results were obtained when we ran a special series of control experiments 1½ years after the practice activity; the purpose of this set of control experiments was to analyze to what extent the two groups were still able to perceive geometric relations and consciously make a visual analysis. Again the most gifted pair of twins, for whom this task was no longer so complicated, gave no sign of any notable difference between them, whereas the other pairs continued to display sharp differences (Table 12).

Table 12

Subject	Voluntary discrimination of figure in uniform field		Mental rearrangement of figures	
	Experiment 1	Experiment 2	Experiment 1	Experiment 2
Pol. M	85	60	100	100
E	33	10	50	20
Lun. M	50	37	100	40
E	37	25	0	91
Kost. M	100	90	75	100
E	100	80	62	90

The first two columns in the table show results obtained in experiments in which a figure was discriminated against a plain background. The columns for this group refer to experiments in which the subjects singled out figures mentally on a checkerboard (first experiment) and from a complex structured background (second experiment).

The last columns in the table refer to experiments designed to assess mobility of perception and the children's ability to shift the position of the perceived figures in space mentally. The first column refers to transposition of elementary geometric figures (first experiment); the second, to arresting hand positions (second experiment).

One need only to examine this table carefully to see that the differences in the way groups E and M approached these problems were still quite pronounced, evening out noticeably only for the third pair

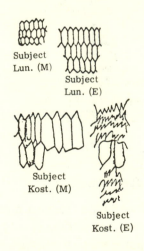

Subject Lun. (M)

Subject Lun. (E)

Subject Kost. (M)

Subject Kost. (E)

Figure 16. Reproduction of geometric relations by twins in groups E and M $1\frac{1}{2}$ years after the end of their practice with constructive activity.

of twins (the most gifted). **Figure 16**
gives only two examples illustrating
the differences obtained between the
two groups in copying figures involving complex geometric relations. In
this figure we see that these differences had vanished for the most gifted
pair, whereas for the less intelligent
pair they remained distinct in both
this and more complex tasks (Figure 17).

Thus, experiments conducted $1\frac{1}{2}$
years after systematic use of developmental games had been stopped showed
that the results obtained in those exercises were relatively long lasting
and that in our main experiment we
not only produced a short-lived skill

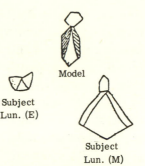

Figure 17. Repro-
duction of geometric
relations by twins in
groups E and M $1\frac{1}{2}$
years after the end
of their practice with
constructive activity.

but also caused a more thorough reorganization of the methods
used in constructive activity and for perception in the child.

* * *

The study we have reviewed was devoted to a psychological
analysis of the proper ways to develop the constructive activity
of a preschool child. In this study, begun by V. I. Kolbanovskii
and A. N. Mirenova and continued by the latter under my direction, we were able to show how much could be achieved if the constructive activity of the child was developed along correct lines.

In contrast to the methods usually employed with preschool
children, which are generally limited to free construction or
building from examples, i.e., passive reproduction of finished
examples with blocks, and do not achieve the required effect,
that is, they do not really develop constructive activity, we used
a different method, which we termed "building from models."

The most essential psychologically distinctive feature of this
method is that the child is given a specific, definite, constructive
task to carry out. He has to build a specific model and has to

find the ways to do it himself, i.e., he has to find the constructive elements from which the model can be built. To do this he
has to transform the direct, spontaneous perception of the model
into a complex process of visual analysis, to develop his perception of geometric relations among these elements, combine them
in his mind, and mentally shift the position of particular figures
relative to one another. By obliging the child to do these things,
our method was able truly to develop the principal components
of a child's constructive activity.

Our results demonstrate persuasively that our version of constructive play is truly developmental in that it achieves radical
changes in the constructive activity of the child and activates
new forms of more complex processes. The effect of play of
this kind is quite lasting, persisting for some time. There is
every reason to assume that if these psychologically designed
kinds of constructive play were introduced into preschool instruction, they would bear tangible results in the development
of constructive activity in the preschool child.

Notes

1) Detailed results of this study were published in A. N. Mirenova & V. N. Kolbanovskii, Tr. Mediko-Biol. Inst., No. 3, and
in A. R. Luria & A. N. Mirenova, [Collection of studies on medical genetics, dedicated to Professor S. N. Davidenko], and Tr.
Mediko-Genet. Inst., Vol. IV.

2) These twins differ from dizygotic twins, which develop
from two egg cells and are ordinary brothers and sisters born
at the same time. Monozygotic twins are always of the same
sex and look alike. In contrast, dizygotic twins may be of different sex and often do not look at all alike. There are a number
of special genetic methods to determine if twins are monozygotic.

3) First the children had to copy this drawing from memory,
and then from the real object.

Translated by
Michel Vale

O. K. Tikhomirov

THE FORMATION OF VOLUNTARY MOVEMENTS
IN CHILDREN OF PRESCHOOL AGE

The development of movements in both phylogenesis and ontogenesis is closely coupled with a change in the nature of their
afferentation and thus with a change in the level of regulation.

The specific uniqueness of human voluntary movements lies
in the participation of a verbal system in their construction.
This participation relates to both the afferent and the efferent
components of voluntary movement. The specific stimulus that
evokes voluntary movement is speech, which does not simply
replace the direct signal, but facilitates the abstraction and
generalization of direct signals. If elaboration of so-called
voluntary movements in animals requires analysis and synthesis of afferent impulses coming from the working muscles
(Miller, Konorsky, Skipin), then in establishing truly voluntary
movements in human beings it is characteristic for this reverse
proprioceptive afferentation from the completed movements to
be subjected to analysis and synthesis at the level of the second
signal system with the aid of speech. Only as a result of this
process is it possible for the higher forms of cortical regulation to become "self-regulating"; and only this kind of verbal

From A. R. Luria (Ed.) Problemi vysshei nervnoi deyatel'
nosti normal'novo i anormal'novo rebenka [Problems of higher
nervous activity in normal and abnormal children]. Moscow:
APN RSFSR, 1958. Pp. 72-130.

participation in the organization of motor behavior makes this behavior really conscious and voluntary.

It is essential that we ask how such self-regulation is formed in the child and through what stages it passes.

We began with the fact, established in the work of T. V. Yendovitzkaya and N. P. Paramonova, that in 3-4-year-old children relatively complex connections in the verbal system can be established (so that the child can repeat an instruction given to him), but that these still do not regulate direct action. This is explained by various age-dependent features of the child's neurodynamics: by the diffuseness of the nervous processes, which tend to irradiate, which have relatively poor mobility, etc. Hence, at an early stage the speech a child masters in communication with an adult still does not regulate the child's behavior. As N. P. Paramonova has shown, only continuous speech reinforcement on the part of the experimenter can guarantee that a 3-4-year-old will carry out an instruction correctly.

Our investigation, however, centered on the role of the child's own external speech in regulating his motor reactions. A word is a complex stimulus that, like any stimulus, creates an auxiliary excitation center and can, by this means, evoke an auxiliary motor impulse; speech also completes a system of connections that have a selective influence. Viewing speech in this way, we analyzed the nature and interrelation of these various influences of the child's own speech at different ages. To do this we focused only on the simplest form of the child's speech and tried to show ontogenetic changes in the influence of spoken words on the regulation of motor responses.

The experiments consisted of two series. In the first series the subject was told to carry out, silently, a movement in accordance with a verbal instruction. In the second and more basic series the subject carried out the same movements, accompanying them with speech responses. Then the first series was usually repeated. (1)

In trying to trace the relative role of the various components of the child's speech in regulating motor responses we accompanied these responses with various kinds of speech.

In order to determine how well the child could regulate the execution of motor responses with the aid of voiced speech and to analyze the relative role of the various components of external speech in this regulation, we put the child in different experimental settings, giving him different kinds of preparatory instructions.

In the simplest task the child had to squeeze a rubber bulb each time a signal was presented and to refrain from squeezing it when there was no signal.

A more complex task was to react differently to two different signals: when one signal was given, to squeeze the bulb, and when another signal was given, not to squeeze it, i.e., the instruction set up a simple differentiation between the stimuli.

Finally, to study how well children differentiate successive, complex, motor responses, we told them to squeeze the bulb twice in succession in accordance with an instruction.

In all these experiments we obtained data showing that speech has varying influences on the execution of responses; thus the organization of motor responses by means of speech must be based on different mechanisms.

To analyze these mechanisms, which make possible the organizing of the motor response, we carried out a special group of experiments that compared the role of speech in organizing motor responses with nonspeech modes of motor response organization.

We hypothesized that a child's carrying out a preparatory spoken instruction is impeded by inadequately differentiated proprioceptive impulses from the motor responses, which are needed to form a reverse afferentation. We hypothesized further that the creation of auxiliary, exteroceptive, reverse afferentation could organize the action and that at this specific developmental stage the child's own speech could serve as a means of auxiliary afferentation.

The data obtained in the experiments to confirm these initial hypotheses will be presented in the present article. As we have said, the experiments were conducted in accordance with the method of preparatory instruction.

The stimuli in the experiments were flashing lights of different colors located in front of the subject. The subject's motor response was a squeeze on a rubber bulb with the fingers of his hand. The motor responses were recorded on a continuously moving paper tape. The apparatus recorded all the details of the motor responses and their relations with the signals.

The subjects were preschool children, aged 3, 4, or 5 years. All the children could discriminate the signals on the basis of their color. The experiments were conducted individually in one to six sessions. Each session lasted 15-30 min.

Overcoming the Direct Influence of a Stimulus

In most 3-4-year-old children simple responses to a signal, which can be evoked with the aid of a preparatory verbal instruction, are performed with mistakes, such as squeezing the bulb not only during the presentations of the signals but also in the intervals between them. This is presumably explained by a diffuse irradiation of excitation arising from the stimulus under the conditions of the experiment.

In experiments by N. P. Paramonova (2) it was shown that the difficulties in carrying out a preparatory instruction by a 3-4-year-old child were often overcome by the introduction of continuous speech reinforcement of the motor responses. Continuous speech reinforcement of the child's motor responses (in the form of an experimenter's evaluation of the actions) was presumed to facilitate mastering those neurodynamic difficulties manifest in the child's carrying out the instruction incorrectly. These data raised the question of how to analyze the role of speech accompaniment of a motor response if the child himself spoke while carrying out the preparatory verbal instruction, i.e., the question of the transition from external regulation of the response by the experimenter to the initial forms of self-regulation managed by the child himself.

As shown in the work of M. R. Peskovskaya (3), 3-year-old children manifest a divergence between the execution of motor

and speech responses to a signal. If in simple motor responses
to a signal a child frequently responds between signals, then
substituting speech responses for motor ones markedly reduces the number of intersignal responses. This is explained
by the great mobility of the child's verbal system at this age.
This mobility of the verbal system can be used to organize
motor responses by uniting verbal and motor responses: with
each presentation of the signal the child says "Squeeze!" or
"Must!" and gives a motor response. This method led to a
sharp decrease in the number of intersignal motor responses.
Thus, in these experiments it was possible to achieve a concentration of excitation arising from the stimulus with the aid
of the child's own speech.

We repeated these experiments and obtained analogous results. We shall give here only one illustration. Figure 1A
shows a section of the protocol of the experiment with subject
Andrei Ch., age 4 years, who is instructed: "Squeeze at the red
light; but when there's no light, don't squeeze." But the subject continues to squeeze after the signal and between signals
in spite of the frequently repeated instruction. In 44 presentations of the signal he gives 14 extraneous responses (32%).
But when he says "Squeeze," the signal meaning of the stimulus, the number of mistakes in the first stage drops sharply;
and then the subject generally acts without making any mistakes
(Figure 1B). In the next session he carries out the instruction
silently (Figure 1C), and the number of extraneous responses
increases. Thus the diffuse irradiation of the excitation between signals is largely overcome with the aid of the subject's
own speech.

On the basis of these observations we centered our attention
on the nature of the influence of the child's own speech response
that accompanies and organizes his motor responses.

We view speech as a complex stimulus having a twofold influence. Speech can have a direct influence by virtue of its
verbalization and a mediating influence by virtue of the system
of selective connections, which is actualized under the influence
of speech. These different forms of the influence of speech can

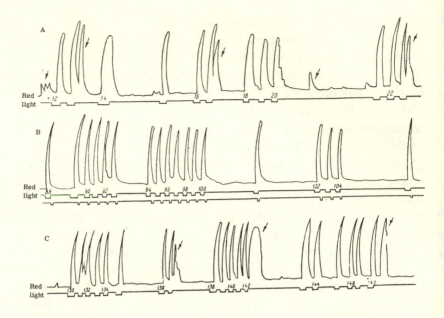

Figure 1. Andrei Ch., age 4 years. A. Carrying out the instruction "When the red light comes on, squeeze; and when there is no light, don't squeeze." B. The same, with speech ("Squeeze"). C. The same, silently.

be traced on the ontogenetic level and in a system of tasks of varied difficulty.

In these experiments using simple responses, mastery of the intersignal motor responses was achieved by the child's saying each time a word that formulated the signal meaning of the stimulus ("Squeeze"). But the mere effect of movement regulation by means of this word tells us nothing about the nature of the word's influence, about how this effect is achieved.

We hypothesized that for 3-4-year-olds the comparatively simple task of squeezing [a rubber bulb] in response to a signal permits the word "Squeeze" to have not a selective, but a simpler, impulsive influence, creating an auxiliary center of excitation that facilitates concentration of the excitation arising from the stimulus.

To confirm this hypothesis we modified the experiment so that saying the signaling stimulus "Squeeze" or "Must" was replaced with the syllable "tu" at each signal.* Hence in this series of experiments the same instruction was given to the subject as before ("When the light comes on, squeeze; and when there is no light, don't squeeze"), but the nature of the verbal accompaniment was different. The subject had to pronounce the syllable "tu" at the appearance of the signal and simultaneously squeeze the bulb.

The results of these experiments showed that in replacing the utterance of the signal meaning of the stimulus with the pronunciation of a syllable that did not constitute a direct signal stimulus meaning, we obtained the same regulating effect on the motor response.

Let us take as an example an experiment with Lena F., age 4 years, 1 month. The subject was instructed "When the red light comes on, squeeze; and when there is no light, don't squeeze." In spite of the fact that the experimenter repeated the instruction several times, Lena responded in the intervals between groups of signals (Figure 2A, after 22, 25, 29). In 36 signals there were 11 intersignal responses (31%). After this, a series was carried out in which the subject was instructed to command herself with "tu" at every signal and to squeeze (she was shown how to do this in advance). In this series she carried out the instruction almost without error (Figure 2B). When she later once more carried out the instruction silently, she again made intersignal motor responses (Figure 2C). Thus, with the aid of "impulsive" speech a child could regulate motor responses while carrying out an instruction and master completely or partially the diffuse irradiation of excitation from the signals.

Let us summarize the results obtained in these experiments on overcoming intersignal motor responses by means of impulsive speech: in 13 of 20 children there was a reduction in the number of intersignal motor responses in the series in

---

*"Tu" in Russian is a nonsense syllable. — Ed.

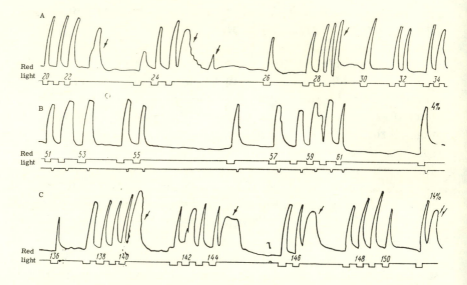

Figure 2. Lena F., age 4 years, 1 month. A. Carrying out the instruction "When the red light comes on, squeeze; and when there is no light, don't squeeze." B. The same, with speech ("tu"). C. The same, silently.

which movements were accompanied by speech. Hence the data obtained in these experiments confirm our initial hypothesis that, under the described experimental conditions, the child's speech acts not so much as a system of selective connections but as a means of creating an auxiliary afferent impulse. The inadequate regulation of the motor responses made in accordance with the single instruction of this series is due to the as yet undeveloped proprioceptive signalization coming from the executed movements. As becomes clear from questioning, the children are not aware of the incorrect movements. Under these conditions a child's speech responses, by creating a supplementary afferentation of the motor act, which comes from a more flexible and controllable system, make the act more controllable and voluntary.

Furthermore, we observed substantial age-dependent and individual differences among the children. In certain 3-year-olds (usually children with poorly developed speech and with perhaps generally retarded development) we were generally unable to carry out the experimental series in which speech accompanied motor responses because it was impossible to create a stable system of speech-motor responses. In these children speech often simply ceased. On the other hand, in older children — 5-year-olds — the instructions were carried out right away without mistakes, even silently; and the inclusion of external speech was superfluous.

Between these two extremes were children who made mistakes while carrying out the instruction silently but whose errors were reduced when an external speech impulse was added. But even among these children we could observe age-dependent increments in the effectiveness of the supplementary speech impulse.

Table 1 presents the average percentage of intersignal responses in the series with and without speech accompaniment for children 3-4 and 4-5 years in age. In this table it is clear that there is a general tendency for the number of intersignal responses to decrease with age, possibly because the nervous processes are becoming more concentrated. It is also clear that relative to 3-year-olds, 4-year-olds display better regulation of their responses with the aid of a speech impulse.

Table 1

Experiments with a Simple Response

Intersignal motor responses in carrying out instructions under various conditions (%)

Age	Silently	With impulsive speech	Silently
3-4 years	71	29	31
4-5 years	50	11	17

We set up the basic group of experiments with simple responses so that after the instruction had been carried out silently, the subject immediately had to make motor responses
accompanied by a supplementary speech impulse. We constructed this type of experiment in order to facilitate creation
of a single speech-motor response system.

To ascertain the relevance in speech-regulated movements
of purely speech-type responses (as opposed to motor responses), we conducted an additional group of experiments in
which a series with motor responses was followed, first, by a
series with only speech responses to a signal ("tu!"), and then
by a series with motor and speech responses together.

The results of these additional experiments show that if a
child is told to pronounce the syllable "tu" in response to a signal, then for almost all children the number of intersignal
speech responses is significantly less than the number of intersignal motor responses. This is presumably explained both by
the great flexibility of the subject's speech system and by the
different structure of the speech response, the reverse afferentation of which has an exteroceptive aspect. These factors
make it possible to utilize the more developed speech responses
as a means of regulating motor responses. Data from the additional sessions are presented in Table 2. These experiments
also showed that whereas five of six 3-4-year-olds responded
between signals, only one of six 4-5-year-olds made intersignal responses. This demonstrates the age-dependent development of the neurodynamics of the verbal system.

The question arises: Why does a speech accompaniment organize motor responses? What is the mechanism of this influence? To answer this question let us turn to the latency of
the motor responses. The data indicate that when a child carries out an instruction silently, as a rule the latency of the
motor responses is less than the latency of certain speech responses to a stimulus. (4) Because of this, in the series in
which the motor and speech responses were combined there
was an increase in the latency of the motor responses, often
by one and a half or two times. When the instruction was

Table 2

Comparison of Motor and Speech Responses
in Experiments with a Simple Response

	Intersignal responses (%)	
Age	Motor	Speech
3-4 years	41	10
4-5 years	28	1

Table 3

Latencies of Simple Motor and Speech Responses
and of Speech-Motor Responses

	Average latency of responses in carrying out instructions under various conditions (sec)			
Age	Motor responses	Speech responses	Motor-speech responses	Motor responses
3-4 years	0.6	1.3	1.1	0.7
4-5 years	0.4	0.9	0.7	0.5

subsequently carried out silently, the latency again decreased
(Table 3).

In this way movements accompanied by speech are slowed
down and become, as it were, less impulsive. This speech-
based regulation permits many children to increase the general
tone of inhibition and to master the tendency toward extraneous,
impulsive, motor responses, a tendency connected with diffuse
irradiation of excitation arising from the stimulus.

* * *

It is essential to analyze how the child's motor responses acquire the necessary flexibility under the influence of auxiliary speech afferentation, how they come to depend on a verbal instruction and not on the dynamics of the motor act itself or on a direct signal influence. It is essential to analyze as well how, with age, the movements lose their direct dependence on a signal and are incorporated into a new system — into the system of speech regulation, by means of which the movements acquire a truly independent and voluntary nature.

We begin with a concept of motor-act structure that distinguishes a preparatory afferentation from the signal that evokes the response. (5) In established voluntary actions the preparatory afferentation is a system of verbal connections set up by a preparatory instruction, and the direct signal has only an actuating influence. It is possible, however, that at earlier stages of development these relations can be quite the reverse: the traces of the instruction turn out to be too weak and do not form a preparatory afferentation of the movement, and the direct stimulus not only actuates but also regulates the movement.

To study these relations we carried out several modifications of our usual simple-response experiments. To obtain a simple response to a signal in accordance with a preparatory instruction we explained and showed a child several times how to squeeze the rubber bulb. The subject was told and shown that he must squeeze and then immediately release his grip. Moreover, he was told and shown that he must squeeze only once in response to each signal. Before beginning the main experiment, we checked to see how the child responded to the direct order "Squeeze once." For younger children (age 2-3 years) this task still represented some difficulty; but most of the children (of age 3-4 years), after a reinforcing of the instruction, responded correctly, i.e., they squeezed the bulb and immediately released their grip, and squeezed it only once, as specified by the instruction.

We compared the execution of movements required by an instruction in response to a signal under two sets of conditions that differed in principle. In the first case the subjects were

presented with comparatively brief signals (1-1.5 sec). Under
these conditions the subjects generally responded as instructed:
Squeeze, and immediately release. It is important to emphasize that the brief duration of the signals provided a favorable
condition for carrying out this kind of movement: the signal's
appearance evoked the beginning of the motor response, and
the signal's offset evoked the termination of the squeezing.
Here the influence of the signal, as it were, coincided with the
influence of the instruction.

In the second case the very same instruction ("Squeeze the
bulb and immediately release it") was carried out under conditions in which, in addition to the short signals, longer signals
(3-4 sec) appeared randomly from time to time. When a long
signal appeared, the subject had to terminate his motion before
the end of the direct signal; the influence of the signal thus
came into conflict with the requirements of the instruction. It
was shown that under these conditions the motor responses depended greatly on the duration of the signal. With a short signal the subject could easily carry out the instruction to
squeeze and immediately release the bulb; but with longer signals carrying out the instruction turned out to be greatly impeded; and many subjects, having squeezed the bulb when the
signal appeared, stopped squeezing only when the stimulus
ceased. The motor response acquired a strongly expressed
tonal nature. In all 5-year-olds and in some 3- and 4-year-
olds this phenomenon ceased after several repetitions and
demonstration of the instruction. In some cases the phenomenon was stable and did not cease after demonstration and repetition of the instruction.... Hence in some cases the instruction, not the direct signal, defined the nature of the motor response. In other cases, with the long signals, the direct signal (which conflicted with the requirements of the instruction)
defined the nature of the motor responses.

In a series of other cases the movements' dependence on
direct stimuli lay in the fact that with the presentation of extended signals, the movements acquired a rhythmic nature and
sometimes continued after the signal was terminated. Correctly

carrying out the order "Squeeze once," a subject then given a
long signal would squeeze the bulb several times. In such
cases the movements are controlled not by the verbal instruction, but by the direct signal itself. Repeated demonstrations
and repetitions of the instruction did not eliminate this phenomenon in many subjects. The stimuli that evoked a wave of diffuse excitation and, so to speak, imparted impulses to the
movement during the duration of their presentation turned out to
be a stronger factor than the trace effect of the instruction.

Thus, when a signal conflicts with the requirements of an
instruction, the subject's difficulties are presumably explained
by the fact that the traces of the verbal instruction do not form
a sufficiently stable afferentation to oppose the direct influence
of the stimulus. If this is so, we should be able to strengthen
the speech afferentation of the motor response by requiring
the subject to say a word that will give additional afferentation
and an auxiliary impulse to the movement. To confirm this
hypothesis we conducted a series of experiments in which the
motor responses were combined with the impulsive speech response described above. When the signal was presented, the
subject had to pronounce the syllable "tu" and squeeze the
bulb. When this was done, the selective motor response was
broken off by pronunciation of "tu." Hence, in the conflict between the direct signal and the traces of the verbal instruction,
the instruction was reinforced by pronunciation of the syllable.
It turned out that this method could be used to overcome the
movements' dependence on the duration of the signal.

Let us consider an experiment with Valya S. (age 4 years,
4 months). She can correctly carry out the instruction "Squeeze
and immediately let go" in response to a direct order and short
signals; however, upon presentation of longer signals she begins
to assimilate the movement to the signal, and tonal responses
arise (Figure 3A, Nos. 13-14). When the subject is again
shown that it is necessary to squeeze, she again correctly carries out the instruction in response to the direct order "Squeeze"
(Figure 3A, after No. 14), but upon presentation of longer signals, makes tonal responses. After this series is conducted in

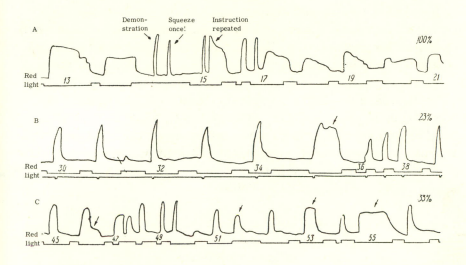

Figure 3. Valya S., age 4 years, 4 months. A. Carrying out the instruction "When there is a red light, squeeze and immediately let go." B. The same, with speech ("tu"). C. The same, silently.

which the motor responses are combined with impulsive speech; when the signal is presented, the subject has to say "tu" and squeeze the bulb. Accompanying the motor responses with the spoken syllable leads to a change in the nature of the movement. It no longer depends on the duration of the signal. In response to both short and long signals the subject can correctly carry out the instruction to squeeze and immediately release the bulb. This change in nature in clearer in Figure 3B (Nos. 30-34, 38-39). Only in isolated cases does the subject, in spite of the speech accompaniment, make tonal responses (3 mistakes in 13 signals). When the instruction is again carried out in silence, the number of errors increases markedly once more, but the instruction is nevertheless carried out better than before (Figure 3A). This experiment shows that with the aid of a speech impulse it is possible to organize the execution of motor responses and to overcome their dependence on the signal. We have already mentioned the fact that tonal movement in response to a long signal occurs because the verbal instruction does not create sufficiently stable afferentation of the motion; when there is a conflict between the signal and the requirements of the instruction, the signal not only plays an actuating role but directly energizes the movement. Under these conditions the strengthening of the required afferentation by pronunciation of the syllables aloud at the instant of movement has an organizing influence on the movement and makes the movement independent of the stimulus and thus subordinate to the instruction.

Table 4

Age-Dependent Changes in the Role of Speech
Accompaniments in Overcoming the
Direct Influence of Motor Signals

	Mistaken responses to long signals in carrying out instructions under various conditions (%)		
Age	Silently	With speech	Silently
3-4 years	90	49	85
4-5 years	93	33	51

Experiments with a simple response and extended signals show that an auxiliary speech impulse plays a regulatory role in overcoming the dependence of the movement's nature on the direct signal in all children, to one degree or another. There are also age-dependent changes in the effectiveness of the auxiliary speech impulse, as is clear in Table 4. The average number of mistakes in a series in which the movement is accompanied by speech is reduced from 49% in 3-4-year-olds to 33% in 4-5-year-olds. Subsequent development leads to the instruction's being carried out correctly even when it conflicts with the direct signal.

*   *   *

In the simple-response experiments we obtained data on the organization of motor responses by pronunciation of the signal meaning of the stimulus (the series on overcoming intersignal responses) and by impulsive speech (the series on overcoming intersignal motor responses and dependence of the movements' nature on direct signal duration). The experiments clarified the role of the impulsive influence of speech in overcoming the direct influence of a stimulus on movement, both in the form of direct assimilation of the movement to the signals and in the form of its aftereffects (intersignal responses). There was, however, no comparison of the selective and impulsive influences of speech on the regulation of movement. This will be done in the next series of experiments.

Analysis of the Interrelation of the Impulsive and the Selective Influences of Speech

In the simple-response experiments we saw that a child's speech responses can overcome both direct subordination of movements to a signal and the excitatory irradiation that is characteristic of the child's neurodynamics. All this took place only in the cases in which the child's speech acted impulsively.

However, the nature of speech is twofold. Speech as a complex stimulus can have a direct and impulsive influence, but it can also actualize a system of selective connections. How is this latter influence realized in the child? How are the various forms of the influence of speech interrelated at various ages? In order to answer these questions it was necessary to set up an experiment in which the impulsive and the selective influences of speech could be separated, including conditions under which they could have directly contrary effects. . . .

In a new series of experiments, children had to work out a system of differentiated responses to the preparatory verbal instruction "When the red light comes on, squeeze; and when the green light comes on, don't squeeze." This instruction was repeated by the experimenter several times and was repeated by the subjects. The repetition of the instruction was usually carried out correctly, although not independently, and in a questioning form, in fragments. In the motor responses it generally turned out that the connection set up in the verbal system by the preparatory instruction did not completely regulate the flow of the motor responses. The excitation in response to positive signals was diffuse and broadly irradiated and led to disinhibition of the differentiation. The subject squeezed the bulb not only during the positive signals but also during the inhibitory signals. Thus, the trace influence of the instruction was clearly inadequate to overcome the diffuse irradiation of the nervous processes, which was manifest in the disinhibition of differentiation during the presentation of inhibitory signals following a series of positive signals.

We then wondered if it would not be possible to strengthen the inadequate trace effect of the preparatory verbal instruction by pronouncing the signal meaning of the presented stimulus aloud each time. This was done in the following way: The subject was instructed to pronounce its signal meaning each time the stimulus was presented — to say "Squeeze" or "Don't squeeze" or simply "Must" or "Must not" and correspondingly to squeeze the bulb or refrain from squeezing it. Thus, in these experiments we wanted to trace the influence of pronouncing the signal meaning of the stimulus, i.e., the influence of the selective speech connections of the child himself, on the flow of his motor responses in carrying out an instruction.

In this way we set up a collision between the selective and the impulsive influences of the child's accompanying speech. If the words "Must not" influenced selectively, they would create an inhibitory effect; if they influenced impulsively, they would evoke a supplementary disinhibition.

The experiments showed that in children aged 3-4 years the impulsive influence of speech was paramount: a speech accompaniment not only did not decrease but often increased disinhibition of the differentiation during presentation of an inhibitory signal.

Let us examine a specific session (with subject Lena S., 3 years, 9 months). In accordance with the preparatory verbal instruction "When the red light comes on, squeeze; and when the green light comes on, don't squeeze" we tried to set up a differentiation. The subject made motor responses not only to the positive signals but also to the inhibitory signals, i.e., there was disinhibition of the differentiation, as is clear in Figure 4 for presentations of the green light Nos. 2, 4, 6, 8, and 10.

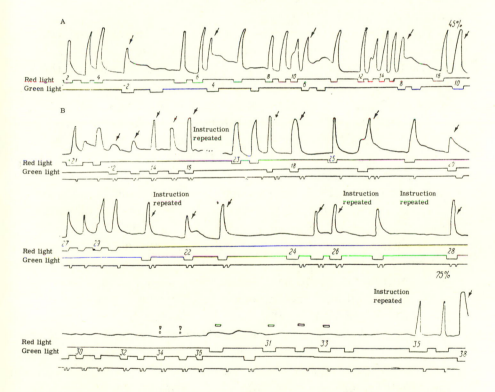

Figure 4. Lena S., 3 years, 9 months. A. Carrying out the instruction "When the red light comes on, squeeze; but when the green light comes on, you must not squeeze." B. The same, with speech ("Must," "Must not").

One should note that in a series of inhibitory signals presented after positive signals, the subject usually makes an erroneous motor response only to the first of the inhibitory signals (Figure 4, Nos. 2, 6, and 8). In Nos. 3, 7, and 9 in Figure 4,
the differentiation is not disinhibited. This indicates that along
with the irradiation of the excitation we have retention of the
speech traces, which make it possible to overcome this disinhibition in the subsequently presented inhibitory signal. Hence
there is a defect here specifically in the efferent phase. The
question thus arises: Can speech aid in strengthening the inhibitory connection?

To confirm this we conducted a series of experiments with
pronunciation of the signal meaning of the stimulus. It turned
out that in spite of pronunciation of the signal meaning of the
inhibitory stimulus ("Must not"), the subject squeezed the bulb
when the inhibitory signal was presented (Figure 4, No. 12).
On presentation of several inhibitory signals in succession, the
subject, saying "Must not," responded erroneously to every inhibitory signal (Figure 4, Nos. 12-16).

Thus, during silent carrying out of an instruction disinhibition of differentiation occurs only at the beginning of a series
of inhibitory signals; but in a series in which the signal meaning of the stimulus is pronounced aloud, there is a continuous
disinhibition of the differentiation. After presentation of signal No. 16, the instruction is repeated; but in the subsequent
presentations of inhibitory signals (Nos. 17-21), the differentiation is disinhibited: the subject says "Must not" but simultaneously squeezes the bulb. After signal No. 21 the instruction is again repeated, but the inhibition is not extinguished.
After signal No. 26, the instruction is once again repeated,
but this does not change the picture (Nos. 27-28). Only with
the repetition of the instruction after stimulus No. 28, i.e.,
after many repetitions of the instruction in a continuous presentation of only inhibitory signals (eight signals), is the differentiation reestablished. On presentation of inhibitory signal No. 29 the subject says "Must not" and, finally, does not
squeeze. The same thing happens on presentation of signals

Nos. 26-30. After this the positive signal is once again presented (No. 30), and the subject says "Must" and does not
squeeze in response to presentation of a positive signal. This
also happens in response to signals Nos. 31-34. After repetition of the instruction, on presentation of positive signals
Nos. 35-36 the subject says "Must" and makes a motor response; and then in response to inhibitory signal No. 32 says
"Must not" yet once again makes a motor response.

Thus, in the experiments in which the signal meaning of the
stimulus is pronounced aloud, the words "Must not" evoke a
motor response to an inhibitory signal; but with the extinction
of this response the word "Must" also ceases to evoke a motor
response to a positive signal. Hence any regulation of motor
responses by the semantic aspect of the voiced speech that accompanies the responses to both stimuli is clearly absent. We
observed this absence of regulation in most of the children; in
a third of the children the number of errors even increased
when speech accompanied the motor response.

How should we interpret this? Why does a child saying the
words "Must not" respond with an action that is just the opposite of his words (squeeze the bulb); and why when this incorrect response extinguishes does he fail to squeeze the bulb
while saying the word "Must," i.e., again act contrary to the
meaning of the word?

Let us analyze the response to the positive signal from the
beginning. On presentation of the positive signal the subject
who follows instructions says "Must" and squeezes the bulb.
Like every word, the word "Must" has to be viewed as a complex stimulus that can have both a direct and impulsive influence and a selective influence. The selective influence of the
word "Must" is positive — "Must squeeze the bulb"; the impulsive influence of the word is also positive: the verbal response is achieved, and creates a corresponding center of excitation. Thus, the selective and the impulsive influences of
the word here coincide in sign. Because of this we do not know
which aspect of the word produces regulation of the motor responses to the positive signals.

This is not at all the case with the second half of the instruction. On presentation of an inhibitory signal the subject says
"Must not." The selective influence of this phrase is inhibitory ("Must not squeeze the bulb"); but, like the first word, it
evokes a center of excitation in the speech part of the cortex,
since the speech response is made and is not delayed. Hence
the selective and the impulsive influences of the words have
opposite signs. They not only do not coincide, as in the first
case, but are in conflict. For this reason we can suppose that
when the child says "Must not" and simultaneously squeezes
the bulb, the words have a regulatory influence on the motor
response not by means of any systematic, selective (inhibitory)
connections, but simply because they serve as a supplementary
center of excitation.

Thus, in 3-4-year-olds in the complex speech responses
"Must not," in which there is a conflict between the selective
and the impulsive influences of the words, the stronger component is more often the direct and impulsive influence of
speech, which regulates the flow of the motor responses, pro-
ducing disinhibition of the differentiation in spite of the meaning of the words. In cases of stable disinhibition of differentiation under the influence of the words "Must not," by means
of many repetitions during continuous presentation of inhibitory signals, we could achieve a situation in which the subject,
pronouncing these words, did not squeeze the bulb, i.e., in
spite of the positive, impulsive influence of the verbal response,
the subject made an inhibitory motor response. In this case
the response was formed as a result of direct reinforcement
of the inhibitory process, and was not under the influence of
the selective effect of the words. In subsequent presentations
of the positive signal, the subject said "Must" but still did not
squeeze the bulb, i.e., he made an inhibitory motor response
contrary to the speech response. Here, as well, the direct,
impulsive influence of the word predominates. On the whole,
the data from the experiments attempting to regulate a system
of differentiated responses by means of pronouncing the signal
meaning of stimuli show that, in a majority of 3-year-olds and

in half of the 4-year-olds, the number of mistakes increases
in the series in which the motor responses are accompanied
by speech.

The fact that when there is a conflict between the selective
and the impulsive influences of a word the regulation of motor
responses is effected by the latter aspect of the word indicates
that in 3-4-year-olds the nonspecific influence of speech (in
the experiments with simple differentiation) dominates under
these conditions. This is presumably connected with the fact
that there is an as yet inadequate differentiation of the word's
specific aspect — its meaning. The verbal system does not
dominate the system of selective connections.

We have described the inhibitory influence of the words
"Must not" in the experiments with simple differentiation.
There are, however, difficulties other than those we described.
A second difficulty lay in uttering the words "Must" and "Must
not" and in combining them with the movements. In several of
the children, usually 3-year-olds, we observed difficulties in
combining the speech and motor responses into a system and
in switching over from one type of speech response to the other.
These observations demand special and more careful analysis.

Only in several, usually older, subjects did we observe par-
tial regulation of motor responses with the aid of pronunciation
of the signal meaning of the presented stimuli. We shall return
to these findings at the end of the present section.

*   *   *

In the simple differentiation experiments, disinhibition of the
differentiation in the pronouncing series is explained by the
direct, impulsive influence of the speech accompanying the inhibitory response. Hence it is logical to ask how an instruction
will be carried out if there is a "reduction" of this conflict.
In order to eliminate the conflict between the selective and the
impulsive influences of the speech response "Must not," we
set up the following experiment: The subject was told that on
presentation of a positive signal he must say the word "Must"

and squeeze the bulb, and on presentation of an inhibitory signal he must remain silent and not squeeze the bulb. In this
way conflict in the speech response was eliminated: to the
positive signal the subject responded verbally and squeezed
the bulb (in other words, a positive motor response corresponded to a positive articulation), and to an inhibitory signal
there was no speech response and the motor response was inhibited. It turned out that this produced a dramatic improvement in carrying out the instruction.

Let us consider an experiment with Gena P. (age 3 years,
7 months). The subject was given the preparatory spoken instruction "When the red light comes on, squeeze the bulb; but
when the green light comes on, you must not squeeze the bulb."
This instruction often produced disinhibition of the differentiation during presentation of an inhibitory signal following positive signals (Figure 5, Nos. 11, 13, 14, 16 — presentations of
green light).

After this we conducted a series in which the speech and
motor responses were brought together, i.e., in which the subject pronounced the signal meaning of the stimulus ("Must
not," "Must"). Now the subject, pronouncing the corresponding
part of the instruction, had either to squeeze the bulb or else
refrain from squeezing it. It is clear from the figure that the
experiment did not give the desired results. The subject, although saying "Must not" on presentation of an inhibitory signal, nevertheless simultaneously squeezed the bulb (Figure 5B,
Nos. 25-30, 31-36). Thus, pronouncing the signal meaning of
the stimuli leads no longer to isolated mistakes, as in series
A, but to continuous disinhibition of the differentiation. This
disinhibition is stable and is not extinguished by many repetitions of the instruction (Figure 5, after Nos. 27, 30, 31). We are
dealing here with the same situation that we spoke about above:
the words "Must not" act as a supplementary impulse and
evoke, in spite of their meaning, a continuous disinhibition of
the differentiation.

We then conducted a series in which the subject was told to
pronounce the signal meaning only of the positive stimulus and

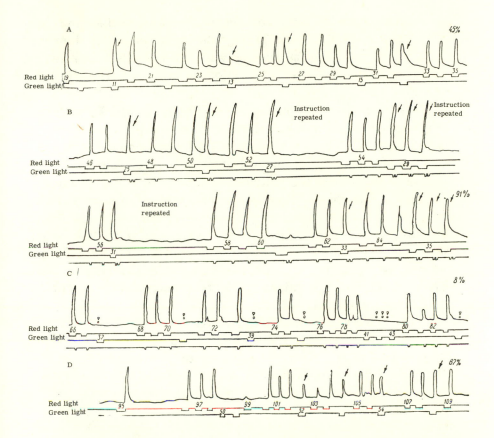

Figure 5. Gena P., 3 years, 7 months. A. Carrying out the instruction "When the red light comes on, squeeze; but when the green light comes on, you must not squeeze." B. The same, with speech ("Must," "Must not"). C. The same, with the inhibitory link ("Must"...) being passed over in silence. D. The same, silently.

to remain silent when the negative stimulus was presented. It turned out that under these conditions disinhibition of the differentiation on presentation of an inhibitory signal following positive signals was almost completely extinguished. In Figure 5C it is clear that on presentation of [positive] signals Nos. 66-84 the subject, saying "Must," squeezed the bulb and, on presenta-

tion of [negative] signals Nos. 37-44, remained silent and did
not squeeze the bulb. In 12 signals there was only 1 error
(8%). After this, the instruction was again carried out silently,
and again there was disinhibition of the differentiation (Figure
5D, Nos. 52-55).

Thus, comparing the results of series A, C, and D, we see
that carrying out the instruction is disrupted because of the
weakness of the trace influence of the verbal connections and
that reinforcement with the aid of pronunciation (series D) improves carrying out the instruction and leads to regulation of
the motor responses. However, a comparison of series B and
C shows that such regulation is extremely limited, because it
is realized only under conditions in which the actualized aspect
of the speech response coincides in sign with the motor response: to a positive signal a speech and a motor response are
made; to an inhibitory signal both the speech and the motor response are inhibited.

These observations confirm the hypotheses that the influence
of speech still has here a relatively simple nature and that
speech acts primarily as a supplementary impulse regulating
the flow of the responses.

*   *   *

If motor-response regulation in the process of establishing
a differentiation on the basis of a preparatory instruction is
achieved only when the meaning of the sign "Must" coincides
with its direct and impulsive influence, the question then arises
as to which aspect of the word "Must" actually achieves this
regulation: Is it the system of selective connections underlying
the word, or is it a supplementary impulse connected with the
word's pronunciation? Perhaps there is essentially no meaning, in general, of the pronounced word apart from the fact of
its pronunciation.

To answer this question we made a series of observations.
The subject was told to pronounce the nonsense syllable "tu"
and to squeeze the bulb when the positive signal was presented

and to refrain from both motor and voiced responses on presentation of inhibitory signals. We conditionally called such speech "impulsive" speech. In this way this series analyzed the nature of the influence of a conditioned speech impulse on the flow of the motor responses in isolation from the pronunciation of the signal meaning of the stimuli, as in the previous series. We assumed that under these conditions we could utilize the supplementary speech impulse as a means of regulating the motor responses.... We found that 20 children aged 3-5 years, in carrying out the instruction, had an average of 45% mistakes (responses to the inhibitory signal); but for speech alone the average was only 4%. This is explained by the great mobility of the verbal system and by differences between the structure of the speech and the motor responses (see P. 238). As the experiments showed, the more integrated impulses from speech responses could be successfully used as a means of regulating the child's movements.

Let us consider an experiment with Larisa T. (age 3 years, 8 months). A simple differentiation was established on the basis of the preparatory spoken instruction "When the red light comes on, squeeze; but when the green light comes on, you must not squeeze." Although she squeezed the bulb on presentation of a positive signal, in several cases the subject also squeezed mistakenly on presentation of the negative signal (Figure 6A, Nos. 12, 19, 21 to green light).

Then the subject was told to say "tu" and to squeeze when the positive signal appeared and on presentation of the inhibitory signal to remain silent and not to squeeze. In this series the instruction was carried out almost without error (Figure 6B). When the instruction was again carried out silently, disinhibition of the differentiation occurred once more (Figure 6B, Nos. 42, 52, 54, 56).

Thus, with the aid of a simplified speech (even "voiced") impulse of what was to be done on presentation of positive signals we were able to achieve an almost error-free execution of an instruction, something that was quite impossible when it was carried out silently. How are we to interpret this finding?

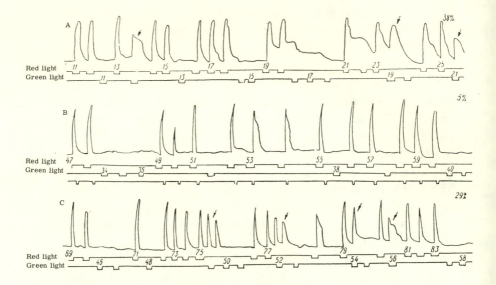

Figure 6. Larisa T., age 3 years, 8 months. A. Carrying out
the instruction "When the red light comes on, squeeze; but
when the green light comes on, you must not squeeze." B. The same,
with speech at the positive signal ("tu"). C. The same, silently.

The instruction, which sets up verbal connections, creates
preparatory afferentation of the movement, as a result of
which the red light evokes a motor response and the green
light evokes an inhibition of movement. But the situation is
quite different in cases in which the verbal connection, closed
by a preparatory instruction, is stable enough to oppose the
diffuse irradiation of excitation arising from the stimulus,
manifest in disinhibition of the differentiation, and in which it
can thus make the excitation process selective. In our subjects
the memory traces of the verbal connections produced by the
preparatory instruction frequently were weak, did not restrain
the diffuse irradiation of excitation, and did not provide afferentation of the motor act.

Under these conditions the voiced impulse "tu," which is uttered in response to a positive signal and not uttered in re-

sponse to a negative one, strengthens the speech afferentation of the motor responses. We should emphasize that the supplementary speech impulse is selective: it is made only in response to the positive signal. Such selectivity of the impulse is facilitated both by the generally greater mobility of the neurodynamics of speech and by the fact that with regard to the subject's speech response, there is no continuously acting stimulus such as those coming from the bulb in the subject's hand. In this way, using a supplementary signal and the reverse afferentation that arises from it, we were able to achieve improved execution of the prior instruction.

Consequently, in the experiments involving pronunciation of the signal meaning of only the positive stimulus ("Must"), the regulatory influence on motor responses was realized not so much by the system of selective connections underlying the word as by the supplementary speech impulse that created auxiliary afferentation. Moreover, these findings are relevant to understanding the mechanism of the nonspecific speech influence in the pronunciation experiments. Specifically, the mere utterance of the words "Must not" creates an impulse toward movement in spite of their inhibitory meaning.

Let us summarize the data obtained in the experiments on regulating movement by means of a supplementary voice impulse (Table 5). We observe regulation of responses in 29 of 30 children, although it is expressed differently in different children. The regulation is expressed as a reduction in the number of mistakes in the series involving combining the responses. In this case there were usually two types of mistakes: the first was disinhibition of speech responses, i.e., on presentation of an inhibitory signal, the child said "tu" and squeezed the bulb; the second type of error occurred when the child retained a differentiated system of voiced responses but nevertheless inhibited his motor responses. Although speech responses occurred without error in a majority of children (25 of 39), combining these responses with movements increased the number of errors in the speech responses themselves (these errors occurred in 14 of 19 children).

Table 5

Experiments with Simple Differentiation. Regulation of
Responses by the Impulsive Influence of Speech

Responses to an inhibitory signal in various
series of experiments (%)

Age	Single motor responses	Single speech responses	Motor and speech responses combined	Single motor responses
3-4 years	47	4	20	34
4-5 years	58	2	25	60

Analysis of the data shows that with increasing age there is
a change in the number of cases in which motor inhibition is
connected with speech inhibition on presentation of an inhibitory signal. In 3-4-year-olds an average of 47% of the total
number of cases of motor inhibition coincides with speech inhibition, whereas in 4-5-year-olds the proportion of such
cases is down to 25%. These data indicate an age-related
change in the stability of speech responses.

Thus, in several children 3-4 years of age we observed a
sharp difference between the influence of semantic and impulsive speech. Uttering the signal meaning of the stimulus only
increases disinhibition of the differentiation, owing to the fact
that the words "Must not" do not act selectively, but impulsively; accompanying positive responses with impulsive speech
and remaining silent for the inhibitory signals creates the
necessary auxiliary afferentation of the movement and dra-
matically improves the execution of the instruction.

*   *   *

A question remains, however, as to the mechanism by which
the auxiliary speech impulse exerts its influence.

In order to achieve an understanding of this regulation, we compared the latency of the positive responses. It turned out that the latency of the motor response to positive signals was less than that of the impulsive speech response. In the 4-5-year-olds,* when the motor and speech responses were combined there was usually an increase in the latency of the former; but when the instruction was once again carried out silently, there was a decrease in the latency of the motor responses to the positive signal. This is shown in the data in Table 6.

Table 6

Experiments with Simple Differentiation. Changes in the Latency of Motor Responses Combined with Speech

Age	Latency of motor and speech-motor responses on presentation of positive signals (sec)			
	Single motor responses	Speech responses	Motor and speech responses combined	Single motor responses
3-4 years	0.5	1.0	0.3	0.6
4-5 years	0.4	1.0	0.6	0.6

We can conclude that the regulatory role of the auxiliary speech responses that accompany the motor responses amounts to a reduction in the impulsiveness of the movements, to a certain restraining or inhibiting of the motor response that results in a reduction of the disinhibition of the differentiation as the child attempts to carry out a preparatory verbal instruction.

*   *   *

*Added by author in a personal communication to the editor (1975).

The experiments in which the signal meaning of every stimulus was spoken aloud in association with differential motor responses have shown the predominance of the impulsive influence of the word.... However, one ought not to conclude that disinhibition when speech accompanies the motor response implies speech has absolutely no selective influence.

In several children about 4 years old we encountered a paradox: disinhibition of the differentiation, which was observed in the preliminary silent execution of the instruction and which sharply increased when the movements were coupled with speech responses to every signal ("Must" or "Must not"), was suddenly and completely extinguished when the instruction was again carried out silently in the subsequent series of experiments. An analysis of the latency of the incorrect responses to an inhibitory signal in this series of experiments shows that all the mistakes in carrying out the instruction silently share one feature: their latencies are relatively short (0.5-0.6 sec). These are, so to speak, premature, impulsive responses of the child. These mistakes are quite different from those in the series with combined movement and speech, which are inhibited under the influence of the speech impulse of the motor responses. These disinhibited responses have a latency of two to three times greater than that of the impulsive responses (1.7-2.0 sec) and roughly coincide with the latency of the speech response itself.

It turns out that the nature of the mistakes in the series combining responses is directly connected with how the instruction is carried out silently when the pronunciation of word(s) is eliminated. If the pronunciation series has mistakes of disinhibition only under the influence of speech and the impulsive responses are extinguished, then the instruction in the subsequent series will be carried out correctly. If in the same pronunciation series there are, in addition to inhibition errors, impulsive squeezings (with short latencies), then even after verbalization has been eliminated, the instruction will still be carried out with many errors (Table 7).

In the first case we have this picture: The predomi-

Table 7

Hidden Influence of Pronunciation in Simple Differentiation
Experiments. Dependence of an Instruction's Execution
on the Nature of Mistakes When a Verbal Response
Accompanies Movement

Subjects	Indicators	Experimental series		
			With speech	
		Silently		Silently
Serezha O. (4 years, 6 months)	Disinhibited responses (%)	43	80	0
	Latency (sec)	0.5	-- 1.6	--
Serezha K. (4 years)	Disinhibited responses (%)	37	77	66
	Latency (sec)	0.6	0.6 2.0	0.6

nance of the impulsive influence of speech leads to an increase
in the total number of mistakes in the series in which the responses are combined. The verbalization, however, facilitates
strengthening of the selective connections thanks to which the
impulsive motor responses to the bulb are extinguished. The
effect of strengthening these connections is also expressed
when there is no more verbalization: the impulsive squeezings
do not arise. Eliminating verbalization leads to extinction of
the disinhibition errors that arise from speech. In short, the
instruction is carried out correctly.

Thus, already in 4-year-olds we observe a selective influence
of the spoken word, but it is still masked by the predominant,
impulsive influence and is expressed only as an afteraffect of
the utterance.

*   *   *

In analyzing the data from the experiments with 3- and 4-year-olds we have shown that it is possible to achieve regulation of motor responses by using the simple impulsive influence of speech. However, such regulation by means of the system of selective connections energized by speech is quite often impeded, especially when it conflicts with the impulsive influence of speech. Furthermore, with some 4-year-olds the number of mistakes is reduced by uttering the signal meaning of the stimuli "Must" or "Must not." It is natural to assume that in still older children, uttering the signal meaning of two stimuli will produce a clear effect of motor-response regulation, i.e., the direct and impulsive influence of speech will no longer predominate; and instead the system of selective connections that are energized under the influence of speech will predominate. To analyze this question the experiments with simple differentiation we described above were carried out with 5-year-olds.

The experiments showed that the instruction to make differential responses to different signals was more easily mastered by 5-year-olds; the traces of this instruction were more stable; and, under the usual conditions (moderate rate, long signals), they were able to regulate motor responses in a sufficiently stable way. With 3- and 4-year-olds we had only to accelerate the rate of signal presentation (intervals of 2-3 sec) to increase the number of disinhibited differentiations. With 5-year-olds this could be done only by combining a rapid rate of signal presentation with a reduction in the duration of the signals themselves (to 0.5-0.75 sec). Hence, with age a narrowing in the zone of difficulty for carrying out the same instruction occurs.

However, we are interested primarily in the nature of the influence of the child's own speech in overcoming difficulties in carrying out motor responses guided by a preparatory instruction.

It turned out that, under these conditions, in 5-year-olds speech has already begun to play a specific role and that even when there is a conflict between its impulsive and selective influences, speech continues actively to regulate motor responses.

Let us take as an example the experiment with Natasha K. (age 5 years, 10 months). She is given the instruction "When the green light comes on, squeeze the bulb; but when the red light comes on, you must not squeeze."

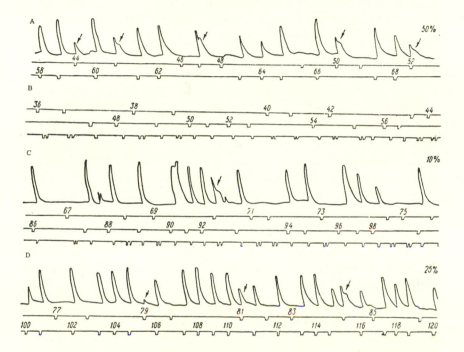

Figure 7. Natasha K., 5 years, 10 months. A. Carrying out the instruction "When the green light comes on, squeeze; but when the red light comes on, you must not squeeze." B. Speech responses to the signals ("Must," "Must not"). C. Combining speech and motor responses. D. The same, silently.

The instruction is correctly repeated and carried out. However, when the rate of presentation is accelerated and the duration of the signals is shortened, mistakes resulting from disinhibition of the differentiation occur. Hence in Figure 7A we see that the subject responds incorrectly to signals Nos. 5, 44, 45, 47, 50, and 52. To the 30 inhibitory signals she makes 15

mistakes (50%). Furthermore, replacing the motor responses
with speech responses reveals a greater preservation of the
speech ones. Combining the movements with speech leads to
a sharp reduction in the number of mistakes (Figure 7C). In response to 21 inhibitory signals there are only 2 mistakes (10%).
In subsequent silent execution of the instruction the number of
mistakes again increases (to 25%).

Thus, pronunciation of the words "Must not" in response to
an inhibitory signal leads to a result that is quite the opposite
of that we observed in 3-year-olds. In spite of the conflicting
nature of the speech response "Must not," in spite of the impulsive disinhibitory influence of this verbal response, we see
in operation here the system of selective connections underlying speech, which by this time has become sufficiently stable
to allow effective regulation of motor responses.

Certain data from these experiments point to a mechanism
for this regulation. Comparative analysis of the latency of
speech and motor responses to a positive signal indicates that
the average latency of speech responses is always greater (by
$1\frac{1}{2}$-2 times) than the average latency of motor responses. Addition of speech to motor responses to a positive signal leads
to their retardation, to an increase in the latency of the motor
response; the movements now begin to flow, as it were, under
an increased tonus of the inhibitory process, which reduces
the disinhibition of differentiation. At least in some cases, under the influence of the accompanying speech there is a decrease in the variance of the latency of the motor responses
(by a factor of two or more). Even with a very crude recording
of a very excited child we could observe a decrease in the variance of the amplitude of motor responses to a positive signal
(Table 8). This decrease in the variance of the amplitude of
motor responses and in latencies presumably indicates that
under the influence of speech, there is a concentration of the
nervous processes in which the regulatory influence of speech
is manifest and which leads to a reduction in the number of
cases of disinhibition of the differentiation.

Thus with children 5-7 years of age, under conditions in

Table 8

A Simple Differentiation Experiment
(Natasha K., 5 years, 10 months).
The Regulatory Role of Verbal Responses
Accompanying Motor Responses

Experimental series	Mistaken responses to an inhibitory signal (%)	Motor responses to a positive signal		
		Latency		Amplitude
		AM*	V*	V
Silently	50	0.4	13	15
With speech	10	0.5	7.5	6

*AM — average latency of the motor response (sec).
V   — coefficient of variance (%).

which connections set up by an instruction do not completely regulate the flow of motor responses, it is possible to strengthen this regulation by accompanying each motor response with a speech response. In the accompanying words ("Must not") the dominant aspect is no longer the impulsive influence but, instead, the selective and semantic influence.

The data from simple differentiation experiments with 5-year-olds indicate that nearly all children experience, though in differing degrees, a reduction in disinhibition of differentiation under the influence of pronouncing the signal meaning of the stimuli "Must," "Must not." These data indicate the presence in 5-year-olds, in the given experimental situation, of a selective, regulatory influence of speech.

In Table 9 we summarize the dynamics of the age-dependent changes in the influence of saying "Must not" to the inhibitory stimulus. This table gives the average number of mistakes (as a percentage) in three basic series of experiments with children 3, 4, and 5 years old. In 3-year-olds verbalizing the meaning of the stimulus only decreases the differentiation,

Table 9

Age-Related Changes in the Role of Pronouncing
the Signal Meaning of Two Stimuli in
Experiments with Simple Differentiation

		Responses to an inhibitory signal in carrying out an instruction under various conditions (%)		
Number of children	Age (years)	Silently	With speech	Silently
10	3-4	40	60	37
10	4-5	56	52	42
10	5-6	57	30	38

which is explained, as we said above, by the impulsive influence of speech; in 5-year-olds oral speech reduces the disinhibition, because of the selective influence of speech.

Having established the existence of a selective influence of
accompanying speech in older preschoolers, we proceeded to
analyze the degree to which this accompanying speech necessarily participates [in the responses]. Perhaps it is sufficient
merely to reinforce the connection between the corresponding
speech responses and the signal in order to strengthen the instructions having regulatory influence so that this influence
becomes adequate for regulating movements without the child's
having to respond verbally each time. To confirm this hypothesis we returned once again, after a series of experiments
with several speech responses, to investigating several motor
responses and then to combining them with speech.

It turned out that with older children (age 8-11 years), under
the conditions of a simple differentiation (with positive signals)
and when a considerable number of mistakes had been made,
only one instance of the speech responses ("Must," "Must not")
led to a sharp reduction in disinhibition of the motor response

(Table 10). This phenomenon is quite weakly expressed when
conditions have been made more difficult because of short signals, and the regulation then obtained is achieved only by accompanying the motor responses with speech each time.

Table 10

Influence of Practicing Speech Responses
on Subsequent Motor Responses

Disinhibitions of differentiation in
various experiments (%)

Number of children	Before practicing speech responses	After practicing speech responses	Combining motor and speech responses
8	48	22	9

Carrying out a preparatory spoken instruction requires that
at least two conditions be met: a stable connection is necessary, first, between the stimuli and the words that form the
signal meaning of these stimuli and, second, between those
words and the corresponding movements. When these two
conditions have been met, the instruction can be carried out:
every stimulus, being mediated by the verbal connection of
inner speech, evokes the required response. The speech response's preparatory role is evident in the fact that under
relatively simple conditions, the connection "word-movement"
is already stable in older preschoolers. Thus, when the speech
responses are practiced, we observe a direct projection into
motor responses; but the connection "signal-word" is still insufficiently reinforced, so that a single repetition of the preparatory instruction is inadequate. Saying the words "Must"
or "Must not" aloud when the signal is presented is required
to reinforce the signal meaning of the stimuli. From speech

that accompanies movement the child moves on to speech that
precedes movement.

From the results of experiments in establishing a simple
differentiation guided by a preparatory instruction we can draw
several conclusions. In these experiments the essential feature is analysis of the interrelation of the impulsive and the
selective influences of speech. It turns out that this interrelation changes with age and passes through a series of stages.

In the first stage, which applies basically to very young children and occasionally to 3-year-olds, there is no regulatory
influence of the connections underlying the word; the impulsive
influence of the word is dominant. Regulation of positive motor
responses by a speech impulse is hindered by difficulty in creating a system of speech-motor responses. In the second
stage, i.e., in 3-4-year-olds, a clear regulation of motor responses is formed with the aid of an auxiliary speech impulse.
Words, which form the signal meaning of the stimulus, act not
selectively, but impulsively, and hence regulate motor responses only when the impulsive and the selective influences
are of the same sign. When they are of opposite sign, the impulsive influence of the words dominates; and for this reason
adding the response "Must not" to an inhibitory signal leads
to disinhibition of a delayed motor response.

In the third stage, i.e., in 5-year-olds, movement regulation
is effected by a system of selective connections activated by
words. Even when the impulsive and the selective influences
of words conflict, the specifically selective influence predominates, which organizes the realization of motor responses in
carrying out an instruction.

Subsequent development presumably consists of an ever-
increasing selective influence of speech, no longer as external
speech, but in the form of inner speech or traces of connections
established according to the preparatory instruction that have
become so stable that it is unnecessary to use external speech. . . .

Notes

1) This methodological principle was presented in the

article by E. D. Homskaya, [The role of speech in the compensation of disturbed motor reactions]. [Problems of the higher nervous activity of normal and abnormal children]. Vol. 1. Moscow: APN RSFSR, 1956.

2) N. P. Paramonova, [On the formation of mutually acting signal systems in the child]. [Problems of the higher nervous activity of normal and abnormal children]. Vol. 1. Moscow: APN RSFSR, 1956.

3) See the article by A. R. Luria, [The role of speech in the formation of voluntary movement]. [Materials of a conference on psychology]. Moscow: APN RSFSR, 1957.

4) We conducted experiments, with V. Rozanova, in which we analyzed the latencies of speech responses. See V. Rozanova, [The study of motor and speech responses in preschool children]. Department of Psychology, Moscow University, 1957.

5) See [Problems of higher nervous activity]. Moscow: USSR Academy of Sciences, 1949.

PART THREE

Neuropsychology

A. R. Luria

L. S. VYGOTSKY AND THE PROBLEM
OF FUNCTIONAL LOCALIZATION

Forty years ago, in the mid-1920s, a young Soviet psychologist, still under thirty, came to the Clinic of Nervous Diseases, at first to observe, later to conduct his own independent research. His name was L. S. Vygotsky.

Unlike many others, including Professor G. I. Rossolimo, the director of the clinic, he had not come to conduct psychological tests for perfecting diagnoses of brain diseases. His task was incomparably greater: he saw the analysis of local brain infections as a basic means of solving fundamental questions of the structure of mental processes and of the material substratum of complex forms of mental activity. Some years later he wrote: "It seems to me that the problem of localization, like a common channel, includes examination of both the development and the disintegration of higher mental functions." This was in a lecture he read six weeks before his death: "The problem of the development and disintegration of higher mental functions" (Problema razvitiya i raspada vysshikh psikhicheskikh funktziy. In L. S. Vygotsky, Razvitiye vysshikh psikhicheskikh funktziy [Development of higher mental functions]. Moscow: APN RSFSR, 1960. P. 383).

Vygotsky approached the problem of localizing mental functions from a well thought out, innovative viewpoint, which from

---

From Voprosy psikhologii, 1966, 12(6), 55-61.

the outset was opposed to the basic psychological and neurological tenets of the time.

Psychology in the 1920s was dominated by the idea that human mental life was a complex of "functions" or "properties" common to man and animals. Leading psychologists of the time regarded sensations and perceptions, attention and memory, judgment and deduction, emotions and voluntary actions as natural manifestations of the working of the nervous system, or at best as processes with a reflex structure whose mechanisms were carefully studied in the conditioned reflex activity of animals. This came only shortly after the period of domination of dualism, when the crucial question for psychology had been whether mental and physiological phenomena were "parallel" or "interactive." Therefore, the naturalistic approach to mental phenomena, which had been the point of departure for both German Gestalt psychology and American behaviorism, not only was approved but even endorsed by the most progressive wing in psychology.

Naturally enough, however, after successfully solving a number of important questions of the mechanisms of elementary mental processes (sensations and the simplest forms of perception, involuntary attention, and spontaneous memory), the "naturalist" psychologists could not begin to approach questions of the mechanisms that underlay specifically human higher mental functions. How can one understand the mechanism of a voluntary act? What are the characteristic ways in which voluntary attention and active memory work? How can one approach scientific analysis of abstract forms of thought that allow man to penetrate the deepest connections of reality? At the time an attempt was made to answer all these questions by idealistic "descriptive psychology" — understood as the "science of the spirit [dukh]" — which took up these questions while rejecting their genuinely scientific, materialist analysis.

Our young Soviet psychologist's point of departure differed radically from these views.

In Vygotsky's view, higher mental functions, which the naturalistic school had refused to study, must not be just the subject of causal analysis: such an analysis must be the <u>basic task</u> of scientific psychology. To retain the natural scientific approach and reject this examination would mean to arrest scientific progress and direct it along false lines. The spiritualist psychological approach is just as unacceptable, however: to retain the question of higher forms of consciousness and will but reject scientific analysis of the genesis of these phenomena would be to substitute fideistic philosophy for science.

Vygotsky saw the way out of "the historical crisis of psychology"* in a radical reappraisal of basic psychological concepts. "Higher mental functions" must have an origin; but this origin must not be sought in the depths of the spirit or in hidden properties of nervous tissue: it must be sought outside the individual human organism in objective <u>social history</u>. In forming society and using tools, man created new, indirect forms of relationship to the external world to which he had formerly accommodated himself and which he now controlled. The formation of language during the process of social development provided him not only with a new, previously unknown method of communication but also with a new tool for ordering his mental processes. The higher mental functions that originated in social labor and speech enabled man to rise to a new level of organization in his activity. By adapting the methods created for verbal communication to his own needs, he developed forms of intelligent perception, voluntary attention, active recall, abstract thought, and voluntary behavior that had never existed in the animal world and that have never, to any extent, been demonstrated to be primordial properties of the "spirit."

To approach human mental life from this angle entailed a radical reorganization of all the basic areas of psychology. Perception and memory, imagination and thought, emotional experience and voluntary action ceased to be considered natural functions of nervous tissue or simple properties of mental life. It became obvious that they have a highly complex structure and

---

*He made a special analysis of this crisis, but it has not been published.

that this structure has its own sociohistorical genesis and has acquired new functional attributes peculiar to man. Speech activity ceased to be regarded as an isolated process only indirectly connected with perception, attention, memory, and thought. It actually became possible to explain the processes of abstract thought and voluntary action scientifically. What had previously been considered isolated "functions" or even irresolvable properties now emerged as highly complex functional systems formed in the past and changing in the course of lifetime development. When communicating with adults, reorganizing his behavior on the basis of objective activity and speech, and gaining knowledge, a child not only acquires new forms of relationship to the external world but also works out new ways of regulating his behavior and establishes new functional systems enabling him to master new forms of perception and recall, new ways of thinking, and new methods of organizing voluntary actions.

Vygotsky's ideas radically altered our view of the nature and structure of mental processes. Fixed and immutable "mental functions" were transformed into complex and mobile functional systems that change during development; psychology emerged from its constricting naturalistic boundaries and became the science of the social formation of natural phenomena.

One question, however — perhaps the most essential one — remained open: How is the material substratum to be understood? What conceptions of the working of the brain should underlie our view of the material bases of mental activity?

The problem of localizing mental functions in the cerebral hemispheres (and the question of the cerebral bases of mental activity was formulated in precisely this way) underwent a period of acute crisis in the 1920s, reflecting to a large extent the general crisis in psychology. On the one hand, neurology continued to assert its naïve ideas of the localization of complex mental functions in limited areas of the cerebral cortex — ideas originally crystallized in the great discoveries of the 1870s. On the basis of the simplified views of mental functions then current in psychology, neurologists assumed that in addition to the cortical sensory and motor "centers," analogous centers could be found for more complex mental processes. As a result of the writings of Lissauer, Henschen, and Kleist, the idea of "perceptual centers," "calculational centers," and "conceptual centers" in the cerebral cortex did not seem the least bit extraordinary.

Naturally enough, however, these views of restricted localization gave rise to serious doubt. Aware of the complexity of human higher mental processes and taking into account the well-known clinical fact that they could be disrupted by injuries in widely varied locations, many neurologists assumed that complex forms of mental processes were the result of the activity of the brain as a whole. Some of these authors, adhering to the holistic viewpoint (Monakov, Grunbaum), under the noticeable influence of the Würzburg school of psychology, were indifferent to all attempts to examine more closely the cerebral apparatuses connected with higher forms of mental activity. Others, supporting Gestalt psychology (K. Goldstein), tried to construct a hypothesis of an excitation structure evenly distributed throughout the cortex and to see the basis of complex forms of human mental activity in these featureless "structural" processes. While accepting a restricted localization of elementary physiological processes in limited areas of the cortex, they rejected in practice all concrete analysis of the critical zones that take part in the execution of complex forms of human mental activity. "Revolving in a vicious circle of structural psychology," wrote Vygotsky, "examination of the localization of specifically human functions vacillates between the poles of extreme naturalism and extreme spiritualism" (loc. cit. P. 386).

The idea of higher mental functions as social in origin, systematic in structure, and dynamic in development, which Vygotsky took as his starting point, naturally could not be contained in the patterns described: a new, radically reorganized approach to their cerebral localization was required.

The fact that no mental function could be understood as a simple "property" of mental life forced, from the outset, rejection of the idea that higher nervous processes were represented in the cortex in the same way as elementary physiological "functions"; however, concrete ideas about their complex differentiated composition had already rendered fruitless the concept of the brain as a single, undifferentiated whole at the foundation of such functions.

The ideas that Vygotsky arrived at made him think that "localization of higher nervous functions can be understood only chronogenically, as the result of mental development," that the relationships characteristic of the separate parts of the brain that fulfill higher mental functions "are formed during the process of development," and that "the human brain possesses new localized principles compared with an animal's brain" (loc. cit. P. 382). This discovery required a much fuller and more concrete analysis of the functional organization of human mental processes, for without this all attempts at solving the problem of localization would be impossible.

In his earlier experiments (see his Izbrannyye psikhologicheskiye issledovaniya [Selected psychological investigations]. Moscow: APN RSFSR, 1956; and Razvitiye vysshikh psikhicheskikh funktziy) Vygotsky had already considered the fact that a child's mental development is not a simple maturing of natural "instincts," but occurs in the process of objective activity and communication with adults. The child masters the tools developed in human history and learns to make use of external means or signs to organize his own behavior. Whereas an animal's responses are produced by stimuli arising from its external or internal environment, a child's actions very quickly begin to be directed by signals he himself creates and obeys. The child's direction of his attention by means of his own speech signals and his organization of his activity through the regulation, first, of external and, later, of internal speech serve as examples of mediated organization of his mental processes. Only gradually does this overt activity, which relies on the external environment, contract and acquire a covert character, turning into those internal mental processes that can appear as simple and irresolvable "mental functions" but actually are the product of highly complex historical development.

Naturally such a mediated, "instrumental" type of behavior, which is peculiar to man and absent in animals, makes one assume a new principle in localizing higher mental processes as distinct from those forms of cerebrally organized behavior found in animals. This is why Vygotsky speaks of the role of "extracerebral connections" in localizing functions connected with specifically human areas of the brain (Razvitiye vysshikh psikhicheskikh funktziy. P. 391). These are formed in man's external activity, in the use of tools and external signs, which are so important to the formation of higher mental functions. Human practical activity is impossible to imagine without an objective, as is verbal thought without language and its external devices, speech sounds, letters, and logico-grammatical constructions, created in the course of social history.

Social history ties the knots that produce new correlations between certain zones of the cerebral cortex; and if the use of language and its phonetic codes gives rise to new functional relationships between the temporal (auditory) and kinesthetic (sensorimotor) areas of the cortex, then this is the product of historical development relying on "extracerebral connections" and forming new "functional organs" in the cerebral cortex (see A. N. Leont'ev, Problemy psikhicheskogo razvitiya [Problems of mental development]. Moscow: APN RSFSR, 1959).

However, the fact that in the course of history man has developed new functions does not mean that each such function relies on a new group of nerve cells and that new "centers" of higher nervous functions appear, such as those so eagerly sought by neurologists during the last third of the 19th century. The development of new "functional organs" occurs through the formation of new functional systems, which has never happened in animals and which is a means for the unlimited development of cerebral activity. The human cerebral cortex, thanks to this principle, becomes an organ of civilization in which are hidden boundless possibilities, and does not require new morphological apparatuses every time history creates the need for a new function.

The study of systematic localization of higher mental functions thus removes the contradiction between the ideas of restricted localization and notions of the brain as a single entity. Each specific function ceases to be thought of as the product of some

center; on the other hand, the function of the brain as a whole
ceases to be presented as the work of an undifferentiated and
uniform mass of nervous tissue. Both ideas have been replaced
by that of a system of highly differentiated cortical zones working simultaneously and accomplishing new tasks by means of
"intercenter" relations. These ideas, established by Vygotsky,
have provided the basis for the study of systematic or dynamic
functional localization that now, 30 years after the author's death,
have been thoroughly incorporated into modern science. (See
A. R. Luria, Vysshiye korkovyye funktzii cheloveka [The higher
cortical functions of man]. Moscow State University, 1962.)

One vital aspect of Vygotsky's study of systematic localization
of mental functions still requires concrete experimentation, however. This is the question of dynamic change in the correlation
of cerebral "centers" during development and disintegration,
which opens up new horizons for extended study of "chronogenic
localization" of functions in the cerebral cortex. Neurology had
never considered the possibility that the same functions could,
at different stages of development, be performed by different
parts of the cortex and that the interaction of different cortical
zones could vary at different stages of development. This is the
conclusion Vygotsky reached after careful study of the developmental pattern of higher mental functions in ontogenesis. This
was a completely new idea for neurology.

In tracing the early stages of ontogenesis, Vygotsky showed
that the first steps in forming higher mental functions depended
on more elementary processes that served as a base. Complex
concepts cannot be developed if there are insufficiently stable
sensory perceptions and ideas; voluntary recall cannot be
formed if there is no stable substratum of immediate memory.
In later stages of mental development, however, the relationship
between elementary and complex processes changes. Higher
mental functions developing on a base of elementary mental processes begin to influence the base, and even the simplest forms
of mental processes are reorganized under the influence of
higher mental activity; it is enough to recall the part played by
verbal classification in color perception to understand the full

depths of this process.

These facts compelled Vygotsky to assume that the relationship between separate cortical zones changes during development and that if, initially, the formation of "higher" centers depends on the maturity of the "lower," ultimately the "higher" organize and influence the "lower" in fully formed behavior. This inverse correlation of cortical areas at different stages of development, according to Vygotsky's theory, means that injury to one particular cortical area may lead to extremely different syndromes at different stages. If injury to the cortical zones in question in the early stages of development leads to underdevelopment of the higher sections forming on this base, after maturity it is the lower systems dependent on these zones that are affected by injury. This assumption makes it clear that injury to the gnostic zones of the cortex in early childhood leads to general mental underdevelopment, and that in an adult it produces isolated symptoms of agnosia that can — within certain limits — be compensated for by the undamaged higher systems of the cortex.

The assumption that a change occurs in relations between centers in subsequent stages of ontogenesis added a new dimension to the study of dynamic localization of mental functions; but only the next generation of investigators will be able to estimate the full import of this brilliant theory.

Vygotsky's research of the late 1920s on the development of higher mental functions, the changes occurring in them under abnormal conditions, and their disintegration in the presence of cerebral injury laid the foundations for a new area of science, neuropsychology, which has only recently become established. His last work, published posthumously, "Psychology and the localization of mental functions" (notes for a lecture he was fated never to deliver), was the first and most comprehensive program for investigating the functional organization of the human brain, the organ of human consciousness.

This was one of the greatest contributions to science of that outstanding investigator L. S. Vygotsky.

Translated by
William M. Mandel

A. R. Luria and E. Yu. Artem'eva

TWO APPROACHES TO AN EVALUATION OF THE RELIABILITY OF PSYCHOLOGICAL INVESTIGATIONS
(Reliability of a Fact and Syndrome Analysis)*

1

A psychologist faced with the problem of ensuring the necessary degree of reliability of a fact he has discovered usually proceeds along a scientifically well-established path. He defines the problem, isolates the relevant area of investigation, finds a procedure adequate to the problem, and collects the number of cases necessary to ensure the reliability of the discovered fact. The criterion of reliability in these cases is the amount of data the investigator has at hand and the amount of variability in the results obtained. It is generally accepted that when the facts at hand are completely homogeneous, a relatively small number of experiments is sufficient to ensure reliability, whereas if the variability of the obtained data is relatively great, the number of observations required to ensure the statistical reliability of

---

*This paper was prepared for presentation at the XIXth International Congress of Psychology, held July 27-August 2, 1969, in London, and was obtained by the editor directly from Professor Luria. It reflects one of the primary concerns of the psychology group at Moscow University — the need to increase mathematical sophistication in the conduct of psychological research. — Ed.

a fact must be increased considerably.

However, this procedure, which is classical for almost all spheres of science, is not the only one; and there are numerous fields in which this classical procedure is inapplicable. One of these is clinical psychology; another is a new branch of psychology, namely, neuropsychology.

Neuropsychology is concerned with the analysis of cerebral mechanisms of mental processes, and its primary subject matter is the case in which circumscribed local brain lesions cause specific changes in mental processes. An analysis of patients with local brain lesions has established that the temporal region of the left hemisphere plays an essential role in ensuring complex forms of verbal (phonemic) hearing; that the parieto-occipital region of the left hemisphere is involved in the synthesis of incoming visual and tactile impressions into simultaneous spatial structures and in the formation of complex forms of verbal (symbolic) syntheses; and that the frontal lobe is intimately involved in the programming and regulation of human behavior.

However, a fundamental difficulty always arises in any neuropsychological investigation. A neuropsychologist always deals with a relatively small number of cases. For example, a relatively "clean" local lesion of a certain brain area that does not involve neighboring zones of the cerebral cortex and is not accompanied by general cerebral disturbances is so unlikely that it is effectively impossible to ensure the reliability of an observation by accumulating an amount of reproducible material that is statistically sufficient.

Does this circumstance preclude the possibility of the neuropsychologist's obtaining reliable facts, so that neuropsychology must be relegated to the fate of a descriptive branch of knowledge that can never approach the reliability of a genuine scientific investigation?

To accept this view would be to renounce any attempt to find scientific means of acquiring reliable knowledge in an entire, important sphere of science.

There are numerous important considerations that convince us that such a view is totally unwarranted and that the reliability of a neuropsychological investigation, as of any clinical investigation, can, indeed, be ensured, albeit in a totally different way, which is a function of the very nature of this sphere of knowledge.

A neuropsychological investigation is based on the premise that any mental activity is a complex functional system reflecting the joint activity of a whole group of cerebral (and in the first instance, cortical) zones, and that every area of the brain has its own highly specific function, which plays a necessary and specific role in the effective performance of complex forms of mental activity. From this premise we may infer that by disrupting this role, a lesion of any area of the brain gives rise to an immediate primary defect, which in turn produces a series of secondary or systemic disorders and disturbs the normal process of that form of mental activity in which this functional system was active.

Thus, as we have already demonstrated elsewhere (A. R. Luria, 1967, 1962, 1966, and others),* a lesion of the cortex of the left temporal region results directly in the disturbance of complex forms of verbal (phonemic) hearing, which is a primary symptom of such a lesion. However, disturbance of phonemic sound necessarily entails a disturbance of all forms of verbal activity, which is impossible without the participation of intact verbal hearing. Consequently, these patients are necessarily unable to perceive speech addressed to them with adequate clarity, to name objects without error, or to write, although mental processes that do not involve phonemic hearing (e.g., written calculations, spatial orientation) remain intact.

The same holds true for lesions of the left parieto-occipital region of the cortex. The structure of this region, which is an "area of overlapping" of cortical sections of the visual, auditory, tactile, and vestibular analyzers, makes it an important apparatus for the synthesis of successive incoming impressions into simultaneous spatial structures, thereby ensuring, as an eminent neurologist phrased it, the possibility "of unifying isolated stim-

---

*References were not supplied in the manuscript we received from Professor Luria. — Ed.

uli into a simultaneous whole" and "of converting a consecutive
review into a simultaneous panorama." Hence it is natural that
when this section of the cerebral cortex is damaged, the possibility of relying on such "simultaneous spatial structures" van-
ishes; and the patient begins to experience notable difficulties in
orienting himself in the perceived space, in distinguishing between right and left, or in simultaneously comprehending the
spatial relationships among a group of objects. This defect is
an immediate, primary result of the particular lesion.

However, such a lesion unavoidably leads to secondary or systemic disorders of all types of mental activity that are not able
to take place without simultaneous synthesis. Consequently, patients with a lesion of the parieto-occipital region of the left
hemisphere are not able to decipher a geographical map or geo-
metrical patterns, whatever their complexity. They begin to experience serious difficulties in mental computations and are no
longer able to comprehend logico-grammatical constructions
exhibiting a complex system of relationships (A. R. Luria, 1947,
1962, 1966). These difficulties are a secondary or systemic result of a primary focal lesion, and processes that are not incorporated into such "instantaneous spatial structures" remain intact in these cases. An analysis of primary defects from local
brain lesions and of their relationship to secondary systemic
disorders is also the paramount method of neuropsychology, by
virtue of which a neuropsychologist is able to describe the set
of symptoms or "syndrome" of mental disorders resulting from
the local brain lesion.

This method of "syndrome analysis" of brain lesions, which
essentially reproduces the method employed in any clinical investigation, is of prime significance: it is a second method of
ensuring the reliability of an observed fact, and can be ranked
on a par with the first method — the classical method — with
which we began our discussion.

There are many features of this method that are quite unique
and that render it fundamentally different from the first, classical method.

In itself, a "primary symptom" does not exhibit any signifi-

cance and can have many causes. An elevated body temperature
may be the result of any one of dozens of causes, and does not
in itself indicate an underlying infection, intoxication, or other
phenomenon. Even less does the high temperature have a causal
association with any specific system of the organism. A physician can advance a hypothesis as to the nature of a disease and
suggest a sufficiently probable analysis of it only by correlating
an elevated temperature with a whole series of other symptoms.

The difficulties a patient with an as-yet-unknown brain lesion
experiences in repeating closely similar phonemes (such as b
and p, or d and t) suggest that these difficulties can be traced to
a disturbance in phonemic hearing. However, the plausibility of
this hypothesis is very slight. Indeed, the difficulties experienced by a patient in repeating similar phonemes can with equal
probability be caused by difficulty in switching from one pho-
neme to the other, by defects in articulation, by general inactivity, etc. The observed symptom itself is always amenable to
many interpretations, and its definitive significance can finally
be established only by comparing it with other symptoms or, in
other words, by "syndrome analysis." Thus, if a patient experiencing difficulties in repeating similar phonemes also exhibits
the same difficulties in writing them or in discriminating word
meanings, confuses similar-sounding words, has trouble in
naming objects, or makes phonemic mistakes in selecting words,
without, however, showing any signs of a pathological inertness
in movements, difficulties in articulation, or diminished activity,
it is much more probable that the observed syndrome is a manifestation of an underlying disturbance in phonemic hearing.

The same holds for the second example given above.

A disturbance in spatial orientation is not sufficiently reliable
grounds by itself for postulating a lesion of the parieto-occipital
sections of the brain. This syndrome may be the result of memory disorder, defects in programming of the patient's activity,
inactivity from which the patient becomes increasingly susceptible to any direct stimulus, etc. The significance of a hypothesized lesion of parieto-occipital brain systems is substantially
enhanced only after the neuropsychologist turns to an analysis

of other types of mental activity and discovers that the patient is able to perform without difficulty tasks not requiring intact spatial patterns, retains adequate goal-directedness and activity, has an intact verbal memory, but experiences difficulties in perceptual and in motor and symbolic processes that require intact spatial patterns for their fulfillment.

This means that neither a description of a single symptom in one patient nor its repeated observation in a large number of patients increases reliability in the analysis of a fact under study. A single symptom is always open to multiple interpretations (A. R. Luria & M. Yu. Rapoport, 1964), and the necessary reliability can be ensured only through syndrome analysis.

Consequently, a neuropsychologist (in contrast to a psychophysiologist and general psychologist) is seldom able to eschew a careful study of "secondary" symptoms not directly related to the object of his study. On the contrary, he makes such a <u>comparison of a whole group of processes (some disturbed, some intact) the primary method of his investigation; moreover, the greater the number of such symptoms, whether negatively or positively correlated, he has at his disposal, the greater is the reliability of his hypothesis.</u>

It would be erroneous to think that a comparison of interrelated symptoms and syndrome analysis, which is the chief method of neuropsychology, can only increase the probability of an accurate local diagnosis of a lesion.

The main value of this method lies in the fact that it allows one to go from a description of the clinical picture of a patient's disorders to an analysis of the fundamental conditions or <u>factors</u> behind the observed group of symptoms.

However, such a "factor analysis," which is conducted on one patient by correlating a large number of symptoms and which substantially increases the reliability of a hypothesis, is not limited to a simple description of the observed symptoms. This method can be utilized to its fullest only by a qualitative analysis of those symptoms that exhibit a maximum correlation and are necessarily associated with each other.

As we already indicated in one of the examples above, if a

lesion of the parieto-occipital section of the left hemisphere inevitably gives rise to symptomatology that includes disordered
spatial orientation, considerable difficulties in calculation, and
disturbances in the comprehension of complex logico-grammatical structures, the investigator can assume with high probability
that all these disorders conceal a <u>common factor</u> that is directly
involved with the function of posterior sections of the cerebral
cortex and that breaks down when they are injured. A precise
characterization of this factor requires a psychological analysis
or, in other words, a careful study of the disturbed processes
and an attempt to find some common constituents without which
these processes could not run their normal course. In the example we have given, an investigation made it possible to isolate
the factor responsible for <u>formation of simultaneous spatial patterns or relationships</u>; moreover, this factor is disclosed by a
qualitative analysis of each of the processes enumerated and is
corroborated by the necessary appearance of the entire group
of symptoms described for a circumscribed local brain lesion.

This illustrates a close similarity between the method of
"syndrome analysis" and the method of "factor analysis," which
is widely used in psychology. However, the procedures used in
the former are fundamentally different and permit a high degree
of reliability to be achieved with a comparatively small number
of cases — sometimes even a single case.

2

After pointing out that syndrome analysis can considerably increase the reliability of a psychological investigation and pave
the way for isolation of "factors" even when the number of subjects is small, we should give a more precise formulation of the
formal foundations of such a possibility. It would be desirable
to employ a procedure for evaluating reliability of inferences
that would most fully reflect the formal aspects of the logic
evolved by a clinician or neuropsychologist in many years of
practice. A convenient instrument for such a procedure would
appear to be some modification of Bayes's formula by which the

a posteriori probabilities of a hypothesis after the occurrence of a certain event are evaluated:

Let A_1, A_2, A_3, ..., A_n be a system of nonintersecting hypotheses constituting in their totality a reliable event; B, an event that either may or may not occur empirically; $P(A_1)$, $P(A_2)$, ..., $P(A_n)$, a priori probabilities of the hypotheses; and $P(B/A_1)$, ..., $(P(B/A_n)$, the probabilities that event B will occur if the corresponding hypothesis is true.

Then

$$P(A_1/B) = \frac{P(A_i B)}{P(B)}$$

$$= \frac{P(B/A_i)\, P(A_i)}{P(B)}$$

$$= \frac{P(B/A_i)\, P(A_i)}{\sum\limits_{j=1}^{n} P(B/A_j)\, P(A_j)} \tag{1}$$

We will use the Bayes approach to discuss two different but interrelated problems of neuropsychology:

(1) knowing a set of manifest symptoms, to evaluate the reliability of an inference concerning the location of a lesion;

(2) knowing the location of a lesion, to distinguish a set of symptoms forming the essential factors of which a syndrome is constituted. This problem seems to be very closely associated with the detection of a set of symptoms necessary for an optimum increase in the probability of a hypothesis concerning an actual location.

Let us turn to a solution of the first problem.

Again, assume A — a hypothesis concerning lesion location,

A — a hypothesis of any other location,

B_1, ..., B_n — observed symptoms,

C_1, ..., C_m — factors responsible for the symptoms,

D_1, ..., D_k — a factor-ensemble: factors on the next level of generality, perhaps already unequivocally associated with the lesion.

. . .

Let us construct a hierarchical procedure for establishing the reliability of the hypothesis A of location; first, we determine the reliability of the existence of the factors underlying the symptoms (the roots of the symptoms) and then the reliability of uniting the factors into a factor-ensemble corresponding to the given lesion and the reliability of the location hypothesis itself.

Let the actually observed symptoms known to us be

$B_1, \ldots, B_n$

  C — the hypothetical factor,

  $\overline{C}$ — all other factors that can explain the symptoms,

  $P(C)$ — the probability of how often the given factor occurs,

  $P(B_i/C)$ — the probability that symptom B_i occurs if the hypothetical factor C occurs (as a rule, $P(B_i/C) = 1$),

  $P(B_i/\overline{C})$ — the probability of a symptom's appearing jointly with other factors.

The probability $P(C)$ and $P(B_i/\overline{C})$, generally speaking, must be determined from records; but, as will be shown below, in most cases very rough estimations of the type "symptom B_i occurs jointly with factor C less often than without it" (the type familiar to every empirical researcher) are sufficient to establish reliability. Since at this stage of observation we employ independent tests and do not know whether B_i and B_j are associated or not, we assume their independence in the aggregate of sets of outcomes corresponding to C and $\overline{C}$, which is the assumption least favorable to our hypothesis.

 Then

$$P_0(C) = P(C)$$

$$P_1(C) = \frac{P(B_1/C) \cdot P(C)}{P(B_1/C) \cdot P(C) + P(B_1/\overline{C})\,(1 - P(C))}$$

$$P_2(C) = \frac{P(B_1/C) \cdot P(B_2/C)\, P(C)}{P(B_1/C)\, P(B_2/C)\, P(C) + P(B_1/\overline{C})\, P(B_2/\overline{C})\,(1 - P(C))} \quad (2)$$

$$\ldots\ldots\ldots\ldots\ldots\ldots\ldots\ldots\ldots\ldots\ldots\ldots\ldots\ldots$$

$$P_n(C) = \frac{P(B_1/C)\, P(B_2/C), \ldots, P(B_n/C)\, P(C)}{P(B_1/C)\, P(B_2/C), \ldots, P(B_n/C)\, P(C) + P(B_1/\overline{C})\, P(B_2/\overline{C}), \ldots, P(B_n/\overline{C})\,(1 - P(C)).}$$

Let us examine a numerical example illustrating a readjustment of the probability of the hypothesis postulating the presence of factor C:

Let $P(C) = 0.5$, $P(B_i/C) = 1$, $P(B_i/\overline{C}) = 0.5$, with B_1, B_2, ...,
B_{10} occurring empirically,

$$P_0(C) = 0.5$$

$$P_1(C) = \frac{0.5}{0.5 + 0.25} = 0.7$$

$$P_2(C) = \frac{0.7}{0.7 + 0.3 \cdot 0.5} \approx 0.82$$

$$P_3(C) = \frac{0.82}{0.82 + 0.18 \cdot 0.5} \approx 0.9$$

$$P_4(C) = \frac{0.9}{0.9 + 0.1 \cdot 0.5} \approx 0.94$$

$$P_5(C) = \frac{0.94}{0.94 + 0.03} \approx 0.997.$$

After the hypotheses postulating the presence of factors have been tested, or at least after $P(C/B_1, ..., B_n)$ have been found, we pass to a discussion of the reliability of the hypothesis A itself, postulating location.

Let A be our hypothesis, and C_1, ..., C_m factors. If $P(A)$, $P(C_i/A)$, $P(C_i/\overline{A})$ are known, then analogous to formula (2)

$$P_m(A) = \frac{P(C_1/A), ..., P(C_m/A) \, P(A)}{P(C_1/A), ..., P(C_m/A) \cdot P(A) + P(C_1/\overline{A}), ..., P(C_m/\overline{A}) \, P(\overline{A})}. \quad (3)$$

Here, since C_1, ..., C_m have a probability near but not equal to unity, the true reliability (let us call it α) of the inference is somewhat lower than that which we obtained. Actually,

$$\alpha = P_m(A) \, P(C_1/B_1, ..., B_n), ..., P(C_n/B_1, ..., B_n). \quad (4)$$

If the number of factors is relatively small and they are reliable to 99.9%, error is negligible; and a correction for $P_m(A)$ is unnecessary ($\alpha \approx P_m(A)$). If, however, $P(C_i/B_1, ..., B_n)$ is far from unity, a correction is necessary.

If the factors are not independent, but combinations of factor-ensembles appear, the true reliability is even greater since in this case

$$P(A/C_1, \ldots, C_m) = \frac{P(C_1, \ldots, C_m/A) \cdot P(A)}{P(C_1, \ldots, C_m/A) \cdot P(A) + P(C_1, \ldots, C_m/\overline{A}) \, P(\overline{A}) \geq P_m(A)}.$$

We observe that our approach differs from the well-known idea of calculating the probability of a disease when symptoms assumed to be independent are manifested. Without speaking of the difficulties in establishing the initial values and in the interpretation of the results of such a calculation, its results are weaker than those examined here. Let us illustrate this with a numerical example.

Assume that two symptoms B_1 and B_2 are observed and that it is known that they can be explained (or perhaps cannot be explained) by one factor, C. The reliability of location A must be determined with a significance of 90%. Assume that

$$P(A) = 0.5 \quad P(B_i/A) = 1 \quad P(C/A) = 1 \quad P(B/C) = 1$$
$$P(C) = 0.8 \quad P(B_i/\overline{A}) = 0.6 \quad P(C/\overline{A}) = 0.05 \quad P(B_i/\overline{C}) = 0.45$$

then $P(B_i/\overline{C})$ can no longer be assigned arbitrarily, but must be compatible with the other probabilities.

Then

$$P(C/B_1B_2) \approx 0.995$$
$$P(A/C) \approx 0.952$$
$$\alpha = 0.952 \cdot 0.995 \approx 0.947$$

i.e., A is, practically speaking, reliable (90% significance).

Let us now find $P(A/B_1B_2)$ by assuming independent symptoms.

$$\alpha = P(A/B_1B_2) \approx 0.74,$$

and the inference cannot yet be considered significant at the 90% level.

We now pass to the second type of problem a neuropsychologist faces. Assume that only one patient is observed and that the location A of the lesion and the set of symptoms $B_1, \ldots, B_n$ detected by a specific set of tests are known. It is desirable to isolate adequately a set of factors circumscribing the lesion. Assume that such a problem can be solved as follows: the symptoms are concretely analyzed, as a result of which the assumed set of factors $C_1, \ldots, C_m$ is elucidated and estimates of $P(B_i/C_j)$, $P(B_i/\overline{C}_j)$ are obtained. As in the first problem, $P(C_j/B_1, \ldots, B_n)$ are calculated by formulas analogous to (2);

and α, the reliability of the location A, is found.

$$\alpha = P(C_1), \ldots, P(C_m) \frac{P(C_1, \ldots, C_m/A)\, P(A)}{P(C_1, \ldots, C_m/A) \cdot P(A) + P(C_1, \ldots, C_m/\overline{A})\, P(\overline{A})}.$$

If the estimated frequencies of occurrence of the sets of factors elsewhere than at the given location are known, the sets of
factors and their specific interrelation (see the sets A and $\overline{A}$),
which together optimize the tendency of α toward unity, can be
found. These sets and this interrelationship are the best coor-
dinates for detecting a lesion and, consequently, are in some
sense its best descriptive characteristics and factor-ensembles.
Then the sets of symptoms and their interrelations, which give
the optimal increase in probability $P(C_j/B1, \ldots, Bn)$, can reasonably be assumed to be the symptomatology of the factor C_j,
and the combination of such sets for all C_j in the factor-ensembles
to be the symptomatology of a lesion in the particular location.

Translated by
Michel Vale

A. R. Luria and L. S. Tzvetkova

DISTURBANCE OF INTELLECTUAL FUNCTIONS IN PATIENTS WITH FRONTAL LOBE LESIONS

It is well known that lesions of the posterior (parieto-occipital) and frontal lobes of the brain lead to structurally disparate disturbances in intellectual functions.

Whereas in patients with posterior (parieto-occipital) lobe lesions the orienting basis of intellectual activity is preserved and only individual intellectual functions (such as the possibility of simultaneous comparison of different descriptions) are disturbed, patients with frontal lobe lesions exhibit a contrary picture. Individual functions are potentially preserved, but the orienting basis of an intellectual act is often affected, and the selectivity of intellectual processes governed by a particular program is disrupted [1, 2].

We have previously restricted outselves to an analysis of disturbances in solving arithmetic problems. In the present report we shall explore disturbances manifested in another type of intellectual function, i.e., those involved in outlining and recounting a written text. Particular attention has been given to an analysis of the orienting basis of this type of activity.

The patients were presented with a relatively simple text. They were to read it through and recount it orally. Then they were asked to outline their recitation. Thus they were placed in a situation that required a special orientation toward the con-

From Voprosy psikhologii, 1967, 13(4), 102-106.

ceptual structure of the text. For a control, the same patients were asked to relate some event in their lives and to outline this account.

The study involved a comparative analysis of patients with parieto-occipital or with frontal lobe lesions.

It is recognized that work with a written text, like other intellectual tasks, demonstrates the most essential aspects of an intellectual act. For a coherent account of any event, it is first necessary to set out certain ideational points of reference to establish the pattern of narration; then the individual episodes must be distinguished and coordinated with each other, showing their interrelatedness. This preliminary analytic-synthetic activity is immediately transformed into a detailed narrative.

The construction of an outline of a perused text represents the most complicated requirements for the orienting basis of an intellectual act. To compose such an outline it is necessary to divert one's attention from the direct exposition of the material and to break the text down into its ideational components. Each of these components acts as an ideational reference point in constructing an outline. These points may be delineated only in the final result of an active, conscious process to extract the essential point of the material (A. A. Smirnov [4]). All these processes (breaking down the text into components, isolating the ideational points of reference in the text, and determining the points of primary and secondary importance and the relationship between them) are the principal elements in any intellectual activity.

The analysis of a text according to its ideational components and the extraction of the main thought from each of these, i.e., the ability to ignore unessential details, is an active process requiring a preliminary orientation to the material and the maintenance of a goal-directed, analytic-synthetic activity.

In our study we found that in work with a written text, as in the solution of arithmetic problems (see reference 3), the disturbance of the process reveals sharp differences between patients of the two test groups.

Patients with frontal lobe lesions exhibited striking defects in work with a written text.

These defects were already apparent in the simple <u>recounting of the perused text</u>.

Descriptive texts containing several trains of thought were often recounted fragmentarily by these patients: only isolated, sometimes unrelated, facts were presented. They were unable to discern the chief thought of the text, to distinguish a unified pattern of exposition; and sometimes they included in their account incidental associations that occurred to them while reading and consequently were unable to give a unified, consistent presentation of the perused material.

The disturbances characteristic of these patients were also manifested when they recounted relatively simple narrative texts: sometimes these narrations followed the text very closely, often the individual fragments of the exposition were unrelated, and sometimes the sequence of the exposition was interrupted by incidental associations that occurred to the patients as they read the text.

A careful analysis showed that all these defects were attributable to the fact that these patients did not make a special effort to analyze the ideational structure of the text; the exposition followed the formal plan of the text, rather than an outline formulated by the patients. This was especially noticeable when the patient was asked <u>to make his own outline</u> of narration first and then to relate its content. Often the patient was totally incapable of performing such a task.

> For example, patient Bog. (56 years old, higher education, senior scientific assistant) had been admitted to a rehabilitation course after removal of a tumor from a posterior area of the left frontal lobe. The patient clearly manifested a frontal lobe (posterior area) syndrome, with inactivity, lack of spontaneity, clumsy perseverations, and inertness of stereotypes occurring in the motor and the speech apparatus. The patient was asked to read and recount orally a story by G. Skrebitzkiy and V. Chaplin, "Look out the window." The patient al-

most word for word recounted the content of this story,
but was completely unable to outline it.

When asked to formulate an outline of the story, the patient said: "Outline ... well ... yes ... the first point, that
is ... of course! The first is ... look out the window ...
(pause) ... well, and then the second is — look out the window (laughs) and there you will see ... the whole window
is decorated with white designs and the trees also ..."
(then the patient again glided off into a simple exposition
of the story's content).

Patient Urb. (30 years old, secondary education) underwent several operations in 1960-63. First a tumor (oli-
godendroglioma) in the anterior area of the right frontal
lobe was removed; this was followed by extirpation of a
tumor from the posterior area of the right frontal lobe;
and finally, another tumor in the posterior-medial area
of the left frontal lobe was removed.

This patient, like the previous one, was able to com-
municate the content of stories quite accurately, in great
detail. For example, he had no difficulty in recounting
L. N. Tolstoy's story "The eagle"; but he failed completely in his attempts to outline the story. To the tester's
questions "How did the story begin? What was the main
thought in the first part of the text?" the patient answered,
"About an eagle and his nest." When asked to give an outline of the story, the patient immediately passed to a
simple recounting of the text: "Next the people simply
took away his fish, the devils, and went away. The eagle
is our tsar, and that's the way they treated him! He flew
back to his young without the fish, and there they were
peeping, asking for something to eat; but the eagle was
tired...," etc. (Extract from report of July 12, 1963.)

Analogous difficulties were observed in patients of this group
when they attempted to narrate some known or experienced
event. They were able to narrate a known episode or series of
episodes, but they were unable to formulate a preliminary out-

line; and they were incapable of relating a story in accordance
with an outline. Hence, to write a composition on a slightly
known theme requiring preliminary reflection and the construction of a basic plan of exposition was completely beyond the ca-
pabilities of these patients.

> The same patient Bog. related a journey to the South.
> "I traveled to the South. The South, the land of plenty,
> beautiful country. Yes, I went there. There grow the
> plane trees, beeches, hornbeam, rosalia . . . there is the
> sea. Where you can bathe and get a tan . . . ," etc. This,
> however, is the outline he made for this same story.
> "(1) The South is a land of the sun. (2) The South is the
> land of happiness. (3) My journey (pause) . . . that's all."
> In response to a request for a more detailed outline from
> the moment of departure, the patient wrote: "(1) My jour-
> ney to the South. (2) My journey to the land of plenty.
> (3) My journey . . . (pause) . . . that's all."
> Further attempts to encourage the patient to make an
> outline were fruitless.
> The same phenomena was observed in patient Bor. (50
> years old, secondary-school teacher), who had had a tu-
> mor removed from the left temporal lobe in 1963. When
> asked to relate something about the North, she said: "The
> North means the cold and lack of fruit . . . that's all; what's
> more . . . " (pause). When requested to relate something
> more detailed, she retorted: "Well, what are more de-
> tails? . . . I simply can't . . . I will tell about Shadrinsk; I
> lived there and know the place, but don't know how to tell
> about it . . . There is much snow, severe frost . . . there are
> difficulties with water . . . you must wait your turn for a
> bath . . . there are many dogs . . . every house has a mean
> dog . . . the houses are of wood. They fell trees. That's all."

Thus, when working with a written text, as when solving arithmetic problems, patients with frontal lobe lesions are incapable of isolating essential relationships and cannot compose a

preliminary outline. The orienting basis of intellectual activity leading to the construction of a plan for further exposition is profoundly disturbed in these patients.

Patients with parieto-occipital lesions displayed a totally different syndrome.

In contrast to patients with frontal lobe lesions, patients of this group exhibited pronounced defects in both the nominative function of speech and in its logico-syntactical structure. This is sharply reflected in the detailed narrative speech of the patients. Sometimes they have difficulty in constructing a sentence, and even more in constructing an entire coherent narrative. For this reason, these patients experienced considerable difficulty in fulfilling the task of reciting a perused text. But in contrast to patients with frontal lobe lesions, they managed a story outline with relative ease. Even though they still exhibited the described speech defects, they were aware of the central point in each ideational unit, frequently expressed this in two or three words, and were able to formulate an outline, although with considerable speech difficulties.

> Patient Bub. (39 years old, higher education), with residual symptoms of thromboembole in the left medial cerebral artery and a syndrome of gross semantic aphasia, spatial disorientation, acalculia, and defective oral expression, was examined by the same procedure. After several attempts to give a coherent account of the content of a story about the adventures of Odysseus, the patient was still unable to fulfill this task. However, he quite rapidly composed a precise outline of the story, consisting of the following points: "(1) Odysseus — a brave and clever man; (2) The journey of Odysseus; (3) His encounter with Cyclops; (4) Scylla and Charybdis; (5) Odysseus and the people." (Extracts from report of January 12, 1963.)

The same phenomenon was observed in patient L., who had had an arachnoid endothelioma removed from the left occipital parasagittal area in 1961, after which a syndrome of spatial disorientation, pronounced semantic and anamnestic aphasia, and acalculia persisted.

The patient was asked to tell about a journey to the South. She experienced considerable difficulty in fulfilling the task. "In the South ... it is hot ... there is ... vegetation ... especially southern ... there ... it ... Oh! Good heavens! Really, I know all about it; I've seen it ... but I can't say anything. There are tropical plants ... and ... and there are ... people live ... there ... Oh! I can't!" (refusal).

The speech of the patient was interrupted by pauses and accompanied by pronounced emotional responses.

But when asked to make an outline of the story, the patient wrote, formulating each point with difficulty: (1) Departure from Moscow; (2) Sketch of the landscape along the way; (3) Approaching southern regions; (4) Characteristics of nature and the beauty of the South; (5) Return home.

Analogous phenomena were observed in her attempts to cope with an outline for a story on a theme based on her personal experience. For example, when she was asked to make an outline of a story on the theme "The North" she said: "First, how it all began ... this ... How should I say it? ... well, anyway ... the excursion, no ... no ... no excursion, the preparation for departure to the North. And then, the second point, well ... the beginning ... how should I say it? Well, let's say the beginning of the journey. The next point ... that we ... no ... well, yes, I have it, the interesting things met along the way. Next, arrival, so, then ... the forests. No, that's not what I mean, I want to tell about ... no, about the arrival in the North. How beautiful it is, different from where we live, unusual ... this can be expressed in the outline as ... northern beauty. And then ... who lives there, what's the correct way to say it? The inhabitants of the North, right? And now, something must be said about the animals," etc. (Extract from report of February 25, 1962.)

The data obtained demonstrate quite convincingly the essence
of the difficulties experienced by patients with parieto-occipital
lesions and make it possible to establish the fundamental differences in the intellectual processes of patients with parieto-
occipital and of those with frontal lobe lesions. Whereas in patients with parieto-occipital lesions the orienting basis of intellectual activity remains intact and the main defects are associated with disturbances in the ability to formulate the subject
verbally, patients with frontal lobe lesions retain this ability,
and the main defect is found in a disturbance of the orienting
basis of intellectual activity and the ability to program that activity, i.e., to extract a system of ideational relationships as a
guide for subsequent exposition.

References

1. Luria, A. R. [Disturbance of the structure of an action in
frontal lobe lesions]. Dokl. APN RSFSR, 1962, No. 5.
2. Luria, A. R., & Khomskaya, Ye. D. [Disturbance of intellectual operations in posterior lobe lesions]. Dokl. APN
RSFSR, 1962, No. 6.
3. Luria, A. R., & Tzvetkova, L. S. [Neuropsychological
analysis of problem solving by patients with local brain dam-
age]. Moscow: "Prosveshchenie" Publishers, 1966.
4. Smirnov, A. A. [Psychological memoirs]. Moscow: APN
RSFSR, 1946.

A. R. Luria and L. S. Tzvetkova

NEUROPSYCHOLOGICAL ANALYSIS OF THE PREDICATIVE STRUCTURE OF UTTERANCES

A few years ago, one of the authors (A. R. Luria, 1947, 1948, 1962, 1963) described a special form of speech disorder, oc-curring as a result of local injury to a posterior area of the left frontal lobe, that he called dynamic aphasia.

This speech disorder is very similar to the speech adynamia noted by early investigators (Kleist, 1930, 1934; Pick, 1905; and others), and could be described as follows: The patient retains the motor and sensory components of speech and can easily name objects and repeat words and even sentences, but is to-tally unable to utter independent, expanded statements. His ac-tive speech is manifestly disturbed. When the major part of the above-mentioned brain area is damaged, the patient is unable to construct even simple phrases. In less severe cases various difficulties arise as soon as the patient attempts to compose a coherent story, describe a situation, or employ speech in an oral conversation.

Although comprehension remains as fully intact as motor speech, the patient is unable to use speech for spontaneous com-munication and thus, for all practical purposes, is without speech. When he is asked to describe a picture or relate a story, he makes unsuccessful attempts, saying: "Yes ... and ...

From A. A. Leont'ev (Ed.) Teoriya rechevoy deyatel'nosti [The theory of verbal activity]. 1968. Pp. 219-33.

how should I say it? ... what the devil! ... No, I don't know ..."
[da ... i ... kak by eto skazat' ... chert voz'mi ... net ya ne znayu].

We recall a patient with a bullet wound in the lower part of
the posterior area of the left frontal lobe who tried to compose
an oral composition on the subject "The North." After 10 min
of unsuccessful attempts, he was able to say only: "There are
bears in the North." With further encouragement, he added:
"Which I shall tell you about."

Another patient with an analogous syndrome who attempted to
present a more elaborate composition on the subject "The
North" proved to be totally incapable of doing so and solved the
problem by reciting Lermontov's well-known poem "In the Wild
North."

The syndrome of dynamic aphasia does exist, but its detailed
mechanisms are still unclear. The purpose of the present experiment was to attempt to collate certain data for an analysis
of the disorders underlying this type of speech defect.

The Problem

Let us begin with a few examples of disorders of active
speech in patients with dynamic aphasia; only then will we be
able to formulate a hypothesis and set up a series of experiments to verify it.

Patient Mor (Institute of Neurosurgery, case history
No. 36309) (aneurism of the left anterior cerebral artery
and hemorrhage in the posterior central region of the left
hemisphere).

The patient was asked to relate the history of his illness. "Well ... what the devil ... I ... oh ... no ... this is
terrible ... painful ... no ... (3'35"). [Nu ... chert voz'mi
... ya ... o ... net ... eto uzhasno ... eto gore ... net ...]

Tell us, please, where you live, what you do, and how
old you are. "I ... oh ... well ... I can't ... simply can't."
[Ya ... ok ... vot ... ne mogu ... nikak.]

When the patient was asked specific questions and the

experimenter prompted him, the patient was able to complete the answers.

Where do you work? "Oh...well..." [O...da] I work. "I work as a groom." [Ya rabotayu konyukhom.] How old are you? — "Well...how is it?" — [Vot...kak eto?] I am..."I am 28!" [Mne 28!]

Where do you live? - - -"I live...I live..." [Zhivu... zhivu.] I live... — "I live in the country." [Ya shivu v derevne.] What do horses do in the country? — "O... well...well..." [O...da...da] They work in...They haul... — "Hay." [Travu.]

Who loads the hay in the cart? "The workers." [Rabochiye.] Who pulls the wagon? "The horses." [Loshadi.] What is in the cart? "Hay..." [Trava.]

It is clear that the patient was incapable of composing a phrase, but had no difficulties in finishing a sentence begun by the investigator.

What is the nature of the basic defect leading to a disturbance in spontaneous speech? It is difficult to give a name to this defect. This speech disturbance is not based on a defect in nomination: the patient has no difficulties in naming objects. Nor is there a defect in activity: the patient actively attempts to find the required speech construction, as is clearly manifested in his affective reactions to his own incapacity.

What mechanism could underlie this disturbance?

Disorders in Predicative Functions

There is evidence to indicate that a defect in the predicative functions of speech lies at the basis of this disorder. As Vygotsky pointed out many years ago, the process that begins with a thought and terminates with an expanded statement has an intermediate stage of inner speech that is abbreviated in form and predicative in structure (L. S. Vygotsky, 1934). He hypothesized that inner speech is a mechanism used by the subject for the transition from the initial conception to an expanded verbal statement. There is reason to suppose that it is precisely inner speech with its predicative functions that participates in the formation of the structure or scheme of sentences and that is disturbed in cases of dynamic aphasia.

The first evidence supporting this hypothesis can be obtained in an experiment that determines whether patients with dynamic aphasia are able to find the names of objects (nouns) and the names of actions (verbs) with equal facility. If the predicative function of speech in these patients is, indeed, disturbed, it will be far more difficult for them to find the names of actions than the names of objects.

Fifteen patients with dynamic aphasia and 15 control subjects participated in this experiment. They were asked to give as many names of objects and actions as possible within 1 min (with their eyes closed).

The controls experienced no perceivable difficulties in solving either problem, nor were there any marked differences in the ease with which they found names for objects and actions.

The patients with temporal (sensor) aphasia had serious difficulty in naming both objects and actions; moreover, it was sometimes even less difficult for them to name actions than objects.

The patients with dynamic aphasia can be divided into three groups. The first group was composed of patients with a syndrome of severe dynamic aphasia. They could not find names of either objects or actions, and instead of providing the required names produced verbal stereotypes.

The second group was able to find the names of nine or ten objects within 1 min, but could not name even a few actions.

The third group, made up of patients who showed good recovery from dynamic aphasia, exhibited no disorders in the naming of objects, but experienced marked difficulties in finding the names of actions. The data are given in Table 1.

Table 1

Finding Names of Objects and Actions in 1 Min
(Average Data from Our Experiments)

	Number of object names	Number of action names
Patients with dynamic aphasia (15)	10.3	2.7
Controls (15)	30	31

Table 2 presents data obtained from a group of six patients with dynamic aphasia.

Table 2

Finding Names of Objects and Actions:
Group of Patients with Dynamic Aphasia

	Number of object names	Number of action names
1. Pim. (27237)	10	2
2. Mor. (36309)	8	2
3. Bog. (24725)	11	3
4. Kr. (33957)	12	2
5. Ilm. (33758)	9	4
6. Sklyar. (33755)	12	3
Total	62	16

It is easy to see that it was approximately four times as difficult for these patients to find the names of actions (verbs) as to name objects (nouns).

Below are some examples from our protocols.

Patient Pim. (27237), age 29, student (tumor removed

from the lower part of the posterior area of the left frontal lobe), with dynamic aphasia.

Session 1. Finding names of objects (time - 1 min).
Circle...camel...horse...cow...lamb...blue...

You must name only nouns. "Nouns...table...circle ...sun...sky...rain..."

Session 2. Finding names of actions (time - 1 min).
"O...how is it...go...ride in a bus...go..." [O... kak eto...idti...yekhat' na avtobuse...poyti...]

Patient Kr. (33957), age 45, bookkeeper (meningioma removed from the left premotor zone), dynamic aphasia.

Session 1. Finding names of objects (time - 1 min).
"Horse...dog...camel...duck...tree...oak...pine ...maple...apple...tomatoes...cucumber...now... earth...no, I can't..."

Session 2. Finding names of actions (time - 1 min).
"O...(25")...work...O...now (35")...read..." [Okh...rabotat'...O, seychas...chitat'...]

Patient Mor. (36309), age 28, farm worker (hemorrhage in the region of the left anterior motor artery), dynamic aphasia.

Session 1. Finding names of objects.
"...yes...fog...sky...oh...window...door... frame...o, yes, frame...I can't."

Session 2. Finding names of actions (time - 1 min).
"Oh...no (20")...o...no...(30")...oh...I can't..."

The cases examined by us show that patients with dynamic aphasia exhibit considerable difficulty in finding the names of actions, and we can confirm that the predicative structure of their speech is defective.

Is it possible to assume that this deficiency, which is one of the fundamental causes of difficulties in the free construction of phrases, is, at the same time, the most important symptom in the general picture of dynamic aphasia?

The answer to this question will be given in a series of special experiments.

Disturbances in the Syntactic Scheme of a Sentence

As we have seen, it may be assumed that difficulties encountered in naming actions are an expression of more severe disorders in the predicative form of inner speech.

One of Vygotsky's hypotheses states that inner speech, abbreviated in structure and predicative in function, is an important
intermediate stage between the initial conception and its incor-
poration into an expanded statement. It may be assumed that if
this predicative function of speech is disturbed, an impairment
in the construction of sentences ensues.

Does this actually take place in patients with dynamic aphasia? We can come closer to an answer by checking the impediments in the active, expanded speech of these patients.

As we have already stated, these defects cannot be wholly
attributed to a disorder in initial concept, which does not account for the inability of these patients to enter into an active,
expanded conversation. We can give these patients an initial
concept (for example, a concrete theme on which to compose a
story, such as "The North," or a picture they are to describe),
but this does not facilitate the task of composing an expanded
statement.

Nor is the cause of these difficulties a disturbance in the outward expression of speech; the motor organization of speech
does not cause difficulties for these patients.

We may now return to a deficiency in the predicative function
of internal speech and assume that a result of such a defect may
be disturbance in the linear scheme of a sentence, which is
necessary for the transition from an initial concept to an expanded spoken utterance.

It is quite probable that patients with dynamic aphasia are not
able to find the sentence scheme necessary for an expanded
spoken utterance. Our patients were not able to arrive at a
preliminary scheme that would potentially contain the information on the quantity and sequence of speech elements that were
to make up the phrase. For this reason they were able to utter
individual words by selecting them from all the flowing speech

elements, but were unable to find the necessary scheme of an expanded spoken sentence.

If this was the cause, we can assume a disturbance in subjective generative grammar, whose mechanism now occupies the attention of many prominent linguists (N. Chomsky, 1957, and others).

How can we verify this hypothesis?

There are two possible ways: a negative one, and a positive one.

The first way is to give the patient the individual words that are necessary for constructing a sentence without giving him the linear scheme of the sentence. If this is of no help in constructing a sentence, we can conclude that the difficulties are not caused by lack of the necessary words.

In the second way (positive) we give the patient the linear scheme of a sentence without the individual specific words. If this helps the patient to compose a sentence, we obtain indirect proof that the absence of a sentence scheme is responsible for impediments in active expanded speech. Let us describe data obtained in both experiments.

1. We gave individual words to patients with a dynamic aphasia syndrome and asked them to construct a whole sentence from them.

As a rule the patients were unable to perform the task. Either they attempted to repeat the words or, instead of constructing a new sentence, they reproduced speech stereotypes in which the given words were included.

> Patient Mor. (36309) was given the two words house and hen and was asked to make a sentence that would include these words. After a long pause and unsuccessful efforts he said: "House ... oh ... house ... I can't ... and hen ... house ... oh, my goodness ... here is the house ... and nothing ... " [dom ... o ... dom ... ya ne mogu ... i kuritza ... dom ... o, bozhe moy ... vot dom ... i nichego].
> Patient Bog. (27715) (meningioma in a lower posterior area of the left frontal lobe) was given the word to thank,

[blagodarit'] and in another experiment the word to fly
[letat']. Both times he was asked to construct a sentence
including one of the two words. For a long time (5-7 min)
he tried to do this, repeating the given word, but was unable to form a sentence. He finally recited a fragment
from a well-known poem that contained the words I thank
("For all, for all, I thank you" [za vse, za vse tebya
blagodaryu ya]).

The negative results of these experiments are clear: Patients
with dynamic aphasia are not able to form a sentence even if
individual words are given to them. The task presented to them
cannot induce them to find a scheme for the required sentence;
the patient is able only to repeat the individual words, or must
resort to reciting well-established verbal stereotypes.

2. Let us turn to the second experiment, in which the positive procedure was used.

We asked a patient with dynamic aphasia to give a sentence
expressing a wish (I am hungry; or Give me something to drink)
or formulating a simple graphic situation (a woman cutting
bread; a boy reading a book).

After the patient demonstrated his inability to compose an
expanded sentence, a series of counters was placed on a table.
None of the counters carried any additional information, but the
number of counters in a row corresponded to the number of
words in the required sentence.

This type of experiment gave the patient the external linear
scheme of a sentence without presenting any specific words.

The results of this experiment were striking. A patient who
had previously been incapable of constructing an expanded sentence was able to accomplish this task by touching each consecutive counter with his finger; when the counters were taken
away, he was again helpless.

The linear structure scheme given the patient thus became
a means of compensating for the original defect. Let us look
at some examples.

Patient Mor. (36309), who had a very distinct form of

dynamic aphasia, was able to name objects easily and to repeat words and short sentences, but was unable to utter a coherent statement or employ speech in spontaneous communication. When he was asked a question, he repeated it mechanically, but was unable to find the phrase required for an answer. When he was shown a picture of a horse and wagon filled with hay and asked to relate its contents he responded: "Oh...yes...oh, the devil...a horse...and what else?...oh, the devil!"

When three counters were placed before him and he was asked to compose a sentence by pointing to each of the counters, he pointed to them saying:

"The horse † pulls † the wagon †" [Loshad' † vezet † telegu †].

When four counters were placed before him and he was asked to relate what farm workers do in the country, he pointed successively to each of the counters and said:

"The farm workers † haul † hay † with † horses †" [Kol' khozniki † perevozyat † seno † na † loshadyakh †].

When, however, the counters were taken away and the patient was asked to answer the question again, he was unable to do so and unsuccessfully attempted to find the required words. He was asked to use counters. He took separate bits of white paper, placed four of them in a row, and, pointing to each of them, composed the sentence:

"The trucks-haul-the grain-to the barn" [Gruzoviki-vezut-khleb-k sapayu]. Then he took one more counter and added: "and to market" [i na rynok].

He attempted unsuccessfully to compose a sentence on the weather in exactly the same way:

"The weather...oh, what is this...the weather...no..." [Pogoda...o, chto eto...pogoda..., net...]. However, after taking three counters, he said, pointing to them:

"The weather-today-is splendid!" [Pogoda segodnya prekrasanya!].

The patient was asked to relate the contents of the picture "The Boy in the forest." He said: "The boy (long pause)...the forest...no...I can't."

He was given several counters, which he placed on the table, and pointing to each of them, said, "The boy... went into the forest...to gather mushrooms...and lost his way...He cried...and climbed a tree, etc." [Mal' chik poshel v les...za gribami...i poteryal'sya...on krichal...i zalez na dervo i t.d.]

We have demonstrated a technique for restoring speech with the aid of external supports that give form to the linear scheme of a sentence.

It is unnecessary to review other experiments with patients exhibiting the syndrome of dynamic aphasia: all the patients in our group, which represented varying degrees of dynamic aphasia, presented an analogous picture. We can thus conclude that this experiment was a positive proof of our hypothesis.

The chief disturbance in dynamic aphasia can hence be described as a loss of the linear scheme of a sentence, which, as far as we know, may be the result of disruption of inner speech, abbreviated in form and predicative in function.

Strengthening a Linear Sentence Scheme and Overcoming Preseverations

The restoration of a linear sentence scheme by means of external supports has an additional result that we cannot overestimate. This technique is an important aid in overcoming the pathological inertness of verbal stereotypes or verbal perseverations, which are typical of speech disorders from injury to the anterior brain area.

As has already been noted by one of the authors (A. R. Luria, 1962, 1963) and verified by a series of animal experiments, injury to the anterior brain area has a double consequence: in animals the complex and elaborate programs of action are disturbed, and, in addition, the complex motor stereotypes become pathologically inert.

The same is observable in speech pathology: injury to the posterior area of the left frontal lobe leads to marked perseverations in expressive speech, and we have every reason to suppose that motor perseverations are one of the most important mechanisms in the so-called efferent or kinetic form of motor aphasia (A. R. Luria, 1947, 1963, and others).

Pathological perseverations are especially clearly manifested in cases of dynamic aphasia when injury to the premotor zone affects subcortical motor ganglia.

In these cases, which result in efferent motor aphasia, disruption of active speech is associated with especially distinct perseveration after a word has been uttered.

One of the most important findings is that in these cases the restoration of a linear sentence scheme by means of external supports has a dual result: it restores the possibility of expanded speech and enables the patient to overcome pathological perseverations. Here is an illustration:

Patient Os. (29558), age 47 (tumor with cyst removed from left premotor zone). The patient's movements were "de-automatized," and his speech was severely disturbed. Spontaneous speech was profoundly disordered, and he was incapable of uttering a series of words even mechanically (counting, verse recitation, etc.). He could give an echolalic repetition of one of two words; but when a large series of words was presented to him, he was unable to repeat them, because of perseveration of the first word. Active speech was impossible. He was unable to give an expanded answer to a question, although his understanding of the question remained unimpaired.

Tell me, please, about your condition. "Oh, yes ... it is ... oh, darn it ... yes ... " [Okh ... da ... eto tak ... o chert voz'mi ... da.]

What kind of work do you do? "Oh, yes ... it is ... no ... " [Akh, da ... eto tak ... net ...]

The patient was shown a stick and instructed to ask someone to give it to him.

"Oh ... sgi ... sgiv ... sgivesteck [Akh ... zd ... da ... zdar ... z darushku]. (Contamination: instead of saying

"Give me the stick" [dayte ruchku], the patient inter-
changed the two words in speaking.)

The patient was given external supports (two pieces of
white paper), which were placed on a table at a distance
of 15 cm from each other. He was asked to touch each
piece and say the required sentence. He said: "Give the
stick" [day . . . ruchku]. No perseveration or contamination was noticeable.

The external supports were taken away, and the patient
was asked to repeat the same sentence: "Givestick . . . oh,
no, oh . . . my goodness . . . sgivstig . . . oh the devil . . ."
[Zdarushku . . . o . . . net . . . o . . . bozhe moy . . . zdarus'k . . .
o chert . . .].

As we have noted, in this case the external support method
had a dual result: it restored a linear sentence scheme and,
at the same time, helped to overcome pathological inertness.

We have given some examples of the reorganizing role of external supports in the organization of behavior, which one of
the authors demonstrated many years ago in a series of experiments (A. R. Luria, 1932, 1948).

Attempts at a Physiological Analysis
of the Above Findings

We have demonstrated the role of external supports in the
restoration of a linear sentence scheme, which is lacking in
patients with dynamic aphasia, and in overcoming pathological
inertness in the speech system. Would it now be feasible to
make a few attempts at a physiological analysis of the facts
given and the mechanisms underlying dynamic aphasia?

Let us reconstruct the mechanisms of speech disorder in
this form of aphasia. As has already been noted, we have every
reason to believe that the fundamental mechanism of dynamic
aphasia is a disturbance in inner speech and its predicative
functions. We may even suppose that in this case the transition from an initial concept to a linear sentence structure is

impaired. Is it possible to verify this in a more direct way?
Can we actually demonstrate that in this form of aphasia the
transition from an initial concept to speech activity is indeed
disturbed?

Further experiments are necessary to get closer to the physiological mechanism of this phenomenon. It is well known that
every intention ensures preliminary preparation for action and
that preliminary preparation for a required action is necessary
if the action is to be successfully performed.

In speech activity such preliminary preparation can be seen
in changes in the electromyograms (EMGs) of the speech apparatus in the form of alterations in the initial background of
tongue and lip electromyograms during the preparatory period
for speech. This has been demonstrated by several authors
(Bassin & Beyn, 1957).

Can we use this technique for our purposes?

Is it possible to show that the disturbances in the transition
from an initial concept to speech that we observed in cases of
dynamic aphasia were physiologically concentrated in the motor
output into actual speech or, on the other hand, that they blocked
the process in the preceding stages, when the transition from
an initial concept to speech had not yet occurred? In addition,
is it possible to show the kinds of changes that can be recorded
when we use the above-described external support method and
when the initial restoration of linear sentence structure opens
the way to verbalization of a initial concept? We employed a
technique described earlier by the above-mentioned authors
(Bassin & Beyn, 1957).

Electromyograms of the lower lip (which are indicative even
for a latent speech process) were recorded for patients with
dynamic aphasia. This experiment was carried out both in
cases in which the patients were not able to construct a sentence and in cases in which they were able to overcome this
difficulty by means of external representation of a linear sentence structure.

The patient was asked to prepare for a verbal response without reproducing aloud the required sentence, and in both cases

EMGs of the lower lip were recorded with an Al 'var electro-encephalograph.

It was quite evident in the case of a patient with dynamic aphasia who tried to express a thought verbally that no changes in the background EMG were noticeable.

This is proof that in these patients disturbances do not occur in the motor stage itself, but that the delay in speech impulses is localized in the preliminary stage of the process. In the second case, however, in which external supports were used to restore a linear sentence structure, the EMG underwent appreciable changes.

In this case an intention to utter a sentence results in sharp changes in the background EMG; and separate EMG outbursts, whose magnitudes correspond to the individual components of the sentence in preparation, occur. It is clear that external supports open a pathway for impulses from the speech-motor apparatus.

The data we have presented indicate that an important advance in physiological analysis of the mechanisms of dynamic aphasia is possible. The findings admit the hypothetical possibility that a disturbance in inner speech, with its predicative functions, is typical of dynamic aphasia; that this disturbance leads to disturbance of the mechanism of transition from an initial concept to a linear sentence structure, which, in turn, renders impossible preliminary excitation of the speech-motor apparatus; and that a defect in active sentence construction is the result of such disturbances.

One hundred years ago Jackson advanced his well-known view that "To speak is to 'propositionize' "; and 50 years ago German neurologists made the first inroads into the study of dynamic aphasia. Previously, dynamic aphasia has been regarded as a unique form of aphasia "without aphasia." Only now, through the combined efforts of neuropsychological, linguistic, and physiological analyses, has it been possible to take the first steps toward a description of its mechanism.

Conclusions

A lesion of the anterior section of the speech zone of the left

hemisphere leads to a specific speech disorder that may be
called dynamic aphasia. Patients with this type of disorder retain speech comprehension and have no difficulty in uttering individual words. They readily understand speech, can name objects, and can repeat isolated words and short sentences; but
they cannot employ speech for communication and are unable
to construct a sentence.

For many years the mechanisms of this disorder in structured speech have been unknown. The authors of the present
report have attempted to analyze the mechanisms underlying
dynamic aphasia. They have demonstrated that patients with
this disorder can name objects with ease, but have difficulty
in naming actions, and that the predicative functions of speech
are disturbed.

This suggests the hypothesis that the chief factor in this form
of aphasia is associated with disturbance in inner speech, abbreviated in structure and predicative in function. This fundamental disorder results in disruption in linear sentence structure and in blocking the transition from an initial concept to a
spoken sentence.

The hypothesis was tested in an experiment in which the patients were provided with a linear sentence structure by means
of external supports, which restored the capacity to construct
sentences. Electromyographic recordings showed that this external support method relieved the blocking of the speech innervation necessary for restoring active speech.

References

Bassin, F. V., & Beyn, E. S. [O primenenii elektromiografi-
    cheskoy metodiki v issledovanii rechi] [Materialy sove-
    shchaniya po psikhologii]. Moscow, 1957.
Chomsky, N. Syntactic structures. The Hague, 1957.
Kleist, K. Die alogischen Denkstörungen. Arch. Psychiat.
    Nervenkr., 1930, 90.
Kleist, K. Gehirnpathologie. Leipzig, 1934.
Luria, A. R. The nature of human conflicts. New York, 1932.

Luria, A. R. [Traumatic aphasia]. Moscow, 1947.
Luria, A. R. [Restoration of brain function following combat injury]. Moscow, 1948.
Luria, A. R. [Higher human cortical functions]. Moscow, 1962.
Luria, A. R. [The human brain and mental processes]. Moscow, 1963.
Pick, A. Studien über motorische Aphasie. Vienna, 1905.
Vygotsky, L. S. [Thought and speech]. Moscow, 1934.

Translated by
Michel Vale

A. R. Luria, N. K. Kiyashchenko,
L. I. Moskovichyute, T. O. Faller,
and N. A. Fillippycheva

SYNDROMES OF MNEMONIC DISORDERS
ACCOMPANYING DIENCEPHALIC TUMORS

Recent neurophysiological, pharmacological, and clinical psychological studies have convincingly demonstrated the relationship between the gross memory disorders first described by
S. S. Korsakov [1] and lesions of the medial Papez structures
of the brain [2-6].

Papez's circuit (the hippocampal circuit) includes, in addition to the hippocampus itself, the mammillary bodies, the Vicq
d'Azyr mammillothalamic bundle, fibers from the anterior nu-
cleus of the optical thalamus projecting to the frontal cortex,
the septal nuclei, the fornix, and the links between these structures, which pass through the corpus callosum. It should be
noted that, generally speaking, these structures play an important role in emotional and autonomic responses, regulation of
homeostasis, tonic activation of the cortex, regulation of the
level of alertness, and orienting responses [7, 8]. In other
words, one of the functions of these structures is to supply the
energy necessary for mental processes to take place. Clinical
psychological studies [2-4] have shown that patients with lesions
of structures encompassed by Papez's circuit did not suffer from

From Zhurnal nevropatologii i psychiatrii imeni S. S.
Korsakova, 1973, 73(12), 1853-58.

apraxias, agnosias, speech disorders, or disorders of complex cognitive processes. The syndrome of focal lesions of the medial brain structures consisted of mnemonic disorders, frequently accompanied by disorders in the regulation of emotional and autonomic responses [9, 10]. This observation gave the impression that the memory disorders accompanying different focal lesions in Papez's circuit were all of the same type, although the various clinical syndromes in which they appeared differed. We have studied the significance of the different parts of Papez's circuit in the organization of memory processes and the specific contributions made by lesions of each structure of this system in the development of amnestic clinical syndromes. To stimulate the discussion of these disorders we made a comparison between them and neurophysiological data on the functional state of the brain.

The present article presents the results of a study of 48 patients with focal lesions of only one part of Papez's circuit, namely, the diencephalic region (cases of pituitary adenoma with superretrocellar growth, craniopharyngeoma, and tumors of the third ventricle). For our analysis we chose patients who displayed no signs of intracranial hypertension and for whom it was accordingly possible to link these disorders with the local influence of the pathological lesion in the diencephalic structures as well as with their functional state. All our observations were verified by surgery or autopsy.

To explore the nature of memory disorders accompanying lesions of different parts of the hippocampal circuit we worked out a system of clinical psychological examinations that included the following: (1) recall of elementary sensory stimuli (a modification of Konorsky's method); (2) recall of a series of isolated terms addressed to the visual, auditory, and motor analyzers (sequences of words, pictures of objects, geometric figures, and sequences of finger positions); and (3) recall of semantic structures (sentences, narrations). The conditions surrounding the recall of this material varied: we compared

direct recall, recall after an empty pause, i.e., an interval
(2 min) containing nothing to recall, and recall after a
pause in which some task had to be performed as a diver-
sion. This task could be either of a different type from
the material to be memorized (i.e., addressed to another
sensory modality) or similar to the initial material either
in its characteristics or in the direction of its recall (homogeneous interference). It is known that an experimental
situation is most difficult for a subject when, after recalling one series of elements, he must recall a second series, analogous to the first, after which he must again recollect the first series. If two sets of such material are
alike in both the type of material and the direction of the
recall, favorable conditions are created for detecting
deficiencies in memorization and retrieval. It is characteristic that the influence of interference on the memory
traces of preceding experience, an influence associated
with retroactive inhibition, is also involved in some way
in forgetting in normal persons [11]. Earlier investigations have shown that this type of experimental task should
be able to detect even very well concealed memory disorders [4].

A second part of the study consisted in compiling an ex-
tensive record of different physiological indices: electro-
encephalograms (EEGs), rheoencephalograms (REOs),
electromyograms (EMGs), pneumoencephalograms (PEGs),
the galvanic skin reflex (GSR), and respiration, all of which
together provided a good general idea of the state of the
connections between the brain stem and the cortex, the
regulation of cerebral circulation, and the state of the
functional system responsible for voluntary movements.
These indices were recorded together with a multiple
study of memory processes in a clinical psychological
experiment. It was necessary to make a second study of
memory processes in each patient because of the pecu-
liarities of tumor development, which was accompanied
by fluctuations in the patients' overall functional state.

Patients with lesions in the diencephalic region displayed a quite distinct picture of memory disorders, which was not specific to any particular modality, i.e., it affected visual, auditory, and somatosensory traces equally. Also, the disorders were always particularly distinct when some interference was introduced. Finally, in cases in which the memory disorders were quite gross, they were manifest regardless of the extent of semantic organization of the material to be memorized, but as a rule were not accompanied by active confabulations or any impairment in the structure of memory patterns.

Our case material was broken down into four groups according to the severity and distinctive characteristics of the memory disorders and the clinical physiological syndrome of which they were a part. All degrees of memory disorder, from rapid fatigue to a gross amnestic syndrome with impaired consciousness, were represented.

It is noteworthy that in some of the patients with rather large diencephalic tumors, mnemonic processes were largely intact, indicating that the neural structures in this region were still largely in good functional order. These patients constituted group one. They were still readily accessible to communication, were completely oriented, and were still emotionally flexible, or at times somewhat disinhibited. They had no subjective complaints of memory disorders and performed all tasks flawlessly. The clinical picture included visual and endocrine and metabolic disorders, with no signs of a pathological influence of the lesion on the brain stem.

The second group included patients with an asthenic syndrome and mild memory disorders that were more conspicuous the larger the amount of material to be memorized. However, these difficulties were relatively easily overcome by added verbal promptings. These patients typically displayed fluctuations in their condition, with signs of exhaustion during the course of one examination and for even longer periods of time. Subjectively the patients were troubled by heightened fatigability, weakness, and periodic drowsiness; and they sometimes complained of memory impairment. They were completely oriented

in space and time and to the nature of their illness. Their
emotional responses were completely appropriate to the situation or were somewhat disinhibited. The extent of endocrine
and metabolic disorders was the same as in the first group, and
they showed no signs of pathological influences on the brain-
stem structures.

EEG abnormalities for the first and second groups were
similar: irritative changes were usually recorded against a
background of more or less regular alpha rhythm (frequency
9-10/sec) with a pronounced depression in response to light;
peaked waves, epi-complexes, and beta waves were manifest,
and theta waves were usually recorded from the anterior sections of the brain.

The third group included patients with distinct memory disorders having characteristics of an amnestic syndrome, varying in prominence in the individual case. Memory disorders
were evident even with an ordinary amount of material to be
memorized, and regardless of the level of semantic organization of the latter (i.e., whether two sequences of three words
each, two sentences, or two short narrations were to be memorized). However, added promptings did improve recall. Fluctuations in the general state and in the level of memory disorders were more pronounced and covered a wide range from one
day to the next; it was especially typical that these fluctuations
would occur during the course of the same investigation, and
even during the course of one assignment. In the latter case,
improvements were not spontaneous, but were effected by giving added instructions or by offering emotional encouragement.
The clinical picture of these patients featured a considerable
reduction in activity, languor, adynamia, and heightened fatigability. Often the patients would lie passively for whole days on
end without even reading or listening to the radio. Emotional
responses were monotonic and flattened; the patients were unable to sustain an adequate concern for their illness, and often
underestimated its gravity. Even their rare confabulations
were not spontaneously offered, but given only in response to
a specific question. They were never extended, emotionally

charged, or productive. Orientation in space and time varied in
accuracy. Sometimes changes in sleep patterns were observed.
In contrast to groups one and two, this group sometimes displayed symptoms of damage to the brain stem (paresis of the
upward gaze, pathological reflexes). The EEG abnormalities of
these patients at different stages in the investigation were polymorphous. All featured a reduction in the duration of depression of alpha activity in response to different stimuli, including
light stimuli. It is noteworthy that almost all the patients showed
a prolongation of the depression brought about by a light stimulus if the latter was presented against a background of another
stimulus, especially one that was randomly chosen. This observation is in line with the improvement noted in recall after verbal prompting or after changing the amount of material to be
memorized.

The fourth group of patients included those with the most gross
and stable impairments of memory for current events and, to a
certain extent, for past events. Recall deficiencies were apparent even if only one word or sentence was to be memorized, regardless of whether the interfering task was homogeneous or
heterogeneous. There were some fluctuations in the condition
of memory within the same investigation and from investigations
on one day to those on the next. Usually neither verbal prompting nor a change in the instructions produced any notable improvement in mnemonic functions; indeed, they often led to an
aggravation of the memory deficiency and inhibition of the patient. An amnestic syndrome was always accompanied by disturbed consciousness, with disorientation in time and place and,
especially, gross disorientation in the patient's awareness of
his own illness (often the patient would show not even the least
sign of awareness of his inauspicious physical condition). Persistent and quite monotonic emotional changes and rapid mental
fatigue were observed. This group of patients also displayed
symptoms of a brain-stem lesion in the mesencephalon and
rhombencephalon. The EEG changes in patients of the third and
fourth groups were both especially polymorphous. A marked
reduction in the alpha-rhythm time was combined with the ap-

pearance of long periods of generalized brain-stem bursts, which could be suppressed by supplementary afferent stimuli.

The responses in the various electrophysiological and autonomic parameters to indifferent stimuli and cue stimuli showed a wide range of variations that correlated in magnitude with the depth of the mnemonic disorders. The depression of a normal flow of afferent impulses into the cerebral cortex from nonspecific structures of the brain stem increased in proportion to the extent of memory disorders, and in the last group of patients was combined with pathological influences from the brain stem. It is conceivable that the combination of these pathophysiological factors produced the depression of excitation in the cortex and in the cerebral hemispheres as a whole. The clinical expression of this was the different degrees of memory disorders and disorders of consciousness.

Observations showing the entire range of mnemonic disorders (corresponding to the four groups described above) in one patient are especially interesting within the context of the functional role of the diencephalon in the organization of memory.

Patient C., 34 years old, had been hospitalized at the Institute of Neurosurgery of the USSR Academy of Medical Sciences for a cystic tumor of the third ventricle.

The first time (March 1971) dysmenorrhea, thirst, obesity, and disturbed sleep patterns were noted, in addition to indistinct temporal hypopsia and slightly reduced muscle tone. The fundus oculi was normal, and cerebrospinal fluid pressure was 170 mm H_2O. The EEG showed generalized abnormalities: a reduction in the amplitude of brain waves, disturbances in the basal rhythm, and slight irritation of the cortex. There were synchronous groups of theta waves in the frontal regions. A neuropsychological study showed no signs of agnosia, apraxia, speech disorders, or impairment of cognitive processes; the patient was fully oriented in time and place. The personality of the patient was intact, she had insight into her illness, and her emotions were only slightly blunted. She complained

of memory impairment ("I used to have a good, quick memory, but now I'm forgetful"). A special study of her memory processes disclosed some specific abnormalities: A
routine experiment revealed no disorder of memory; the
impairment appeared under specific circumstances, either
when the volume of the material to be memorized was increased (for example, when three narrations were given
instead of two, as a result of which one was forgotten),
when the recall period was extended (after memorizing
nine of ten words, the patient remembered four words on
the next day, but on the second day was unable even to remember the test), or when the specific memory assignment was eliminated (i.e., the patient was asked to recall
at will any randomly remembered material). The extent
of memory impairment varied from day to day, and
prompting helped recall.

In June 1971 the patient again was admitted to the institute because of a deterioration in her condition: she began
to have severe headaches, debility and fatigue increased,
and she became drowsy. Her range of interests narrowed,
and she stopped reading. Her insight into her illness diminished and emotional flatness increased. Hypomimia
and adynamia were evident. Signs of aspontaneity and inactivity appeared, which, however, were not persistent, but
varied over the course of the day or even within shorter
intervals of time. Hand tremor, bitemporal hypopsia, and
signs of congestion in the fundus oculi appeared. The
EEGs showed a general marked slowing of rhythm and a
predominance of slow activity in the temporal leads. Ven-
triculography with "myodil" showed a tuberous filling defect in the third ventricle, which narrowed the space it
occupied. The outflow from the third ventricle was en-
cumbered. We therefore decided to perform a ventriculo-
cisternostomy.

A neuropsychiatric examination done before the operation showed that the higher cortical functions were still
intact but that the aggravation of hypertensive phenomena

and the local influence of the tumor on the hypothalamic
sections of the brain were accompanied by a worsening of
emotional and mnemonic disturbances. Memory studies
showed that interference had led to contaminations, or to
total obliteration, of memory traces. These symptoms
were even more conspicuous when sentences and narratives were used as the test material: extremely gross
contaminations appeared of which the patient herself was
unaware. She began to forget events that had just occurred.
The state of her memory began to fluctuate over a wide
range from day to day, and she would become quickly ex-
hausted even during a single test. A new task presented
after a short period would liven her up somewhat. On one
day she would recall two sequences of three words after
one presentation, or after three presentations if there had
been interference from a counting task.

Several days later she would recall the same two sequences of three words after one presentation, but after
a counting task she would remember only three words.
The second time she could not remember a single word
after counting, and on the fifth repetition after counting,
she even denied that she had ever performed the task. The
same thing occurred in the recital of narratives: direct
recall of one narrative (about a chicken laying a golden
egg) and then another narrative (about a crow that tossed
pebbles into jars so as to be able to drink himself full on
hot days) caused the patient no memory difficulties, but
it was impossible for her to recollect a previously recalled narrative. This is how she then remembered the
first tale: "The sun shone down on the jars containing
the golden eggs. The jars heated up and the eggs floated
to the top...."

In September 1971 the patient was admitted to the institute for the third time, because of a sudden deterioration
in her condition. She had become apathetic, adynamic,
and had almost constant headaches. She experienced brief
losses of consciousness. There was distinct right-side

hypopsia, with gross paresis of the upward gaze and pronounced choking of the optical discs. Efferent nerves were
paretic on both sides. Bulbar disorders were sometimes
manifest. There were pyramidal signs in the form of
weakness in the limbs on the left side, central paresis of
the 7th and 12th nerves on the left side, Babinski's sign
on the left, and Oppenheim's sign on both sides. Finger
tremor appeared, and at times a grasping reflex occurred.
Her condition fluctuated: the patient was sometimes apathetic and adynamic, and at other times concerned about
her condition. She was oriented in place, but not always
in time. As her condition deteriorated, the patient would
quickly fall asleep if left to herself. But she could be easily awakened, after which she would answer questions in
monosyllables. By this time her memory was extremely
impaired (without confabulations), but her rapid fatigability made it impossible to test her memory processes.
All attempts to increase the patient's alertness so that
the experiment could be performed were unsuccessful.

From this case description it is evident that the four types of
memory disorders found in different patients with diencephalic
lesions can also occur in the same patient at different stages in
the development of the pathological process.

Thus, in diencephalic tumors, the memory impairments are
not specific to a particular memory modality. They are determined basically by the extent to which memory traces are pathologically suppressed by interfering factors.

The range of memory disorders is very wide, from inconspic-
uous impairments to full-blown syndromes similar to the Korsakov syndrome. It is therefore possible to distinguish among
clinical types of disorders, differing in the severity of the memory disorder and in the particular physiological changes in their
clinical picture. The extent of memory disorders does not depend on the size and site of the diencephalic tumor, but is associated with the stage of development of the pathological process and the functional state of the involved brain areas.

The described memory disorders appear in conjunction with general disturbances in the level of alertness and consciousness and are to a considerable extent correlated with clinical and neurophysiological symptoms of depression of the ascending activating system of the brain stem.

References

1. Korsakov, S. S. [Morbid disorders of memory and their diagnosis]. Moscow, 1890.

2. Popova, L. T. [Memory and memory disorders in focal brain lesions]. Moscow, 1972.

3. Luria, A. R., et al. [Memory disorders in the clinical picture of aneurysm of the anterior commissural artery]. Moscow, 1970.

4. Kiyashchenko, N. K. [Memory disorders in local brain lesions]. Moscow, 1973.

5. Scovill, W., & Millmer, B. J. Neurol. Neurosurg. Psychiat., 1957, 20, 11.

6. Milner, B. In C. Whitty & O. Zangeill (Eds.), Amnesia. London, 1966. P. 109.

7. Sokolov, E. N. In [The orienting reflex and orienting-investigatory activity]. Moscow, 1958. P. 111.

8. Bekhterev, N. P. [The physiology and pathophysiology of the deep structures of the human brain]. Moscow-Leningrad, 1967.

9. Bragina, N. N. In [Deep structures of the human brain under normal and pathological conditions]. Moscow-Leningrad, 1966. P. 31.

10. Filippycheva, N. A., & Faller, T. O. In [Materials of the 5th All-Union Conference of Neuropathologists and Psychiatrists]. Moscow, 1969. Vol. 1, p. 270.

11. Smirnov, A. A. [Psychology of memorization]. Moscow, 1948.

A. R. Luria, E. N. Pravdina-Vinarskaya,
and A. L. Iarbus

EYE-MOVEMENT MECHANISMS IN
NORMAL AND PATHOLOGICAL VISION
(Simultaneous Agnosia and Optical Ataxia)

The psychological, psychophysiological, and neurological literature has long since taken note of the intimate relationship
that exists between visual perception of objects and their de-
pictions and eye movements.

We know that the region of the macula lutea, where receptors
are concentrated at maximum density, is the area that trans-
mits maximal information and that most accurately carries out
organized and differentiated vision. Therefore, in order to acquire maximal information, the eye is compelled always to move
to a position in which the retinal image of the portion of the object under examination is in this central portion of the retina.
This shifting of the central visual field to points bearing maximal information constitutes the reflex activity of the eye, which
begins with a signal received by the retinal periphery, and is
carried out by means of a system of visual motor reactions
arising in response to these signals.

Visual analysis, which consists of a continuous process of
singling out the points bearing maximal information and subsequent synthesis of them, requires a system consisting of at
least two stimulated points: one on the periphery of the retina,

From Voprosy psikhologii, 1961, No. 5.

330

serving as source of the signals that promote further eye motion and have the function of orientation, and the other in the central portion of the retina, accepting and transmitting differentiated visual information.

In light of these facts, fundamental interest attaches to those forms of visual pathology in which the visual cortex (to the degree that its cells are in a state of pathological weakness) is incapable of providing reception of the above-mentioned system of visual signals. In the words of Pavlov (1949), the visual cortex "is capable of dealing simultaneously with a single stimulated point, and all other points are as though they did not exist...." In these cases the initial limitation of the capacity of visual reception necessarily leads to profound disturbances of visual movements, of the "optical ataxia" type; and the normal process of visual perception is severely disturbed.

Cases of this type have been described repeatedly in the neurological literature under the names of "narrowing of visual attention" (Holmes, 1919), "simultaneous agnosia" (Wolpert, 1924), "fragmentary perception" (Paterson & Zangwill, 1944), and others. A similar case of injury to the occipital cortex, which results in the subject's being able to perceive only a single object at a time (regardless of its size), has recently been described by one of the present authors (Luria, 1959). A distinctive feature of such cases is that, simultaneously with the narrowing of visual perception in all these patients, "visual ataxia" is observed or, more precisely, a disorder of visual-motor coordination and an inability to shift vision to points bearing maximal information and actively to analyze the object, image, or entire situation seen (Balint, 1909; Hecaen & Ajuriaguerra, 1954; and Luria, 1959).

The connection between the narrowing of visual perception to a single element and disturbances in the active analyzing movements involved in centering one's gaze is of fundamental significance to an understanding of the functional structure of visual perception. Therefore, analysis of this connection — by means of the most exact methods available — may be of significant interest. We shall therefore consider that problem and trace the

nature of the disturbance of the visual act in various forms of
damage to the central visual apparatus.

2

Clinical medicine is familiar with cases in which, as a result
of damage to the visual nerve or the visual conducting pathways,
the field of vision narrows sharply. Various hemianopsias and
concentric narrowings of the visual field, sometimes reaching
the stage of what is called tunnel vision, fall in this category. If
the visual cortex remains intact under these conditions, the patient is in a position to perceive — in the remaining visual field
— an entire system of simultaneous visual stimuli. The remaining visual field is even capable of experiencing a certain functional reorganization, with the production of a new "functional
macula" (Gelb & Goldstein, 1920). In such cases the tracking
movements of the eye not only are preserved intact but begin to
serve as the principal means of compensation for the visual defect.
The following will serve as illustration.

Since 1955, patient D. has been troubled by constant
frontotemporal headaches and impaired vision. The diagnosis was optochiasmal arachnoiditis; and on February 15,
1956, the patient underwent surgery (parting of the arach-
noidal commissures in the optochiasmal region).
Examination of the patient's vision now reveals the following. Visual acuity of both eyes: 0.4 with correction.
Visual field: markedly concentric, narrowing to 10° from
the point of focus (both eyes). Capable of discriminating
colored objects. Fundus: optic papilla somewhat pale,
with borders not quite clear-cut; arteries very narrow,
sclerotic. Despite the fact that the visual field is confined
to 10° (tunnel vision), the patient is capable of orienting
herself completely in space, perceiving objects, images,
and pictures on various subjects. She continues to work
as an archivist, reads, writes, moves in the streets without assistance, and does housework. She compensates for

her visual defect by tracking movements of the eyes,
which continue to be wholly organized in nature, and are
capable of being recorded.

The method of recording eye movements employed in this
case was that developed by one of the authors of this article
(Iarbus, 1956). It consists of attaching a device to the anesthe-
tized temporal portion of the sclera, which records the eye
movements. This device consists of a rubber suction cup to
which a tiny mirror is glued. The light beam impinging on the
mirror from a light source records the eye movement on moving photographic paper.

Recordings made by this method showed that patient D. had
retained the tracking movements of the eye and that they did not
differ from the normal. Figure 1 shows the eye movements in
following the contours of a rectangle (a), and in looking at a
portrait (b). Inasmuch as the patient is incapable of perceiving
simultaneously all the visual material presented to her, she
compensates for this defect by tracking the contours of the
drawing all around. Thus, the tracking movements of the eye
remain, in this situation, the principal means of compensating
for the narrowed visual field.

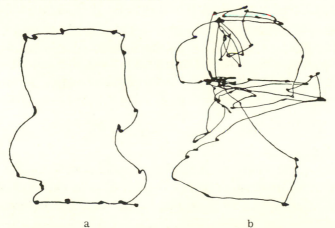

a   b

Figure 1. Eye movements in examination of
a rectangle (a) and a portrait (b). (Patient D.)

Defects in simultaneous visual perception associated with injury to the peripheral portion of the visual apparatus are successfully compensated for by the intact system of the centrally controlled tracking movements of the eyes.

An entirely different picture is seen in certain injuries to the cortical end of the visual analyzer.

3

We have already pointed out the comparatively rare instances (most often of bilateral injury to the occipito-temporal divisions of the brain) in which a pathological state of the visual cortex results in an entirely different type of narrowing of visual perception: the subject finds himself capable of perceiving only one object at a time (regardless of its angular size), and simultaneous perception of more than one object is beyond his capacities. As a rule, the cases of central disorder of the volume of visual perception of this nature described in the literature are accompanied by disturbance in organized tracing movements of the eyes and by opticomotor ataxia.

However, in no case (including that described by Luria, 1959) has the shifting of gaze seen in the patient been subjected to detailed study. This gap is filled in the present communication.

In 1959 and 1960 we had the opportunity to observe a patient characterized by the foregoing combination of symptoms of "simultaneous agnosia" and "visual ataxia" and the associated syndrome of profound disorder of organized visual perception.

We present the data resulting from study of this patient.

General Data

Patient R., 48 years of age, bookkeeper, was admitted to the Institute of Neurosurgery with complaints of a peculiar visual disorder consisting, in his words, of the fact that he could see only one object at a time. Therefore, he was incapable of looking at pictures or going to the theater or the movies, for he was able, in all these cases, to see only disconnected fragments.

Spatial orientation and acts that can be performed only on the basis of visual perception were difficult for him. For example, he would miss a chair he was looking at while attempting to seat himself on it, and was compelled to calculate this act for a long time and to perform it "by feel." He could bend directly over a disposal urn and yet miss it in discarding a cigarette butt. Reaching for an overhead support in a trolleybus, he would miss it and bang the heads of others. All these difficulties could be overcome only when the patient abandoned attempts at visual-motor coordination and oriented himself by proprioceptive perception. According to his description, when walking he had "not so much to see as to sense the way with his foot." When walking down a staircase, he could refrain from holding the bannister, but could not get out of the way of anyone he met. Nor could he read, because he extracted from the text only isolated and unrelated words. He had no trouble in writing isolated letters or syllables, but writing as a process was disordered because he could not simultaneously perceive the line and his pencil, "and one line was written over the next."

In February 1958, R. began to experience headaches, and after a while he found that it was difficult for him to dress: he confused his right and left boots, and was unable to find the sleeves of his jacket immediately. In April of the same year he encountered even greater difficulties in reading: he found himself capable of recognizing only single letters and could not immediately grasp combinations of them. His handwriting also changed. The progress of the disease led to considerable disturbances in visual perception and the patient's orientation in space; and after a brief stay in one of the regional hospitals, R. was sent to the Institute of Neurosurgery because of suspicion of a tumor of the occipito-parietal portion of the brain. In the institute, the following was observed. The patient maintained contact, knew where he was, and had good time orientation. Sometimes he displayed affective outbursts in inadequate relations with people in his environment, but usually he very quickly recognized that he was wrong and begged pardon for his improper reactions. His memory of past events was not entirely intact, and he was

not always capable of providing a coherent history of his disease.
R. went to examinations willingly and repeatedly added, on his
own initiative, various details descriptive of the results obtained.

Neurologically three things were observed in the patient:
sluggishness of pupillary response to light with convergence,
fundus normal, visual acuity 1.0 (bilateral). Examination of the
visual field was difficult because the patient invariably perceived
but a single object (this will be described below in detail), but
the impression was left that the field had been somewhat narrowed, and that R. oriented better in the right half of the field.
Optokinetic nystagmus was sluggish on the left and barely noticeable on the right. Reflex nystagmus was sluggish. There
were mild defects of binaural hearing, and mild bilateral pyramidal symptoms. No disorders of sensation were observed except for some disturbances in discriminative sensitivity of the
skin of the right wrist and of the lungs, but there were pronounced disorders in sense of localization of painful stimuli of
that same wrist. Posture tests were difficult because of the patient's problems with simultaneous perception of space. Tests
for different motions in succession and evaluation and performance of rhythms presented no difficulties. The patient's
speech was not disordered. He was capable of repeating series
of words and numbers, and could name objects without difficulty.
Acoustic analysis of words was intact. Oral counting was performed with ease within the limits of simple assignments, but
written counting was very difficult because of visual defects.
There were clearly defined difficulties in simultaneous perception, and digital agnosia was present. Considerable difficulties
were seen in Head's tests, in orienting on a geographic map, and
in terms of the position of the hands of a clock. Disorders in
understanding logical relations in grammar (of the type of semantic aphasia) were quite pronounced. Blood pressure was
140/190. Wassermann test was negative, as was the blood Cys-
ticercus antigen with cerebrospinal fluid complement-fixation
test. The cerebrospinal fluid showed 0.66% protein and 12/3
cytosis. Lange's test results: 3-3-2-2-1-0. Cerebrospinal
fluid pressure 200 mm Hg.

A skull x-ray showed no deviations from the normal. An electroencephalogram (EEG) revealed changes of the diffuse excitation type. The absence of an alpha wave in the occipital regions and the nature of the changes in response to individual and rhythmical light stimuli led to the conclusion that the occipital lobes of the brain were the site of the primary involvement in the pathological process.

All the clinical data — the distributed nature of the cerebral symptoms accompanied by lack of signs of intracranial hypertension — compelled a hypothesis of a vascular brain disease of unclear etiology; and the sluggish pupillary reactions and the degenerative nature of the Lange reaction suggested the possibility of specific endarteritis.

Inasmuch as the most vivid clinical manifestation of the disease took the form of complex optical and spatial disorders, the conclusion could be drawn that the major focus of damage lay in the cortical regions of both parietal-occipital lobes of the brain. This was subsequently confirmed by electroencephalography.

Investigation of Visual Perception

As previously indicated, the major disorders seen in the patient were associated with his visual perception.

From the very outset the patient complained of visual defects, which essentially resolved to the fact that he was capable of seeing only a single object at a time and was compelled to search for the remaining objects or details of a situation. When one of these details appeared, the first object disappeared. Thus, when he rode down the street, he was capable of seeing at one time only one machine in the entire flow of machines in motion, only one person in a crowd, only one house or one window. When he looked through a window he could see the snow falling, but the wall of the house across the way disappeared. As in the case previously described (Luria, 1959), the size of the object perceived played no significant role. The limitation of his visual perception lay in the quantity, not in the size, of the objects perceived.

When the patient was shown various geometric figures for a

brief period, he was capable of perceiving only one of them at a
time, but concluded that he had been shown two. Change in the
distance between figures, displacement in the horizontal or ver-
tical plane, and removal to various distances (30 cm, 1.5 m,
2.5 m, and 3 m), with a change in angular size, did not affect the
results. Each time the patient saw only one figure, and only occasionally noted that "there is also something else" in his visual
field, most often conceiving of the second figure as being like
the first (for example, evaluating a triangle and a circle as two
triangles). However, experiments conducted under more precise conditions, with the figures presented for 1 msec with the
aid of a flashbulb, made it possible to convince ourselves that
the patient perceived simultaneously only a single figure, regardless of its angular size, and that perception of the given
figure plus "something else" was the result of moving his eyes
when the display time was increased.

Experiment 1. Display of figures for 1 msec (figures measured
4° or 5° angle size)

1.	Circle	Circle
2.	1	Unity
3.	Three-segment broken line	(1) Didn't understand. (2) Four. (3) Four, but the bottom vertical was missing.
4.	Rectangle	(1) Didn't understand. (2) A square.
5.	Multiplication sign	A cross looking like a multipli-cation sign.
6.	Triangle	Triangle.
7.	Plus sign	An ordinary cross.
8.	Two circles (one under the other)	A little circle. One? One (2-5). Same thing.
9.	+0	(1) A little cross; nothing else. (2) A little circle; nothing else. (3) A little cross. (4) A little circle.

10. <u>Same thing, but patient</u>   (1) A little cross. (2) A little
    <u>was told there would be</u>   circle. (3) A little circle
    <u>two figures</u>   and, it seems, something
                                          else too. Probably there's
                                          a little cross and a little
                                          circle here.

Thus, perception of individual figures displayed for a very brief period was within the patient's capacities; but short-term display of two figures led to perception of only one of them, even when the patient was told that two items would appear.

Analogous results were obtained when, under the same circumstances, complex objects or images were displayed. Under these conditions, however, the object or image was not immediately recognized. The impression was gained that recognition took shape gradually on the basis of seizing hold of certain individual identifying characteristics.

<u>Experiment 2.</u> Display for 1 msec; image measuring 5°-8° angle size.

1. <u>Carrot</u> (drawing)   (1) Something red. (2) Something red. (3) A carrot.

2. <u>Poppy</u> (drawing)   (1) Something red. (2) Something dark red. (3) A flower.

3. <u>A rooster</u> (drawing)   (1) A spot. (2) A spot.
                                       (3) Some bird — wings and a nose. (4) A chicken or a bird.

4. <u>A cup</u> (drawing)   (1-5) Some figure of light blue color; I don't understand.
                                       (6-8) Some kind of spot.
                                       (9) A cup.

5. <u>A mushroom</u> (large   (1) Something stands out, like
   10°-15° angle size)   a mushroom .... I saw the cap and recognized the

	mushroom .... Didn't see the stem.
6. A pear (drawing)	(1) Pear-like. (2) A pear.
7. Fork (drawing)	Fork.
8. A broom (drawing)	(1) An awl? Something long. (2-3) Screwdriver. (4) A brush.
9. An infant (drawing, 8° angle size)	(1) A Jack (of cards). (2) A clock? (3) A skull? (4) A flower. (5-6) A clock!
10. Scissors (the object)	Scissors; I guessed from one blade.
11. A comb (the object)	A comb.
12. Penknife, half-open (the object)	(1) A blade, probably of a small knife. (2) A small knife bent at an angle.
13. Two cherries (drawing, 20° angle size)	(1-3) Don't know. (4-5) Something red. A flower? (6) Probably a flower. (7) Probably a fountain pen (the stem of the cherry). (8) A flower? (9) A cherry? I recognized it by the stem. One cherry. (10) A flower. (11) A cherry emerges. (12) A flower .... (13) It emerges as a cherry.

The experiment shows that the patient was able, after a very short display, to perceive both objects and their images; but as a rule he recognized them by some identifying characteristic. Hence perception of relatively simple objects and images with clear-cut identifying characteristics was easy, but recognition of more complex objects or images containing a number of details (9, for example) was quite difficult. Adequate perception of images incorporating several identical elements (13, for example) was beyond the capacities of the patient.

These experiments enabled us to conclude that in patient R.

we actually were dealing with a clear-cut case of simultaneous agnosia with reduction of the capacity for simultaneous visual perception to a single meaning-element. It is this defect that explains the fact that, in this patient, complex visual perception proved to be fragmented.

Pathology of Opticomotor Coordination

As in the case previously described (Luria, 1959), the narrowing of visual perception to a single component was accompanied, in patient R., by gross disturbances in opticomotor coordination.

These defects, clearly manifested in the complaints and behavior of the patient, appeared just as clearly in special experimental tests. What was most important, however, was the fact that they were manifested in instances when the patient's movements were controlled by vision, and were not seen when the movements were controlled kinesthetically.

When the patient's body was touched, he was able to localize the point of contact rather accurately (except for the right wrist and forearm) and, with his eyes closed, to place his hand at the point indicated. Localization of contact was quite accurate, and movements (indicating the point of contact) were rather confident. The range of errors did not exceed 1 cm, and no significant difference was seen between the right and left sides. The same experiments conducted with a lag between contact and pointing to the spot yielded only an insignificant increase in error. It was considerably more difficult for the patient to localize the next two points of contact. In these cases the error in localization of the second point of contact increased, but confidence in movement in the pointing gesture did not change significantly.

More complex movements, controlled by the kinesthetic analyzer or performed conceptually on verbal instructions, proved to be just as intact.

The patient readily recognized geometric figures (a circle, quadrangle, or triangle) when they were traced on the skin of his forearm (no significant difference between the right and the left side was seen) and reproduced them with eyes closed and without difficulty, drawing on his skin or in the air. He was capable of reproducing, with eyes closed, the position of a hand or finger in space, and of repeating a rather complex sequence of movements controlled kinesthetically. Hand motions in accordance with an assigned pattern 1-2-3-4 were copied quite accurately after only two kinesthetically presented examples. On the other hand, all visually controlled movements displayed a pronounced contrast to movements kinesthetically controlled.

Like patient V., previously described (Luria, 1959), R. was unable to touch a visually presented dot accurately with a pencil. He said that he could see either the dot or the pencil point, but could not see both together, and his misses of the target were within an area of 6 cm. He could not place a dot in the center of a circle or cross, missing constantly and putting it at various points in the circle (and sometimes outside it). Although he could draw a circle or triangle with eyes closed without difficulty, he was incapable of tracing a figure presented to him visually and distorted the contours in the grossest manner. He was incapable of tracing the outlines of a face if he was offered a sketch including eyes, nose, and mouth, and was not able to place eyes, nose, and mouth within the given oval of a face. He could not do a drawing of any complexity (for example, an elephant or house). Instead of the continuous outline, he presented isolated representations of individual constituents, saying: "My idea of it is perfectly all right, but my hands don't go where they should." He made a satisfactory analysis of the acoustic composition of a word, but was incapable of writing or copying, because the letters came out on top of one another, and lines were not observed at all.

All these data indicate that the patient's opticomotor coordination was grossly disturbed, although kinesthetically controlled movements were intact, and that these disorders were intimately associated with the basic defect of gross reduction in visual perception to a single constituent, as observed above.

Pathology of Visual Tracking Movements

All these data bring us to the final phase of our observations —

analysis of the disorders observed in the patient in the movements of the eye itself, and primarily in the searching movements of gaze. In order to accomplish these movements, as we
have stated above, it is necessary to preserve a system consisting, at the very least, of two stimulated points, one of which
controls the eye movements, shifting the object to the central
visual field, and the other of which directly carries out differentiated visual reception.

Experiments involving recording of the eye movements of the
patient, conducted in accordance with the above-described techniques, yielded clear-cut results.

Fixation of a single point did not disclose any significant defects in eye movements when the requirement was to trace a
single moving point. Eye movements in following a pendulum,
recorded on a photomicrogram, showed a rather regular sine-
wave, indicating that in this movement the patient revealed no
pathology whatever (Figure 2).

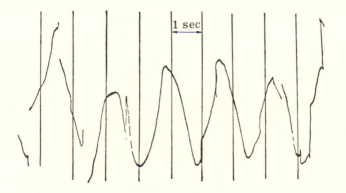

Figure 2. Eye movements in tracking one moving point.
(Patient R.)

We witnessed a sharp contrast to this intact simple act of visual movement as soon as we proceeded to the problem of shifting the eye from one given point to another. In these cases
(even when the two points were only 5° or 6° apart), organized

voluntary shifting of the eyes from point to point proved impossible (Figure 3). The patient, unable to see two points simultaneously, actually now engaged not in shifting the eyes from point
to point, but in ataxic movements of search for the new point.
Therefore, he was unable to find it at once, and constantly lost
track of it; and even long-held display of two points failed to
lead to clear-cut, coordinated movements of the eyes.

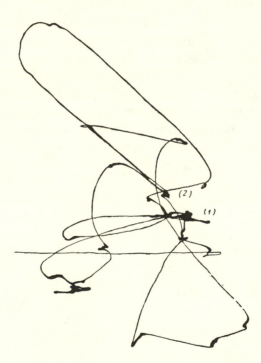

Figure 3. Eye movements when shifting from one
point of fixation to another. (Patient R.)

    This disorder of the self-regulating movements of the eye,
which appeared as soon as the gaze began to be controlled by
two points presented simultaneously, should manifest itself no
less clearly in any act of visual tracking of a system of points
or lines. This was manifested clearly in a series of records
made subsequently.

Figure 4. Eye movements in tracing a rectangle visually. (Patient R.)

Figure 4 presents a recording of the eye movements of the patient when given the assignment of tracing a rectangle with his eyes. In this case the eye movements hardly have the nature of organized tracking of outlines, with the result that a motor "copy" of the figure offered emerges. In the record reproduced, this contour cannot be distinguished, and one is capable of seeing only a number of ataxic movements demonstrating that the patient now finds and now loses the lines he is seeking.

In Figure 5 we present a recording of eye movements in examining a portrait. Whereas in normal vision (Figure 5a) the tracking movements of the eye reproduce the contours of the drawing accurately, yielding points of fixation at its principal points, in the patient (Figure 5b) no copy of the image perceived emerges in the eye movements

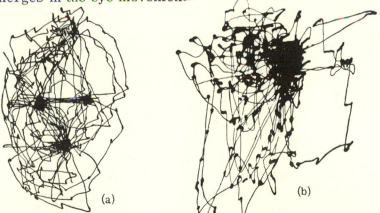

(a)   (b)

Figure 5. Eye movements in examining a portrait:
(a) control (subject examines portrait freely with both eyes and without instructions); (b) patient R.

The patient, although grasping the significance of <u>the complete picture</u>, is incapable of <u>analyzing it</u> visually and of consistently tracking the details constituting it. The "tracker" of the eyes here proves to be so disturbed that, on shifting from perception of the whole to tracking details, the patient begins to experience the same difficulties that arise each time that the visual perception of a single point is replaced by the visual perception of a complex structure.

Analogous data emerged from recording the patient's eye movements in reading. Here, too, he was capable of fixing only isolated points, but not of consistently tracing lines and transferring his eyes from one point to another; reading therefore became a disorganized grasping at isolated components of the text. We cite an example.

<u>Text specimen:</u>

"What is your last name?"   "My name is Ivanova."
"What is your first name?"   "My first name is Nedezhda."
"What is your patronymic?"   "My patronymic is
                              Vasil'evna."

<u>Specimen of patient's reading:</u>

"Read from the beginning." "Vasilina." "My patronymic is Vasilina.... My patronymic is Vasilina."
    "What is your first name? Nadezhda. What is your first name? Nadezhda Ivanovna.... My last name is Ivanova. My first name ...Ivanova? ...that's also my first name ...again it says my first name, but that's what it is.... My patronymic is Vasilina Ivanovna."

These data demonstrate that the pathological condition of the visual cortex, caused by the reduction of accessible visual information to a single element, inevitably results in disordering the entire tracking system of the eye, and that opticomotor ataxia is merely a manifestation of disturbance of this system.

At the same time, these data make possible a direct approach to analysis of the paradoxical observations in visual agnosia

arising in such cases. The patient's intact ability to perceive an
entire image directly (based, it seems, on isolation of the leading meaningful characteristic) disappears as soon as the patient
proceeds to consecutive visual tracking of the components of a
simultaneous structure presented to him. We find that a patient
who is incapable of grasping several components at once is incapable of examining them consecutively: when he directs his
gaze toward a single element, the others disappear, and organized tracking of the entire complex is violated. Thus, the visual
tracker remains intact only when there is a system of visual
stimuli consisting at the very least of two simultaneously stimulated points, of which one activates the orienting oculomotor
reflex, and the other provides precise, differentiated vision.

Experiments in Restoration of Opticomotor Functions

The data on the intimate connection between the two phenomena described above — the reduction in the number of elements
perceived to one, and disorder of the tracking device of the eye
— were confirmed by experiments with the object of achieving
temporary restoration of both these disturbed functions.
Earlier, on the assumption that the syndrome described is explained by pathologically impaired tonus of the occipital cortex,
when this region, in Pavlov's expression, proved to be so weak
that "it was possible to deal simultaneously only with a single
stimulated point," we conducted an experiment on the influence
of caffeine on this weakened cortical function. Significant results were obtained: in a 30- to 40- min period, the volume of
elements perceived simultaneously increased to two or three,
and the phenomena of optical ataxia temporarily disappeared
(Luria, 1959).
We attempted to pursue this approach in the case under discussion, but in this instance employed, in addition to caffeine, a
cholinesterase antagonist — galanthamine — that, according to
Eidinova & Pravdina-Vinarskaya (1959), had proved to be a powerful agent in restoring synaptic conductivity and inducing a
substantial improvement in the functional activity of the weak-

ened cortical cells. The experiments confirmed our expecta-
tions. The injection of 0.5 cc of caffeine in a 10% solution led
to a considerable expansion of the functional visual field. Within
20 min after the injection, the patient began to perceive simultaneously two of the figures suggested to him. There was also
a pronounced improvement in oculomotor coordination. An effect similar to this was obtained upon subcutaneous injection of
1 cc of a 0.25% galanthamine solution. Data involving changes
in visual-motor coordination proved particularly clear-cut.
Whereas before the injection of galanthamine the task of placing
a point in the center of a circle or of drawing a circle around a
point was beyond R.'s capacities, this became possible for him
within 40 min after the injection. Similar results were obtained
in reading. Whereas before the galanthamine injection the patient was able to grasp only scattered words in the text and
moved in disorderly fashion from line to line, afterward he was
able for a while to follow a line in a more organized manner,
and even to move from one line to the next. This continued for a
period, but then the defects typical of this patient began to re-
appear in their previous form.

The inability to obtain lasting recovery of visual synthesis and
visual-motor coordination compelled us to refrain and, for
practical reasons, to abandon direct efforts to restore reading,
and to follow the course of reorganizing the reading process by
inhibiting the disordered eye movements of the patient and proceeding from the fact that kinesthetic afferentation was intact.
To accomplish this, we employed, at the suggestion of L. S.
Tsvetkova, the device of placing a frame around the text that
left but a single syllable exposed (and, subsequently, a word),
which eliminated the disorderly appearance of unconnected
items in the text. This frame was gradually shifted by the patient along the line and, as new components were disclosed, it
made possible a complete process of tracking, based fundamentally on kinesthetic afferentation. The frame was moved to the
next line by pushing it back along the line just read, after which
it was moved slowly to the next. This technique resulted in
slow, but coordinated, reading. It was gradually replaced by

tracking the text with the aid of a ruler below it, and finally with the aid of a finger moving along the line. This approach, the result of which was to shift the leading role in the act of reading to the mechanism of kinesthetic tracking, proved to be the sole means of attaining a certain recovery of the act of reading on the part of the patient.

Conclusion

The normal process of visual perception necessarily includes reflex shifting of the eyes (relative to the object), as a consequence of which those features of the object containing maximum information are fixed by the central visual field. The complex process of examining a picture or real situation presumes a consecutive series of these movements.

The reflex shifting of the eye, with fixation in the central sections of the retina of points bearing maximum information, is possible only if there is a system of simultaneously excited points. Some of these points (peripherally located) constitute the source of impulses inducing reflex shifting of the eye, and others (central in location) bear the function of reception and transmission of visual information.

In cases in which the existence of such a system of simultaneously excited points proves impossible, a secondary disturbance of organized sighting movements arises necessarily, and the integrated process of visual perception disintegrates.

In the present article, which constitutes a continuation of a communication previously published (Luria, 1959), we provide an analysis of a case in which, as a result of bilateral damage to the parieto-occipital divisions of the cortex, the patient was capable of perceiving but a single object at a time. As a consequence of this limitation of the functioning of the visual cortex to the confines of a single stimulated point, one could observe in the patient a gross ataxia in sighting and, as a result, a marked disorder of the self-regulating acts of visual perception.

Use of the technique of recording visual movements, demonstrating that these movements are normal in peripherally in-

duced tunnel vision and are very disordered in centrally originating simultaneous agnosia, makes it possible to approach more
closely an analysis of the role played by eye movements in active perception, and thus to pose a number of significant questions on the psychological and physiological mechanisms underlying visual perception.

References

Balint, K. Seelenlaehmung des Schauens. Monatschr. Psych.
Neurol., 1909.

Eidinova, M. B., & Pravdina-Vinarskaya, E. N. [Cerebral in-
sults in children and tactics for overcoming them]. Moscow:
APN RSFSR, 1959.

Gelb, A., & Goldstein, K. Psychologische Analyse hirnpatho-
logischen Faelle. Leipzig, 1920.

Hecaen, H., & Ajuriaguerra, J. Balint's syndrome. Brain,
1954, 77.

Holmes, G. Disturbances of vision by cerebral lesions. Brit.
J. Ophthal., 1919, 1.

Iarbus, A. L. [A new method for recording eye movements].
Biofizika, 1956, 1(8).

Luria, A. R. Disorders of simultaneous perception in a case
of bilateral occipitotemporal brain injuries. Brain, 1959, 82.

Paterson, A., & Zangwill, O. L. Disorders of visual space perception associated with lesions of the right hemisphere.
Brain, 1944, 67.

Pavlov, I. P. [Pavlovian Wednesdays]. Vol. 3. 1949.

Wolpert, J. Die Simultanagnosie. Z. Neurol. Psychiat., 1924,
93.

Translated by
Michel Vale

ABOUT THE EDITOR

Michael Cole is Professor and Coordinator of Communications
Program, University of California, San Diego. He has been the
editor of the translation journal Soviet Psychology since 1969.
He coedited A Handbook of Contemporary Soviet Psychology,
and has coauthored Culture and Thought: A Psychological Introduction, The Cultural Context of Learning and Thinking, and
many other books and articles. Having obtained his Ph.D. at
Indiana University, Professor Cole taught at Yale, the University of California at Irvine, Hampshire College, and the Rocke-
feller University. His own research is devoted to studying the
influence of cultural environment on the development of cognitive skills.